None but the Braves

A PITCHER, A TEAM, A CHAMPION

Tom Glavine

with Nick Cafardo

Introduction by Greg Maddux

HarperCollins*Publishers*

HarperCollins books may be purchased for educational, business, or sales promotional use. For information please write: Special Markets Department, HarperCollins Publishers, Inc., 10 East 53rd Street, New York, NY 10022.

FIRST EDITION

Designed by Alma Hochhauser Orenstein

Library of Congress Cataloging-in-Publication Data

Glavine, Tom, 1966–
    None but the Braves : a pitcher, a team. a champion / Tom Glavine
  with Nick Cafardo. — 1st ed.
      p.   cm.
    ISBN 0-06-018649-6
    1. Atlanta Braves (Baseball team) 2. Glavine, Tom, 1996–
3. Baseball players—United States—Biography. 4. World Series
(Baseball) I. Cafardo, Nick. II. Title.
GV875.A8G53 1996   96-26043
796.357'64'09758231—dc20

96 97 98 99 00 ❖/RRD 10 9 8 7 6 5 4 3 2 1

To my family: Mom, Dad, Deb, Fred, and Mike
—thanks for all of your support.

To my wife, Carri, thanks for your love and support.
And to my daughter, Amber.
I couldn't have done it without you guys.
—Tom Glavine

To Leeanne, Ben, and Emilee
—my unforgettable triple play.
To Ma, Dad, and Fred, for all you've done for me.
—Nick Cafardo

Contents

Photographs follow page 146.

Acknowledgments

THE AUTHORS OF THIS BOOK WISH TO ACKNOWLEDGE AND thank the many people who provided information and inspiration along the way.

This book could not have come together without the determination and vision of literary agent Stacey Woolf-Feinberg, as well as Bob Woolf Associates agents Gregg Clifton and Jack Toffey, whose diligence kept this project together. Special thanks to the late Bob Woolf, Tom Glavine's long-time agent who would have been proud of Tom's accomplishments. Thanks also to HarperCollins senior editor Mauro DiPreta for his direction and ideas and to his assistant Kristen Auclair.

Thanks to the Atlanta Braves' public relations department—Jim Schultz, Glenn Serra, Thurman Brooks, Phil Civins, and Joan Hicks for their time in researching certain events. Thanks also to the librarians who helped research so many of the events and facts: Dorey Conway of Salisbury, North Carolina, and *Boston Globe* librarians Charlie Smiley and Betty McKeown. Thanks also to NBC for the use of their video library. Thanks to Dom Zminda of Stats Inc. for some of the statistical breakdowns that appear in the book. Thanks to Bill Wanless of the Pawtucket Red Sox and the Richmond Braves for their cooperation.

Thanks to *Boston Globe* executive sports editor Don Skwar, assistant sports editors Joe Sullivan and Robin Romano, baseball writers

Larry Whiteside, Dan Shaughnessy, and Bob Ryan, and administrative secretary Nancy Curley for their support, patience, and advice during this project. Thanks to Peter Gammons for his direction and constant inspiration and to Rob Bradford of Hometown Publications of Salem, Massachusetts, for his transcription of many hours of tape. Thanks to *Boston Globe* computer genius Sean Mullin for his technical assistance. Thanks also to Atlanta scribes Bill Zack of Morris News Service, Thomas Stinson and I. J. Rosenberg of the *Atlanta Constitution,* Rod Beaton of *USA Today,* John Lowe of the *Detroit Free Press,* Steven Krasner of the *Providence Journal,* and Charles Scoggins and Dave Pevear of the *Lowell Sun* for their expert input.

Thanks to that big purple guy, Barney, for entertaining Amber Nicole Glavine so her dad and Nick Cafardo could talk.

Tom Glavine wishes to express his gratitude to Leo Mazzone, Bobby Cox, Greg Maddux, and teammates for adding so much depth to these pages as well as umpire Joe Brinkman, former Red Sox general manager Lou Gorman, Baltimore Orioles farm director Syd Thrift, Toronto outfielder Otis Nixon, and Braves general manager John Schuerholz. Thanks to Jim Bowley of Melbourne, Florida, for childhood memories of Tom.

Introduction

YOU CAN DESCRIBE TOM GLAVINE IN ONE WORD: WINNER.

If you didn't know that prior to October 28, 1995, Game 6 of the 1995 World Series against the Cleveland Indians, you must know it by now.

It was simply a case of a great pitcher pitching a great game at a great moment. And by the second or third inning, I knew we had won. Tom was completely focused, locked in. There could have been people standing a foot behind him heckling and he wouldn't have heard them. He was so in the zone, I don't think he even remembered walking from the mound to the dugout after an inning.

Tom understood the magnitude of the game and it's place in baseball—and Braves—history. And he knew what he needed to do to win. He knew that a lot better than I did when I went out in Game 5 and lost the chance to lock up the championship. I had doubts entering that game, which is perfectly normal, and I thought Glav would also have doubts entering Game 6. I was wrong.

He had beaten the Indians in Game 2 without his best stuff—I've seen him throw fifty or sixty games better than that one—but he still pulled it out, which is the sign of a great pitcher. It also led me to believe that if he was just a little sharper the next time he pitched, then he would have fewer problems and win the game.

Sure enough, he was razor sharp. His pitches were so well crafted that the Cleveland Indians, with one of the best lineups I've ever seen, never got much to swing at. They hit maybe two or three balls hard the entire game, and managed only a bloop single in eight innings. That's amazing in a game that is so important. The only question that remained was, are we going to score and support this masterpiece? David Justice answered that loudly in the sixth inning with his home run, the only run of the game.

I can't think of a more fitting way for the Atlanta Braves to become champs than with Glav on the mound. He has been with the Braves longer than anyone on the team. The rise of the Atlanta Braves began with Tom Glavine, and everything that was done subsequently, all the wonderful things that have happened since, were with him as the centerpiece.

What you probably notice most about Tom on the field is that he wins. When I was pitching for the Chicago Cubs, I'd see him about two or three times a year. We'd come in for a series and he was 7–2. A month later, we'd come in and he was 12–3 and I didn't quite understand why until I became his teammate at the start of the 1993 season.

He wins on heart and he doesn't panic. He pitches according to what's unfolding in the game. He knows how to hold a lead, winning as many games 5–4 as he does 2–1, which is something you don't see that often. Usually when a pitcher has given up three or four runs, he folds and gives up even more, then gets hooked. Not Tom. He gives up two or three runs and he stops himself and says, "That's all I'm giving up today," and more often than not, because of his talent, his drive, and his competitiveness, he succeeds.

An excellent fielder and an excellent hitter, he does all of the little things needed to win. When you need the big play, he'll come through, whether it's bunting the runner over or getting a base hit. Tommy rarely misses an opportunity to help himself with the bat, so he's not your conventional "automatic out" as so many pitchers are in the National League.

With his mound smarts, he doesn't beat himself, but challenges the other team to beat him. The average pitcher in the league beats himself four or five times a year by making a poor judgment. But in the three years I've been his teammate, Tom hasn't made that mistake. Mostly it's because he understands himself as a pitcher, knowing what he does and doesn't do so well.

That's not to say he's afraid to try something new or experiment. Tom's not like that. While some pitchers will struggle against certain hitters and continue pitching the same way, Tom will adjust. He'll go with his fastball and change-up (his bread-and-butter pitches), and if that doesn't work he'll throw sliders and breaking balls.

Knowing all this, it's not surprising that entering 1996, he's the winningest pitcher in the 1990s.

All this success hasn't gone to his head because above all, Tom's a good person. He obviously cares about his teammates after all he's been through with the labor situation. As an effective player representative, you have to be vocal, and Tom was. He took a lot of abuse for his strong stance, and as a team we appreciated everything he did for us. He was chosen to be the mouthpiece, the point person for the press and media, and at times he had to take a public beating for the rest of us.

In the negotiating room, on the field, or in the clubhouse, Tom's our leader. If something needs to be said he'll tell guys what they're doing wrong. And he'll pat someone on the back, sit them down, and have a pep talk to raise their spirits. When Tom speaks, people listen and act.

The first time I ever met Tom as a teammate was a couple of weeks before spring training in 1993 during a mini-camp that pitching coach Leo Mazzone holds in Atlanta. I thought it would be a tough time because I was replacing Charlie Leibrandt in the rotation, and he was the guy the young pitchers—Tom, John Smoltz, Steve Avery, Kent Mercker—learned the game from. But Tom took me in, inviting me to go out golfing with a bunch of them, and I knew right then and there that I would fit in and be accepted.

Tom and I do a lot of things alike. Our approach to the game is the same. We share a commitment to success. We want to be as good as we can be. And we have respect for the game. We don't believe the game owes us anything, but that we owe the game everything we have in life, which is why Tom so respects and fights for the rights of players.

He's dedicated 100 percent to whatever he does. Whether it's pitching or golf or representing players or being a dad and a husband, he doesn't do anything halfway. I think you'll agree with me when you're done reading this book.

He's experienced last place and he's experienced the World Championship and everything in between. You'll experience the anguish and frustration of those early years as well as the triumphant moment of the World Series in the pages that follow.

He's a fighter. He's a competitor. He's a winner.

GREG MADDUX
February 23, 1996

An Atlanta Second

INSTEAD OF LEAPING RIGHT OUT OF MY SKIN AND CHARGING Mark Wohlers on the mound for the celebration, I hung back and sat on the bench for a second after Marquis Grissom had secured the final out of the 1995 World Series safely in his mitt.

This wasn't just any second. This was one of the greatest moments of my life, one I wanted to cherish and stretch out forever. You've heard of a New York minute? This was an Atlanta second.

The 51,875 fans went crazy, rocking the stands of Atlanta–Fulton County Stadium, waving and chopping with their red tomahawks, jumping and screaming—some were even crying they were so happy. I wanted to say, "Go ahead and live it up, you deserve it!"

The tumult crashed over us in the dugout and practically carried everyone out onto the field. My teammates were ecstatic. Some of us had been here from the beginning when the Braves were a National League joke, year after frustrating year, throughout the late eighties, the nineties, and right up to this sweet moment. In the pile of bodies were Mark Lemke, Jeff Blauser, Johnny Smoltz, Mark Wohlers, David Justice, Steve Avery, Kent Mercker—they more than any of the others understood how incredible this moment was.

I was feeling a range of emotions: excitement, happiness, accomplishment, and, most especially, vindication and validation. No longer would we have to hear about how we were the unfortunate bridesmaids or the Buffalo Bills of baseball. We were now, without question, the best. I think we always knew that. But this victory put a stamp on it.

Our team had gone about it the right way, working hard and sustaining a great level of performance from day one to Game 6 of the World Series. Think about that. That's a long time to maintain consistency.

We had to win our division over a 144-game schedule (curtailed from the normal 162 games because of the strike). We had to win the first round of the play-offs against the best hitting team in our league in Colorado, at a ballpark whose altitude turns normal fly balls into home runs. We had to beat a much touted Cincinnati Reds team, which had great team speed, power, and good pitching, to capture the National League pennant. And ultimately, we had to beat the Cleveland Indians, who had gone through their own trials and won 100 games during the regular season.

None of it was easy.

Because I follow Greg Maddux in the pitching rotation, Bobby Cox allowed me to go out there and pitch. And I was fortunate to have pitched the game of my life. When I physically couldn't pitch any longer, I turned to Bobby and my pitching coach and friend, Leo Mazzone, after I came off the field at the end of the top of the eighth, and I said to them, "I've had enough."

I think they were a little surprised. I wasn't asking out. Heck, I would have loved to have been the guy everybody charged after getting the last out. But I didn't want to risk it.

And Leo and Bobby understood.

Bobby said of my decision: "It says a lot for the relationship we have with Tommy, that he would be able to come to us in that spot and tell us the truth. So many other pitchers would have said nothing to their manager. Some of them would have got the job done, and some wouldn't have. And those who weren't true to themselves in a situation like that, how would they be able to stomach it if they'd blown it?"

Let me explain. We had a long bottom of the seventh inning. Marquis got on base with a single and Lemke moved him over with a nice sacrifice bunt. After Chipper Jones's long at bat, Fred McGriff flew out. David Justice worked a walk. They retired us when Mike Devereaux, who had been the MVP of our play-off series against Cincinnati, popped out.

Meanwhile, the temperature had dropped as the game progressed. Just sitting around on the bench, it was inevitable my back and shoulder would stiffen. When I went out there for the eighth inning and took the usual eight warm-up pitches, I had a hard time getting loose.

I got the outs, but I was getting away with a lot of mistakes. I couldn't spot the ball as well as I had earlier in the game because my mechanics were being thrown off by the stiffness and I was also getting tired. I retired Jim Thome on a fly ball to left center field after I fell behind the count, 2–0. He hit a breaking ball that didn't have good location. A bonehead pitch, he easily could have hit a double or a home run on that. This after I handled Jim pretty well earlier in the game by striking him out twice. But I got lucky and we caught the ball.

I didn't feel right in my battle with Tony Peña or with pitcher Julian Tavarez either. Miraculously, I got both out and retired the side, 1–2–3. But it was obvious by then that my breaking pitch had lost its bite, my change-up lacked some movement (instead of breaking naturally away from a right-handed hitter, it was leaving itself more on the plate than I wanted), and my fastball had slowed. If this were just another game during the regular season, I would have just gone as long as I could. Or if it was the second or third inning I might have worked my way through it gradually.

Nothing about the situation was going to get better. God, this was our chance to win it all. What was I going to do, lie to Bobby or Leo and say "I feel great!" and go out there and blow a game like this? As much as I wanted to finish, it would have been unfair to my teammates, who had worked so hard for so long, to take the risk.

I know a lot of people in the stadium and watching on TV probably thought, "What a crazy move by Cox, taking Glavine out." It wasn't him, it was me.

Leo backed me up: "If a pitcher of Tommy's caliber and experience says he's done, then he's done. I'm not going to talk him out of it, because he knows his body better than anyone. I just wanted him to be the guy out there when we won it all."

Bobby, Leo, and I did discuss whether I should stay in to face Kenny Lofton, who was scheduled to lead off the ninth. I had handled him pretty well primarily because he's a left-handed hitter. But the thinking was, why bother when you have Wohlers who can blow his fastball by anyone?

Mark was warming up in the bull pen, and the way he was

throwing I had no reservations handing him the ball. He had been awesome. He's a guy who pitches harder than anyone in baseball. His radar readings are consistently more than 100 miles per hour. For a hitter to go from a guy like me—a lot of off-speed stuff and spot pitching—to a speed demon like Mark, well, that's not an easy adjustment to make suddenly.

You can't put your closer in a tougher spot: 1–0 in the ninth inning and with three outs you can win the championship! But I was confident he would get the job done.

Like me, Mark grew up in western Massachusetts, in the city of Holyoke, where winters can be even more severe than those in Billerica, my hometown in the Merrimack Valley. I figured if we could weather those vicious winter storms, we could weather this.

It seemed every season for the last four years Mark was destined to be our closer, but every year he would lose the job. Until this year. He approached Greg Maddux, who told him what needed to be done to close a game. Mark listened, learned, and worked hard, eventually becoming the pitcher he is today, with command of four pitches and the most wicked fastball in the game. So you understand now why I and the rest of the team weren't too concerned about Mark in this situation.

We all knew that the key to the inning was getting Lofton off the bases. The guy is such a terrific talent and he creates such chaos for a pitcher. He gave us trouble earlier in the series and he was a pain for the Seattle Mariners in the American League championship.

That problem was solved when Rafael Belliard, who did a great job filling in for the injured Jeff Blauser in this series, made a great play on Lofton's pop-up into short center field. Once we got that out, there was a feeling on the bench that "Okay, we're going to do this." Mark was throwing in the high nineties, and it was very evident that even when Indians hitters made contact, they really couldn't extend themselves like they wanted. Mark got Omar Vizquel and Carlos Baerga, a couple of tough hitters, on fly balls to center field.

We were the World Champions!

You have to understand how incredible that sounds to a guy from Billerica, Massachusetts, which is about twenty-five miles northwest of Boston. I grew up in an area that knows all about frustration. Like any other Boston fan, when I was a kid I rooted for the 1975 Red Sox. I was performing the body English right along with Carlton Fisk in the great Game 6 when he stood at home plate and waved his arms so the ball would stay fair and be a home run. I'd heard about the great 1967 "Impossible Dream" season that brought baseball back to Boston and made it forever the most popular sport in the city. But in both '67 and '75, the Red Sox lost in the World Series. And in 1986, I was in the minor leagues following the Red Sox after a long season at Greenville and Richmond, and watched as the ball went through Bill Buckner's legs in Game 6 against the New York Mets.

Even as a kid playing hockey and baseball in Billerica, it seemed every time we were on the brink of winning a championship, we fell a little short. And I had known failure in the early part of my career. When I came up to the majors in 1987, the Braves were a bad team and we remained so until midway through the 1990 season, when I sensed we were turning the corner. Then came the frustration of the 1990s when we were, in my opinion, good enough to win the World Championship every year from '91 on, but for the reasons you'll read about later, we didn't get it done.

So when Marquis squeezed that ball and after I watched while sitting in the dugout with my Braves warm-up jacket on and a towel wrapped around my neck, and soaked in a lifetime of memories, I just let it out. I'm not a real wild person, prone to do real off-the-wall stuff. I think I'm someone who's always in control on the field and off it. But when the crowd let out a deafening roar and my teammates were jumping on each other and hugging, I finally said, "Okay, get out there and celebrate!"

That long second was over.

I have to admit that when I ran onto the field, I was a little cautious. I said to myself, "Don't get yourself caught at the bottom of the pile. Watch that left shoulder!" I've learned that even the most innocent circumstances can spell disaster for your career if you're not careful. Still, I tried to pat and hug everyone. I wanted my teammates, these guys who had fought alongside me for so long, to know how proud I was and how much I appreciated what they'd done for the Braves and the community.

Done sharing the special moment with the fans, we all ran back into the clubhouse, where I threw on my championship hat and T-shirt. I grabbed a bottle of champagne and sprayed everyone in sight. That was half the fun of winning. In 1991 we watched the Minnesota Twins celebrate. In 1992 we watched the Toronto Blue Jays. This was our turn.

I looked all around for my wife, Carri, and mom and dad, Fred and Millie Glavine, but there were so many people in the room, I couldn't find them. Cameras flashed, reporters swarmed, and visitors were everywhere, making it tough to get around.

Somewhere in the chaos I was told I'd won the MVP Award for the series for my two wins. I knew coming in that I had a chance if I won the game and pitched well. Usually, the guy who wins two games wins the MVP Award, especially if he pitches the final game. In many ways it meant more to me than winning the Cy Young Award in 1991. While the Cy Young is a prestigious award—and one I'd love to win a few more times if Greg "Mad Dog" Maddux gives it up one of these years—it's based more on individual achievement. But winning the MVP of the World Series means you've helped your team gain the biggest prize in baseball.

A lot of the media made a big deal out of the fact that I earned $150,000 for winning the MVP because of a bonus clause in my contract. The money was nice, but it's not something I was thinking about. Heck, they could have garnished my pay and I would've savored it just as much—though I would've had to fire my agent. (Just kidding!)

I was presented with the MVP Award by a Chevrolet executive, and they donated a van to charity. It added to all the good feelings.

When Hannah Storm of NBC asked me to do an interview after the presentation, I was happy to do it. Hannah had taken a lot of garbage from Albert Belle, who hates everybody, during the series. She was the victim of one of his temper tantrums just because she was in the dugout before a game trying to set up an interview with Carlos Baerga. She was a professional trying to do her job and she didn't deserve to be disrespected.

She noticed that I had a tear in my eye while I was celebrating. I honestly didn't realize that, but the moment overcame me, I suppose. She asked me how it felt to win the award and stop the best hitting team in baseball and I told her, "I wish I could split this up twenty-five different ways. Everyone deserves a piece of it." Maybe that sounds like a cliché, but I honestly meant that.

Winning the World Championship was the simplest of dreams for me—and the most difficult to fulfill. When I was a kid in the back-yard imitating Carl Yastrzemski or Jim Rice or Fred Lynn, or turning my body 180 degrees like Luis Tiant, I fantasized that I was either hitting the home run or striking out the last batter to win the World Series. When you're that young you never think that's really going to be you people are calling a hero.

And I'm not sure, even well after the fact, that it really happened. I still have to pinch myself, sometimes even double-checking to make sure the championship ring is really mine.

As I was walking back from the press conference, I finally ran into Carri, Mom, and Dad. Carri gave me a big hug and we just stood there holding each other for a while. She was so proud of me. I wished, in a way, my daughter, Amber, had been old enough to understand what had happened. She was home sleeping. Someday, when she's old enough to understand, I'll show her the videotape of the game so she might understand why her dad was so proud of this accomplishment.

Mom and Dad didn't say anything. They didn't have to because I knew exactly how they felt.

This was the culmination of those 5:30 A.M. drives to the hockey rink and the endless number of times I had to be driven to and picked up at baseball practice. I remembered what Mom always said to me: "Someday, it's going to be your turn." Dad was also excited to see the Braves win a World Championship because he was a long-time Boston Braves fan and never got to see them win before they moved to Milwaukee in 1952.

I stayed around the clubhouse—which was almost vacant early into the next morning. Bobby and I were sitting in the trainers room, probably the only place to escape the stench of dried champagne.

As I cut the tape from my ankles, I said to him, "This is all great, but the one thing I would change is the fact that after all we went through we didn't get to spend enough time with each other after this game."

Bobby, wrapped in a towel after showering, looked at me and said, "You're right. I wish it were different. But then again, I don't wish that. We got to win the World Championship at home, in front of our friends and family and fans. That's pretty special." Then, as he shuffled off to change, he told me to get out of there, be with my family, and enjoy myself.

That night, Carri set up a party for us at Time Out, a local watering hole. She and I were the last to arrive, because after the interviews, taking equipment off, and showering, it was about 1:00 A.M. I was stopped in my tracks as patrons—Braves fans—started clapping as I walked in. I smiled and acknowledged them as Carri and I made our way toward a corner where the rest of the players and their families had gathered. The clapping continued, eyes peeled on us, watching everything, not wanting to miss one moment. We only stayed for about an hour, then went home and stayed up a couple more hours with Mom and Dad, who were still pretty excited. It was the first time I'd been able to reflect with my family on what had happened, and that was the most fulfilling time, to spend it with the people you love and who love you and talk about a special moment you'd just all experienced together and how far we'd come from the day when I first tried my hand at pitching at age ten.

It's been pretty awesome to hear what some people in the media and in baseball have had to say about the performance since.

I know that even Joe Brinkman, the home plate umpire who did a terrific job calling balls and strikes, thought I was still throwing pretty well when I came out after eight. Being a National Leaguer, I had never crossed paths with Joe, even in spring training when American League and National League teams play each other. He is a professional umpire and I'm sure he spoke to the National League umps in that series on how I threw the ball and where I spotted it because he was right on it the whole game.

Brinkman's recollection of my performance that night was interesting from an umpire's perspective:

Tommy had a lot of pop on the outside corner of the plate. He just kept popping guys, outside, outside, outside, and kept trying to get more and more of that corner. He can lull you to sleep out there and finally, as an umpire, you have to say, "Okay, that's as much as you're going to get out there." Really he pitched masterfully. Indians hitters were going back to the dugout shaking their heads asking themselves, "Why can't I hit this guy?" I remember the sequence of pitches to Eddie Murray late in the game was pretty. He went outside, inside, and then banged him inside and Eddie struck out. He changed speeds so well that it was very difficult for the hitter to sit on anything.

I would rank that one with big games I've worked. It was the most masterful performance. It was a fitting performance for that series. A fitting ending.

And Bobby had his own observations:

Tonight, Tommy pitched exactly like he did in 1991 in every start out. He was a machine from day one until the end of the World Series that year and did it again tonight. He did it against Colorado,

he did it against Cincinnati, and he did it against these guys. He
knows how to pitch and has the guts of a burglar.

Thanks, Bobby. I think.

The day of the game I really tried my best to make the day as normal as possible. I slept pretty well and I remember Carri waking me
and my telling her I wanted to sleep later. No tossing and turning.
No counting of Albert Belles backward or anything like that. Carri
was relaxed and had that confidence about her that we were going
to win, and her instincts are always right. When I got out of bed, I
just hung around the house, ran around with my daughter, Amber,
and watched *Barney* with her. My parents were coming in from
Boston that day, so I was making sure everything was all right for
them. Occupied, I didn't have time to obsess over the game.

Sometime during the course of the morning, I heard about the
story in the *Atlanta Constitution*. There were big headlines: JUSTICE
TAKES A RIP AT BRAVES FANS! David Justice had criticized the Atlanta fans
for not being as loud or into the World Series as the Cleveland fans.

I knew the story was coming because I'd been interviewed about
David's comments after he made them. But I didn't think it would
turn into such a huge event.

"If we don't win, they'll probably burn our houses down," David
was quoted as saying. "We've got to win. And if we win, it's for
twenty-five guys in here, the coaches and Bobby Cox. It is for us.
Like the song '(You and Me) Against the World.' It's us against the
world. I'm the only guy that will sit here and say it, but there are a
lot of people that feel this way.

"If we get down 1–0 [in Game 6], they will probably boo us out
of the stadium. You would have to do something great to get them
out of their seats.

"Shoot, up in Cleveland, they were down three runs in the ninth
inning and they were still on their feet."

I would never knock David, because he's been a huge part of
our success through the years. He's up-front, not afraid to say what
he thinks, and he always answers reporters' questions honestly.

I just didn't understand what the motivation was to make the
comments he made nor why the media was inflating it into a big
story. I know a lot of people thought David put us in a tough spot. It
was more of a pain in the neck than anything else because we had

to answer so many questions about the comments, and it didn't seem like it was an issue we should have to deal with heading into Game 6. After all, we didn't need a hostile group of fans out there the night we had a chance to win the World Championship.

But I never felt that David's comments put us in any type of bad or awkward position. If I pitched my game and we scored some runs, we'd win. It was as simple as that. Somebody's words weren't about to throw me off my game. If you have it, you have it. How could I have ever made that an excuse if I'd gone out there and got my lunch handed to me? It would have been a lousy thing for me to do. And I would not have blamed anyone but myself.

However, I couldn't see the big difference between how our fans and the Cleveland fans were acting. We had heard coming into the series that Cleveland was going to be such an impossible place to play and that we were going to be so intimidated by the noise the fans made.

What people forgot is that we played in what had to be the noisiest situation I can ever remember, at the Hubert H. Humphrey Metrodome in Minneapolis in the 1991 World Series. That crowd was much more of a factor than the crowd in Cleveland, even though I thought the level of excitement in Cleveland was tremendous. They were grateful fans who were really behind their team. I thought the Cleveland situation was no different from ours in 1991. Like our fans that year, this was the first time Indians fans had gone through this in forty-one years after a long history of losing seasons, and finally they had their team in the World Series.

I don't think it was fair for David, or anyone else, to expect that our fans were going to be as excited as they were in 1991 when it was all brand-new. What we went through in 1991 was special, and that feeling produced by the fans and by the players can never be duplicated. We'd been through two other World Series and another postseason and we were in one again. Until we won it all, how could the level of excitement be like it was in '91? In the back of their minds, our fans were probably a little guarded with their emotions after we didn't win in 1991–93.

Smoltzie and Lemke called a team meeting after batting practice, but since I was pitching, I really didn't want anything to do with it. There wasn't any earth-shattering news coming from it, anyway. The basic message was, "Who cares what's being said?" Orel Hershiser and Omar Vizquel had pissed a lot of us off after Game 5, saying the pressure was on us, alluding to our past losses in the postseason. Smoltzie and Lemke simply said, "The fact of the matter is we've got a chance to win the World Championship tonight so let's go out and do it!"

I drove to the ballpark with Greg Maddux that day, like I always do. Mad Dog, the greatest pitcher on earth (and I don't say that casually), lives a couple of houses down in my development. He had proven to be a great source of strength for me throughout the season. But that day we didn't say a word about the game. We were talking about college football. It was actually on the drive home Friday night after the workout that he gave me a pep talk about the game I was about to pitch.

It was raining and we were making our way slowly through the downtown traffic. I remembered how Steve Avery had pitched Game 4 and won, 5–2. About Ave's victory, Leo said, "Avery couldn't believe they never adjusted to his change-up. So he just kept throwing it." That was comforting, but I was curious what Greg had to say about Game 5 because I felt the Indians had made some adjustments against him to beat him.

"I don't think they adjusted well," Mad Dog said as cars honked and the rain swept over the car. "I was a bit off. It was more me than it was them. Just go out and pitch your game. Don't change anything. Do what you do best and you're going to beat these guys."

That reassured me. And so did something else Mad Dog said after losing Game 5: "At least now, the guy who should be the winning pitcher when the Atlanta Braves win the championship will be out there." When something like that comes from a pitcher like him, it gives you shivers. I'll never forget that.

The next day, game day, we arrived at the ballpark at about 2:30 P.M. The first hour was pretty much your typical get-in-and-start-getting-dressed kind of thing. We got through a deep line of fans who were already perched at the entrance to the auto tunnel that leads down to the locker room.

I went over to the trainers room and shot the breeze with those guys for a while and goofed around with our strength and conditioning coach, Frank Fultz, who likes to tell jokes and keep me loose, but he backed off a little, sensing the magnitude of the game. I was watching a Georgia-Florida football game and then I switched over to Notre Dame during those afternoon hours. Dad got me hooked on Notre Dame football as a kid, an Irish Catholic thing, I guess. It's been a tradition in my family to watch their games on Saturday afternoons. I sipped on a couple of cups of coffee and actually fell asleep for about a half hour in the trainers room.

There was a great mood in the clubhouse. You got the sense that guys knew we were on the verge of beating the Indians. There was a lot of confidence showing around the room.

I know there was a lot of anticipation in the city. Fans were excited by the prospect that we were going to win it all. With that comes a degree of pressure, but in my mind I didn't want to make this out to be a monumental game. In fact, the way I approached it was I told myself this was Game 6, not Game 7. Sure, I wanted to be the guy to win the championship game and the guy everyone ran out to congratulate, but at the same time I could only do as much as I could do. I can't perform miracles. And if we didn't win there was tomorrow. There was a Game 7 and John Smoltz, our money pitcher, was scheduled to pitch.

Lord knows, though, I didn't want that to happen. I remember I put Smoltzie in that position in 1992 when I lost Game 6 and he had to come in and pitch Game 7. All of those things were going through my mind. When you come right down to it, it's a baseball game, and all the talk about what this game would mean for me after the labor issue and what it would mean for the Braves and the city . . . I didn't want to think about that stuff or bring it out to the mound with me. I had to think about how I was going to go about beating the Cleveland Indians, not what I would feel after I beat them.

And so I prepared myself to pitch. The first thing I did was study the weather. I like pitching in cool weather, but obviously not so cool that it's hard to sweat or get loose or you can't get enough perspiration on the ball so that it doesn't feel like an ice ball every time you grip it. It was in the fifties at game time. That was fine.

Believe it or not, a big decision was, do I go with one undershirt or two? I went back and forth on this for a while. No decision on pitch selection during the game was any tougher than this! I thought it was comfortable enough to go with one, but cool enough where I might not perspire as much as I needed to.

Finally, I decided two shirts was the way to go. I wore a traditional-type baseball undershirt with blue sleeves, and I pulled on my lucky blue Notre Dame football T-shirt, which Leo had received in the mail from a man who knew of our love for the Fighting Irish. (Leo's love of Notre Dame simply stemmed from the winning tradition, and so it's no surprise Leo's also a big New York Yankees and Boston Celtics fan. In fact, Lou Holtz, the football coach at Notre Dame, has written notes to Leo and me over the years inviting us to stand on the sidelines during a game. Someday we're going to do it.) I've had the shirt for a couple of years, but I probably didn't start wearing it until after the All-Star break of last year. So I'd had a pretty good run with it.

My locker has remained untouched since 1991. The mainstays are a Bart Simpson doll (I love his humor), a four-leaf clover that someone pressed in waxed paper (how can you throw a four-leaf clover away?), and a trophy (I've always liked the look of trophies). As much as I look at it sometimes and say I need to throw all this crap out, I don't want to touch it and disturb anything that might be working well in there.

I've got a few other superstitions, but I don't carry them too far. My biggest superstition is I always chew a piece of Bazooka sugarless bubble gum when I pitch and I always keep an extra piece in my back left-hand pocket. I also never step on the foul lines when I take the field. Other than that, I don't have many other quirks.

In the bull pen that night I was throwing the ball okay, but I had no idea what kind of stuff I had after my session with Leo, who said, "Everything looks great, kid." Sometimes I know, but there have been times when I've thrown terribly in the bull pen and come out and pitched a shutout. Then there have been other times I come out feeling like Nolan Ryan and I get my butt kicked, so I try not to draw any conclusions. The only thing I pay attention to is my location and hopefully the movement on my change-up and that's it.

I knew that I'd warmed up better than I did for Game 2. I knew I was a lot sharper, but I wasn't totally satisfied with what I was bringing out there.

I took the field and started messing around with the mound like I usually do, trying to find that comfortable spot where I can plant my foot. We've done a lot of work on the mound at Fulton County Stadium over the years and we've gotten it to the point where it's pretty comfortable for everyone—where the slope isn't too severe and you can plant your foot safely and effectively.

Before I threw my first warm-up pitch, I looked up to the stands and looked for Carri and my parents, just to make sure they got in okay.

I could really sense the crowd was into it. Maybe David's comments worked in raising their level of excitement, almost like an "Okay, David, we'll show you" kind of thing. If that was it, that's great.

To start the game, I just wanted to get into a good rhythm. If I've had one problem in my career, it's that I've given up a lot of runs in the first inning and then I settle down. I didn't want to dig a hole for our offense so early in the game, particularly against a great hitting team.

Of course, right off the bat, Lofton is up. He had pretty much shown the world what he can do in Game 1 when he reached on an error by Rafael Belliard and proceeded to steal second and third base, leading to a run off Mad Dog.

But my sequence of pitches to Lofton was pretty good. I threw him a couple of change-ups. He didn't get a good swing at the last one and flew out to right field. When I got that first out and had the peace of mind that he wasn't going to be on base, I really started to relax and settle in. Usually in the first inning, I never show the hitter everything I have. I try to establish my fastball and change-up and then gradually show them my curve and slider.

I struck out Omar Vizquel with a change-up and then I got Carlos Baerga with a nice easy roller right back to me.

Mission accomplished! I wanted to leave the mound feeling confident that I had good stuff, and I definitely felt it. It wasn't that the rest of the game was going to be a breeze, but I knew I had the stuff to beat them that night. All I needed to do was keep my concentration level where it was. And if I did that, I was confident I was going to have a good night.

I walked off the mound, took my jacket from one of the clubhouse guys, and took my usual spot on the far side of the bench away from everyone. I could hear Bobby and Leo and the guys clapping their hands and shouting, "Thataway Tommy!"

I pitched to the minimum twelve batters over four innings. I'd walked Albert Belle to lead off the second inning, but Javy Lopez made a great throw to second base and Lemke made a nice tag to catch Belle stealing.

I didn't mind walking Belle twice in the game because he's the one guy you don't want to give anything good to hit to. I pitched him low and away all night, and in the eighth inning, when I struck him out on a change-up that I got him to fish for, the crowd erupted.

Albert was not a crowd favorite in Atlanta or in any other ballpark except Cleveland. Here was a guy who hit fifty home runs and fifty-two doubles during the regular season. He had hit opposite-field homers in Games 4 and 5. I knew I couldn't let him beat me even if I had to walk him.

Through five innings, I had a no-hitter. The crowd sensed that as I came off the mound after striking out Thome for the second time in the game, on an another change-up.

A no-hitter at any time is pretty exciting for a pitcher (I remember pitching a perfect game in American Legion baseball), but in

Game 6 of the World Series? It can put extra pressure on you. But I never got caught up in it. I knew my sole purpose out there was to beat the Cleveland Indians, no matter how many hits I gave up.

And so I didn't feel any great loss, when, in the sixth, Tony Peña finally stuck his bat out and made contact on a change-up low and away. He hit it hard enough to get it over the infield and soft enough to get it in front of the outfield. It was actually an excellent pitch that I would throw him again in that situation. At least the no-hitter possibility was over and done with and now it was up to me not to fall apart.

I got out of the inning pretty easily and we were heading into the bottom of the sixth in a 0–0 game, but one of the most entertaining 0–0 games you'll ever watch.

I was a little worried that we hadn't scored yet. Dennis Martinez, Cleveland's starting pitcher that night, was out of there in the fifth. We squandered a few opportunities against him and I just wondered whether we were letting too many of them waste away.

But David came up to lead off the bottom of the sixth against a pretty tough left-handed pitcher in Jim Poole. David certainly got his justice! He belted a home run to right field, giving us a 1–0 lead!

Not far from the landing spot of David's homer in the right-field bleachers was a sign that seemed to say it all: WE HEAR YA DAVEY.

During the celebration after the game, David, who had tried to soften his comments earlier in the day, said, "I can't tell you how proud I am of the fans here. They proved me wrong. This is what I was trying to get them to do. I wanted them to be so excited they would burst. This is better than anything the Cleveland fans could have showed. I'm proud now that these are my fans. I know I said this [title] was for us [players], but I was wrong. This is for everybody—the players, the team, the fans, and the city. I'm proud of being here and having won."

It really was poetic Justice and you had to feel good for David. His words certainly reflected how we all felt about winning the World Championship and the role the fans played. They showed incredible patience with us through the nineties and they waited for us to improve in the mid-to-late eighties when we were a laughingstock.

I'm thirty years old (twenty-nine at the time of the game) so I haven't waited as long as a lot of players. Some, like the great Ernie Banks, never got to appreciate the feeling of this moment. Yet, when it all began on a baseball field in Billerica, who knew it would come to this?

2

Home at Billerica

THERE ARE CERTAIN DATES I'LL NEVER FORGET. MY WEDDING anniversary, my daughter's birthday, Game 6. Another memorable date is December 17, 1995: Tom Glavine Day in Billerica. I kid you not. It was a clear, cold day, and Dad and I were riding atop a fire engine. Sirens were blaring and a scattering of people were huddled in their winter coats and hats, waving and cheering. I had been in parades before in Atlanta, in 1991 and then again after we won the World Series, but this was on a smaller scale and a more personal affair.

The fire engine slowed and came to a stop at the Billerica Memorial High School gym. Inside, before a marching band, cheerleaders, and an audience that included several of my high school coaches and teachers as well as my beaming parents, the town officials retired my baseball number—15—and presented me with a street sign that read GLAVINEVILLE.

I was overwhelmed by the gesture made by friends and town officials wanting to show their appreciation for my accomplishments and the positive attention I've brought to the town. It's one thing to receive awards from the team or the league, but to be honored by your hometown? It's something I'll never forget.

It was much more meaningful for me to be recognized for my contributions to the community than for what I do on the playing field. Because when my playing days are over, what am I left with if

I don't have friends and people who love and care about me?

The closeness of the community is why I so enjoy returning there for a visit every winter. Carri, Amber, and I live in Alpharetta, Georgia, now, and we love it, but Billerica will always be home. It's a beautiful town with a population of thirty-seven thousand, set in the picturesque Merrimack Valley about twenty-five miles north-west of Boston, with lots of close-knit neighborhoods, some older and some newer. When it snows, which it does often enough, as you can imagine, it becomes as pretty as a Norman Rockwell paint-ing. It's a place I truly didn't appreciate until I left to make my home in Georgia. And it's more than just the weather that makes these two places different. Georgia has its own beauty, but since I grew up in Massachusetts, it has become a part of me as no other place can.

Billerica is also a place where I can escape from championship fever. After winning the World Series, it's sometimes hard to go places in suburban Atlanta or in the city proper and expect to walk around free of attention. When I go home at least I can walk through the malls and maybe some people will recognize me, but not to the extent they do in Atlanta.

I remember Carri and I went over to Jay Howell's house three days after the World Series, and on the way home we needed to stop to get some groceries. I was worried about going to a grocery store near my home because it seemed everyone recognized me, making it difficult to just run a simple errand. I told Jay, who is a good friend after our playing days together, "I don't want to go somewhere where it's going to be a big project. I just want to get some groceries and go home." Jay said, "No problem. Nobody will recognize you at Kroger's."

Well, he was wrong. From the time I walked into the store to the time I escaped, an hour and a half had passed! I was signing auto-graphs for everyone in the store. Believe me when I say it's a great feeling that there are folks in Atlanta and through the South, and really, all over this country, who are Braves fans. I'd rather have it that way than the way it used to be in the late eighties when nobody cared about the Braves. It makes me feel good. The fans deserve my time and my attention and I'm more than willing to sign an auto-graph or just say hello. It's part of the responsibility you take on when you sign a contract and you put on a uniform and play before more than fifty thousand fans and millions of viewers on superstation TBS almost every night.

But when I go home to Billerica, I can escape that for a while and just relax.

In fact, when I do visit my family around Christmas, I do little except enjoy their company. My parents still live in the house we grew up in on Treble Cove Road, a great neighborhood of Cape- and ranch-style homes that reflect the time period in which they were built. Our house was built by Dad, who has spent his entire life in the construction business, and to this day still runs and operates Fred Glavine Construction.

Mom makes her special holiday dishes—I usually have her unbelievable veal Parmesan a couple of times during a weeklong visit—which I wolf down. It's great when the whole family is around at the same time, but because of schedules it's not easy to get everyone—my brothers, Fred and Mike, and my sister, Debbie, and her family—all together.

Mike is younger and now a first baseman in the Cleveland Indians organization. He's blossoming into a very big, strong player, and from what I'm told, he has the potential to be quite a power hitter. He has the size for it—he's got a couple of inches and thirty pounds on me. I regret that I haven't been able to see him play much, but I just hope I can live up to his image of me as a sports hero. It would be great to see Mike, who was quite a baseball and hockey star in Billerica in his own right, rise and eventually make it to The Show. To play against him would be even better.

My sister, Debbie, is married and still lives in Billerica. My parents often say that she's the one who keeps our family together, and truer words couldn't be spoken. She organizes a lot of our family get-togethers and makes sure that everyone is aware of what others in the family are doing. She's a bit of a worrywart in some ways, concerned whether everybody's all right. My older brother, Fred, whom I looked up to as a young kid because of his athletic ability and the direction he gave me, lives in the Atlanta area and works as a freelance TV producer for TBS, so I get to see him, anyway. But having everybody together is special. We've always been a close, loving family.

My parents and I have tried to keep our relationship the same as it ever was. They have insisted that their lives not change as a result of my good fortune. The house is virtually unchanged—except for the family room I added a couple of years ago, which was the least I could do for Dad, who never wanted anything from me after all he and Mom did.

We used to have this mudroom/porch, closed in at the front of the house, the room where you'd enter the house and take off your shoes and coat, and Dad kept spending more and more time in there. He moved his office into the little room, and it also seemed to be the place where everyone gathered, where you'd pull up a chair and shoot the breeze. Eventually, Dad moved his TV in there, and then the couch and his favorite chair. Dad's construction friends would tease me when I came home in the winter: "When are you going to build him a room?" Well, I figured, why not? So, I built him one and I bought him a big-screen TV so he could watch my games.

I had a running joke with Gerry Callahan of *Sports Illustrated,* who grew up in nearby Chelmsford, which was actually our arch-rival. When he'd see me during the postseason he'd always say, "How's the porch coming?" Well, Gerry, the porch is done.

Dad has been such a big influence on me as a person and in my professional career that to this day when people ask me who my idol is, I say Fred Senior. As I get older and understand what parenting is all about, I appreciate my parents more and more.

As kids we never lacked for anything. This, for sure, is not the story of a kid who grew up in the poor part of town and rose from poverty to become famous. We lived in a close-knit neighborhood. We even used to vacation with our neighbors, the Condons, who are like a second family to us. To this day, my parents still carry on the tradition, which has lasted more than twenty years.

On the Fourth of July we'd always have a block party, closing off our section of the street, and have major barbecues, play all sorts of games, and shoot off fireworks.

We certainly weren't rich, but Mom and Dad provided everything their four children needed growing up. If I needed new cleats or new skates or a new glove, I got them. There were times we couldn't afford some of the luxury items, like the latest state-of-the-art brand-name skates or sticks or the popular baseball glove, but I didn't care.

Dad was a hardworking, straightforward guy. While he wasn't a yeller and never got real upset, he knew how he wanted things done in the house and how we should act. There was never a problem with miscommunication because we all understood what he meant. And when Dad was working, Mom was just as forceful and we respected her the same.

As long as we did well in school, we could play sports. Dad's rule was that before I did anything else after school, I had to get my homework done. There were plenty of times when about a dozen neighborhood kids would hang around the kitchen waiting for me to finish my homework so I could go out and play street hockey. I rarely skipped out without finishing my homework first.

Another rule was, "If you want to play sports, I'll take you wherever you want to go as long as you remain committed." Dad was a great athlete himself, a star high school football player at Billerica, yet he never pushed sports on us. One of the reasons I never played football was that Dad had developed physical problems—such as arthritis in his fingers—as a result of his playing. It was difficult to choose not to play because the coaches wanted my decent southpaw arm on their team.

When Dad came to games—and that was often if not all the time—he sat quietly cheering for me. Neither of my parents were the hollering type. They never heckled or got into shouting matches with the other parents or anything like that. Though if I was getting into a fight in a hockey game, once in a while I'd hear my mom yell, "Knock it off!" She absolutely forbid me to fight, saying, "If you fight, you won't play."

She was always there, too. Even if she was sick she'd find a way to make it to the game, and that was quite a trick for them because Fred was involved in baseball and soccer when he was in high school and Mike was starting to get into hockey and baseball, too. I think she felt that if something ever happened to me and she wasn't there, she couldn't live with herself. Mom never pushed anything on me except my homework. She did the same with my brothers and sister. My lasting memories of her, and I appreciate this more and more as I get deeper into parenthood, is that she was always there to see me start the day off with a good breakfast and to greet me when I came home from school. When I think of friends who come from broken families, I feel fortunate to have Mom and Dad.

One summer after my junior year in high school, and then for the first couple of off-seasons after I'd signed a pro contract, I worked for Dad's company. We poured house foundations and built pools. It was good, tough work, and probably not ideal for a pitcher because I would have to do things like carry a seventy-pound concrete form of part of a foundation across a plank twelve feet in the air—but I was careful. I would take precautions like lifting with my legs so I wouldn't throw out my back or have a hernia problem, and I made sure I didn't lift things of great weight with my left shoulder. I'd seen enough of Dad's construction accidents over the years.

While I didn't much like the hard work, it was neat to watch the building of a house from the ground up. I marveled at the hardness and precision of the work and how my father was able to do this for as long as he did. It also made me realize it wasn't for me. I didn't want to do this the rest of my life, and the insight spurred me to work extra hard on my baseball career to ensure I didn't have to go back and help run the family business.

What bothers me a lot is the misconception that athletes are born with a silver spoon in their mouth. I suppose some were. But that's not true for a lot of guys and that's not true for me. I wasn't afraid to get dirty and work hard even in the middle of January with the temperature ten below zero. When I was a senior in high school, I worked at the high school hockey rink on the weekends. It was only thirty dollars a week, but it was extra money for the movies or for lunch or something. It kept me from having to ask my parents for money all the time.

There are players like Mike Piazza, whose father is a multimillionaire businessman (and Mike probably never had to work a day in his life), but he loved the game and through hard work has become one of the best hitters in baseball. Not bad for a sixty-second-round pick.

And I'll tell you another thing: traveling on buses in the minor leagues for fifteen hours going from city to city and playing baseball in the middle of summer in a southern town with the temperature 120 degrees is no day at the beach either. It didn't surprise me to hear that Michael Jordan bought his team a new bus with all the amenities. Of course, that would never happen otherwise on the money you make in the minors.

There's a lot of frustration and hard work players have to go through before they make it. Most never do. You usually never hear about that, though. Sometimes people just see the glamorous side of being a professional athlete and they wind up resenting the player because he makes a lot of money. They fail to see what he had to do to get there.

Dad and Mom did more than drive me to games and give me work. They were also helpful in giving advice on how I played the game. Always a low-key kid, I was never flashy or anything like that, more serious and respectful. That's the way I was brought up to play and act. Because Dad had been an athlete—he also played basketball at Billerica High—and really understood sports, he was able to spot some things I was doing wrong. But he never said anything right away. He would always wait three or four games, feeling I might be able to figure it out for myself. And if I didn't, he'd say, "Maybe you should try doing it this way." Sometimes I acted like I wasn't listening, because how would it look in front of all my friends to acknowledge what he said? But I was. I would usually try what he said, and if it didn't work, at least he knew I was listening to him.

Even though I was successful at sports, Dad never told me I was a special athlete. I suppose it was his way of motivating me and keeping my head from swelling. He would always pipe up and say sternly, "I don't care how good you think you are, there's always someone out there who is better." And for a kid growing up in Massachusetts playing only twenty baseball games a year when there are kids in Florida and California playing sixty to eighty games a year, my dad's comments made a lot of sense. That motivated me to try harder so I could get to the level of those kids.

I guess I knew I was pretty good because every jump I made I was one of the youngest kids on the team. I once had a Little League coach, Jim Bowley, who told my dad and me when I was about nine years old, "One day I'm going to be watching you play ball in the major leagues!" At the time I said, "Sure, whatever." Dad wouldn't even blink when someone said that, or he sure wouldn't show how happy or proud he was. He probably believed that becoming a professional athlete was a long shot and he wanted me to prepare for something else in life. That's why he stressed good grades so much.

I've heard people comment that I'm one of the most competitive people they've ever seen on the field. I think that's a result of a couple of things. For one, most of the kids in the neighborhood were older, so if I wanted to play, it had to be at their level. And two, Mom and Dad were pretty competitive (Mom was also an athlete in high school), and I guess some of that rubbed off on me.

I should point out that I'm not just talking about baseball. I played hockey from the time I was five years old. Long before I learned how to throw a curveball, I learned to skate. Hockey was my first love.

3

I Could've Played with Wayne Gretzky

HOCKEY WAS AS MUCH A PART OF GROWING UP IN BILLERICA as going to church every Sunday. As with most other kids, as soon as I was old enough my parents bought me skates and brought me to the rink to skate. Or I'd go over to the pond down the street or to Nuttings Lake. I always had a hockey stick in my hand, whether it was for ice hockey or the many street games on the weekends from early morning until darkness.

I went to games at the Hallenborg Rink to watch Billerica High playing Chelmsford, our archrival. Or I'd watch Chelmsford against another pretty hot rival, Austin Prep or Acton-Boxborough. Whenever those games were played, you always saw a little extra fighting, more fans, and more excitement.

That's the first real exposure I had to a rivalry. And by the time I started playing against Chelmsford, it was THE GAME. Everybody would come. Standing-room-only crowds. The play was spirited. Beating Chelmsford usually meant winning the Merrimack Valley Conference and going to face off somewhere down the road in the state hockey tournament. These intense rivalry games were some of the most memorable of my youth.

In a February 20, 1984, game, I got off the quickest goal I ever scored. It was early in the game and the face-off was in the Chelms-ford end. I played center and I was facing off against Jon Morris, who was always battling me for the top scorer spot. As soon as the ref dropped the puck, I snared the puck and shot it in one motion and it flew past their goalie. We took a 1–0 lead and went on to win 4–0.

I remember their coach, Jack Fletcher, saying afterward, "He's unbelievably quick. I've never seen anyone do that to Jon. He's the class of the league."

Everyone always made a lot of my rivalry with Jon Morris, but I never felt it was me against him. I got to know him a lot during our time together at Hockey Night at the Boston Garden, which was a summer program for the top high school players. We got along very well and I admired him and we were supposed to go to the Univer-sity of Lowell together. He was a great player and I enjoy playing against players who challenge me and elevate my game. I feel that way now in baseball whenever I face a great hitter like Barry Bonds or Tony Gwynn.

I mentioned before that hockey was my first love. The game is exciting, in constant movement. As soon as I stepped onto the ice for my shift there was instant activity. As a young kid playing center field I remember Mom yelling out, "Keep your head in the game!" after she spotted me picking daisies between pitches. I think I ulti-mately became a pitcher because I had the ball and could control the tempo of the game.

Even though I was a pretty good center iceman with a nice shot, I always wanted to be a goalie, but when I first started skating, the team I was trying out for already had one. So I became a forward. The rage then was Phil Esposito, who wore number 7. So I wore number 7. I was definitely more of a hockey fan than a baseball fan. More Bruins than Red Sox. The Bruins had Bobby Orr, the greatest hockey player of all time, Espo, Ken Hodge, Wayne Cashman, and all those colorful players. I wouldn't say I tried to emulate them, but they inspired me to improve my game.

We had a long schedule in Billerica Youth Hockey—probably close to a hundred games a year. Obviously, my hockey skills were able to develop pretty quickly. I became a decent player, good enough to be a *Boston Globe* All-Scholastic a couple of years in high school, and I also won the second annual John Carlton Memorial Award, which the Boston Bruins give to the high school senior who combines exceptional hockey skills with academics. I was fifty-eight out of 538 students in my senior class at Billerica High. The award was a thrill because it was presented during a game at the old Boston Garden with all the Celtics and Bruins banners hanging high in the rafters.

I led Eastern Massachusetts in scoring as a senior, with forty-four goals and forty-one assists. My hockey career was punctuated by a few six-goal games. As Dad would say, "Not the flashiest kid on the ice, but at the end of the game you'd look at the stat sheet and he'd done most of the scoring."

I was named the Merrimack Valley Conference Most Valuable Player. I remember after receiving the award, my coach, Roger Richard, said to the *Boston Globe,* "Tom is consistently being watched by opponents, yet he has not taken a penalty this year and has only four penalties in his career. He is the most unselfish player I ever coached."

That was a nice thing for the coach to say. I loved my hockey experience in high school and Coach Richard was a big reason why. We lost in the semifinals of the Division I state hockey tournament two years in a row, but that wasn't important. I got to play with extraordinarily talented hockey players and participated two years in what we called the Super Series against the best high school players from Minnesota.

The first year of the series was played in Billerica. The Minnesota team was a huge favorite, but we beat them 14–3 in the first game, outshooting them 72–23. We won the second and third games, 6–2 and 8–0. Tom Barrasso, who played at Acton-Boxborough and went on to become one of the best goalies in the NHL, came up big for us. Barrasso and Dave Jensen, who was a wing on our team, were number one picks in the NHL. The second year we played in Bloomington, Minnesota, and it was the first time I'd ever flown on an airplane and the first time I'd ever been gone from home for any length of time. We were sluggish in the first couple of games but we won the series. I scored twenty-two points in three games and played on a line with Ken Hodge Jr., who went on to play in the NHL, and Mike Kelfer, drafted by the New Jersey Devils.

When I look back on all of the great players I played against who went on to the NHL—guys like Barrasso, Kevin Stevens, Steve Heinze, Steve Leach, Ken Hodge, and Don Sweeney—I wonder how far I would have gone.

I thought about it even more around the time that Wayne Gretzky was traded from the Edmonton Oilers to the Los Angeles Kings. I thought, "I could have played with 'the Great One' if I had chosen hockey." It was a thrill for me to meet "the Great One" after the 1992 World Series. He had come to watch Game 6, and meeting him was a small consolation for losing the World Series.

Once a Toronto newspaper printed a scouting report on me by some unnamed scout, and it was later reprinted in *Sports Illustrated.* On the third page, the following opinions about my talents appeared: "Good skating ability . . . long stride with good balance . . . good acceleration . . . excellent scorer, smart around the net . . . has several moves and can finish off . . . excellent slap and wrist shots with a quick release . . . tough and durable, will not be intimidated . . . excellent competitor." The scout ranked me number 56 out of 240 draft-age hockey players. Not bad.

I may well have never met this scout because when I was playing hockey in high school, I didn't notice or talk to the scouts like I did in baseball. They usually hid in the rink somewhere, so I had no idea they were around. Later, I found out they did talk to my parents a lot, trying to get them to reveal what sport I was going to play. I knew in order to make it in the NHL, I would have had to gain some weight and strength. Who knows?

One of the most thrilling moments for me was coming home after I'd won the Cy Young Award in 1991. My agent, the late Bob Woolf, set up a skate with the Bruins during practice.

That whole off-season was so hectic. It was grueling, traveling a lot doing banquets and talk shows and making personal appearances at charity events. Bob decided I needed a little relief and set up a little practice session for me. Well, I was pretty excited, but I hadn't put on equipment and skated in years. I was out there with the Bruins, while Dad watched from the stands getting a big kick out of it. It was fun gripping that stick again and taking a few shots, though it was strange to put on all the equipment, some that I never knew existed and had been invented since the time I played hockey. My legs didn't feel that great, but I figured that would happen, not having been on the ice for a long time. Nonetheless, it was a blast. I never put on the skates again, though every now and then I get the urge.

One thing I have to emphasize about my youth sports experience: It was the best. I had coaches who wanted the kids to have fun. Mr. Bowley was that way in Little League baseball and when I got to Senior League—where, by the way, I played for the Pirates, Cardinals, and Braves—Coach Art Streck was also incredibly loose.

The great thing is they knew the fundamentals of the game and how to teach them. But winning or losing wasn't a top priority. For them—and this is the way I feel kids should be taught—you teach kids to do their best, to compete their hardest, and if you win, great, if you lose, so what? I know so many people I've talked to over the years who tell me, "I didn't have a good time playing sports growing up because the coach took it all so seriously." Great. Then why play? There are so few of us who ever make it in professional sports that the attitude should be, have fun, and if you're good enough to make it, you will based on your talent. At least come away with everlasting memories you can share with your children or grandchildren.

When I go out and speak to kids in schools or at clinics, I tell these kids the same thing my dad told me: "The chance of making it is a long shot." I don't want to shatter anyone's hopes because you should always strive for your dream. But I stress trying to be a well-rounded person, and part of that is being an educated person. I tell kids to try and get the most out of their schoolwork and absorb as much as they can so they can be as versatile as possible and have choices when they need to get into the workplace.

Nothing bothers me more than when I read about a college athlete who can't read or write. I ask myself how that can happen. I took advantage of school as a place to learn. I was a good athlete, so I probably could have joked my way through school and focused on my athletics, but I didn't go that route. The programs that were in place for me in high school allowed me to get accepted to some pretty prestigious universities. And like I said earlier, I had to keep my grades up to play. I enjoyed school. I loved my English and health classes, in particular, and of course I loved taking part in gym. The only class I dreaded was physics, but I guess I'm not alone there.

There are kids I've known over the years—and I won't mention names—who were good athletes but never paid attention to their work and now they're struggling through life.

It sickens me that some of the big powerhouse football schools don't demand that their athletes maintain a fairly high grade point average. It's always bothered me that, sure, you make the choice to go to college sometimes based on an athletic scholarship. But your number one priority should be on the education, not the athletics. Until we change that emphasis in the universities, it's going to stay a pretty screwed-up system.

I was at baseball practice on June 9, 1984, when Rogie Vachon, the general manager of the Los Angeles Kings, who was at the National Hockey League draft at the Montreal Forum, called my house and told my mom they had drafted me in the fourth round. I was the sixty-ninth player taken, sixty-eight slots behind Mario LeMieux.

I guess some of the luster of being drafted by a professional hockey team had gone. If I'd been taken in the first or second round, or if the Boston Bruins had drafted me, I guess I might have been a little more excited. Don't get me wrong, being drafted by an NHL team is a great honor.

But by this time I'd become a pretty good high school baseball pitcher. I was left-handed, which scouts preferred. Five days earlier, I'd been taken in the second round by the Atlanta Braves, and before that I'd signed a letter of intent to the University of Lowell. It was close to home and they were pretty good about letting me play both baseball and hockey at a Division I program.

At this point, though, the state high school baseball tournament occupied nearly all of my time and attention. What a bad time to focus on my future!

I'd been recruited heavily to play hockey at several schools in the Northeast, with scholarship offers from RPI, an excellent school and hockey program, the University of New Hampshire, Boston College, and Boston University. I was trying hard to get my SAT scores up because I really wanted to attend Harvard. In a strange sort of way I'm glad it didn't work out because who knows how my life would have changed if I had gone that route? I might have been a president of a company right now rather than playing for the Atlanta Braves, which I guess wouldn't be so bad. But I'll take what I have now, thank you.

Yale was interested, too. My mom still tells the story of how I went to Yale for a baseball tournament my senior year and when I was driving back up after the game I said, "I'm definitely not going to school anywhere down there. You and Dad would never get to see me play. Dad wouldn't be able to get out of work in time to watch me, never mind that it is one of the most prestigious schools in the country!" Staying close to home meant being able to go home when I wanted and having the support of my family in the stands.

The Kings thought I was going to school, so they didn't bother making an offer. They told Mom that if I changed my mind, they'd be waiting for me. Meanwhile, they were going to keep their eye on me and watch my progress.

The Kings actually called me back the same day I was signed by the Braves in late June of that year. They were disappointed. Mr. Vachon was actually a little annoyed that we hadn't told him I was playing baseball, telling my mother, "We're going to keep an eye on him. In a few years he'll be playing for us."

He probably thought I would change my mind and go back to hockey after I tried pro ball, and maybe there were times along the way I felt that way, but never seriously.

Yet my hockey career is a big part of who I am today. As a sport, it's totally different from baseball, but it gave me the mental and physical toughness and concentration I apply to baseball. The same mind-set it took when I was digging for the puck in the corner while trying to hold off an opponent from getting it is basically what it takes when I'm up against a hitter. Early in my baseball career, and even now occasionally, I'd be facing a tough hitter and I'd think, "I wish I could just slam this guy into the boards!"

I felt sad about missing out on college and ULowell because I was looking forward to being a student-athlete, with a chance to play two sports at a higher level. It's always been unique for an athlete to play two sports well at a high level, and I think there was a lot of ego gratification involved as well. Not to mention that the people I dealt with at Lowell were great to me.

At around the same time, I invited the ULowell recruiters to my house and informed them of my decision to sign with the Braves.

The interesting aspect of my baseball/hockey dilemma was that I was the type of kid who would play whatever sport was in season. As soon as hockey was over, I didn't lace up the skates again because it was time for baseball. I grew up with kids who played hockey from the time they were five years old, played it year-round, and by the time they got to high school they were burned out. I made sure that wouldn't happen to me, turning down the invitations I always received for camps and tournaments.

I started playing baseball when I was eight years old as a left-handed third baseman and played some center field. I was ten or so when I started pitching, and then it was because I could throw the ball harder than anyone, right by the batter—if I knew where the ball was going.

Even when I was young, Dad taught me the importance of having an off-speed pitch. That's what he told me right before a play-off game in the Lou Gehrig League when I was about twelve years old.

I started this game in center field, but in the final inning, we were ahead by one run, and the coach told me to come in and pitch. There were two on and nobody out. I struck out the first kid, popped up the next one, and then I had two strikes on two fastballs to the third batter. One pitch away. This sounds familiar to Red Sox fans.

Suddenly I remembered what my dad said: "Take something off it!" I shook off the catcher twice. Obviously, he wanted me to throw a fastball because nobody could hit it, but I took something off it. What a mistake! The change-up was nothing more than a slow fastball and the kid hit it for a double and it scored both runs and we lost the game! It wasn't funny then, but it's something Dad and I kid about even today.

Now I understand what he was trying to say, and my change-up is a bit more successful.

Our high school was known more for its hockey program than its baseball program, so it was quite an accomplishment in my junior year for us to get to the Eastern Massachusetts state final against Brockton, the biggest high school east of the Mississippi River back then. It's a South Shore town steeped in sports tradition, the home of former heavyweight boxing champion Rocky Marciano; middleweight champion Marvin Hagler; football star Ken McAfee, who had a great career with Notre Dame and the San Francisco 49ers; and Greg McMurtry, who was a heck of a baseball player and drafted number one by the Red Sox in 1986, but who signed with the University of Michigan and went on to play wide receiver for the New England Patriots and the Chicago Bears.

Let me stop and say right here that the Eastern Massachusetts state final is in the top five all-time games that I participated in. (As we go along I'll give you the other four.)

Why was it so special? In the tenth inning I went out to play center field after pitching nine scoreless innings in a 0–0 game. In the eleventh inning, the first ball hit to me was a single, and it looked as if it were going to score their winning run. The runner was at second base, one out, when I charged the ball and fielded it. At this point, the runner, the nephew of the late Marciano, was heading around third base. In a seamless flow, I fielded it and threw it to home plate. I remember the runner already had his arms up in the air with a "We won!" gesture! He was running hard, but I hit the catcher on the fly and he was looking at the runner coming in. We had him by fifteen feet! People close to the action saw the runner's expression turn from pure happiness to "Oh, my God, I'm out!" The game, which was held in Rockland, Massachusetts, just ten miles or so from Brockton, stunned the partisan Brockton crowd.

To be able to pitch nine innings, then go to center field and make a throw like that may have been one of the best shows of athleticism in my career.

To top it off, in the thirteenth inning, I singled to lead off the inning and eventually scored the winning run! We won the Eastern Massachusetts championship!

My high school coach, John Sidorovich, was a terrific coach. He stressed being competitive yet having fun at the same time. He pumped me up all the time and made me feel like I was the greatest pitcher on earth and that nobody could hit me. He instilled an attitude in me that I was a good player and that I could succeed at this level and then go up to the next level at either college or the pros.

He also managed to deal with all of the attention I was attracting from scouts in my junior and senior years. He spent a lot of his time speaking with them before and after games so I'd be able to play and just sneak off afterward and do things teenagers did then, like go to the movies with my girlfriend or to the mall and hang around with my friends. Honestly, with sports and school taking up such a huge hunk of time, I didn't have a lot of free time to do much else. I didn't have hobbies, per se, except following the local professional sports teams.

While I didn't notice the scouts at all in hockey, I noticed every one of the scouts at my baseball games. They started coming around my junior year, although my parents say they started noticing them when I was thirteen years old. They'd always be behind the backstop with a radar gun, so I always tried to throw a little extra harder for them, knowing they were back there. I remember at first I had kind of an uneasy feeling, but I got used to it. I noticed, too, that every time I pitched there'd be more and more people coming to our games, and I guess that was a sign they were coming to watch me, which put even more pressure on me.

John never abused my arm. There were times we'd be faced with a big game but he wouldn't use me because I'd pitched two days earlier. He always said, "I'm not going to jeopardize your career for one game." What he did has meant a lot to me. I must also say that in the years since, my pitching coaches along the way have protected my arm as well, keeping me to between 100 and 120 pitches and seven to nine innings. There's never been the abuse you see sometimes in other organizations, where guys are constantly kept out there for 130 or 140 pitches and suddenly they develop arm problems and their careers are never the same.

One side note to my high school baseball career: Our second baseman's name was Gary DiSarcina. Yeah, the same Gary DiSarcina who plays shortstop and hit .307 for the California Angels in 1995. You'll note that when the Angels lost Gary to a thumb injury on August 19, they started to lose their big lead in the American League West to the Seattle Mariners, which is proof positive of how valuable a player he is.

Back then, I probably wouldn't have said to you that Gary was going to be a big leaguer. He was a tall, lanky kid. A great fielder. But he didn't seem to have the power in his bat that he'd eventually show at the University of Massachusetts and then after he joined the Angels organization. But Gary was the perfect example of the late-blooming New England player.

He was great to have behind me in the field because I threw a lot of ground balls and he'd scoop them up out there. Though Gary's best position was shortstop, Coach Sidorovich used him at second base when I pitched because I threw so hard that most of the right-handed batters I faced couldn't get around on my fastball and weren't able to pull the ball, so most of the groundouts went to the right side of the field. I'm happy Gary has made it. It gives me a great sense of pride to see another kid from Billerica in the major leagues. His brother Glenn, an excellent shortstop in the Chicago White Sox organization, also came through Billerica and hopefully we'll see him in the majors some day.

I certainly didn't always win. I pitched a few no-hitters—a perfect game in American Legion baseball—and I struck out eighteen once in a tournament game. Sometimes I'd strike out twelve and walk twelve. I threw pretty hard and that was my meal ticket to professional baseball.

And as my stock began to rise around the country, my senior year became incredibly hectic. It got to the point where my mom was my defense. She would protect me from everyone—the college teams, the scouts from the pro teams—who was calling trying to get a piece of me. I guess in a way it was flattering, but if I had to fill out another form or write another essay, I was going to throw up.

The teams I spoke to the most were the Milwaukee Brewers and the Toronto Blue Jays. The Red Sox were also at the games, but for some reason—I've been told they thought I was going to play hockey—they didn't draft me and that was one of my first disappointments.

I know they picked a catcher, John Marzano, from Temple University in the first round. Maybe they didn't have me as highly rated as the Braves, who really surprised me with their pick. I hadn't seen the Braves at too many of my games, but to be picked in the second round was flattering. A lot of teams had me projected as a first-rounder, but many shied away because they thought I was going to play hockey.

The Red Sox were obviously my first choice. I didn't spend too much time at Fenway as a kid, maybe twice a year. But it was quite a highlight. My most vivid memory was of watching Dwight Evans take outfield practice, because I was so focused on the way people threw a baseball that to watch Evans throw was something spectacular and out of the ordinary to me. I'd watch him time after time picking up the ball and throwing it back to the infield. I was taken aback by the strength, accuracy, and velocity of his throws.

I had been a Red Sox fan for so long and had my heart broken by the World Series loss in 1975 to the Big Red Machine and the one-game play-off loss to the Yankees in 1978 when Bucky Dent sent a Mike Torrez pitch over the Green Monster. I even rooted for them in the '86 World Series when I was in the minors. To see Bill Buckner miss that ground ball killed me.

So yeah, there was a little disappointment in not being drafted by the Red Sox. Not that I'm complaining.

The Braves' New England scout, Tony DeMacio (now working for the Chicago Cubs), had scouted me, and after I was drafted by the Braves that first week in June, he and Paul Snyder, the Braves' scouting director, came to our house on a Saturday to see if they could close the deal.

Dad decided to handle the negotiations himself, though I think there was some advice from agent Bob Woolf, who called us out of the blue and was helpful in pointing out how the negotiating game was played. But Dad handled the negotiations like a pro. They offered us a $60,000 bonus—which was the going rate for a second-round pick—after trying to sell us on the Braves organization and the great Braves players who had created a great tradition: Henry Aaron, Eddie Matthews, and Warren Spahn. He told us how I would have the best instruction in the game and how the Braves were heading for better things.

Dad tells the rest of the story better than I can:

> I was sitting in my favorite chair in the kitchen when I received the offer. Instead of responding, I just looked out through the window for a while. I looked back at Mr. Snyder and Mr. DeMacio and said, "I guess Tommy will be going to school." They asked me to think about it while they walked around the neighborhood and I said that wouldn't be necessary and I repeated, "Tommy will be going to school." They asked when they could get back to me and I said "next Saturday." They said, "Oh no, we'll get back to you sooner." They called back a couple of days later and they offered Tommy $80,000 and we took it.

That extra money was important because if the career didn't work out after a couple of years, we would have the money to go to school.

I was at a party with some friends, celebrating our graduation from high school, when Dad called and told me he had accepted their offer. I was happy that it was finally over and that the decision had been made. I knew what we were looking for and if we got it, I'd given the okay to accept it. I came home from the party pretty excited and thanked Dad for the job he'd done. Soon the phone started ringing off the hook, mostly the local media calling to ask if we had signed. It was a big day.

Mr. Snyder said of the talks later: "I thought we were going to lose Tommy to hockey. That was always our fear when you have a multisport star like that who has many options. But we were fortunate to seal the deal and he's lived up 100 percent to the expectations we had of him that day in 1984. It's very rare to be that right about a kid that age. He just had something special about him."

That something *wasn't* the courage to leave home.

Sweating It Out in the Minors

ON JUNE 27, 1984, MY FAMILY DROVE ME TO LOGAN AIRPORT, A trip that would forever change my life. I was leaving home to join the Bradenton Braves. I was eighteen years old, just a few weeks after graduating high school.

Mom, Dad, and Debbie followed me to the gate, where we talked and had some of the most uncomfortable moments I'd ever experienced. Dad was quiet and outwardly accepted my going off to become a man, so to speak, but I knew inside he was hurting saying good-bye to his boy, knowing what we meant to each other.

Mom looked like she was going to cry, and I could tell, without her having to say a word, everything she was feeling and thinking. Her son was leaving home, and after years of watching over me, making sure I had everything, this moment had to sting. They gave me a little talk about remembering the things they'd taught me, and to choose my friends carefully. In other words, "Don't do anything stupid just because you're away from home."

And Debbie, well, she was crying uncontrollably. She was pretty bummed out by the whole thing and I was bummed out that I was leaving her. Everyone should have a sister like Debbie, who really looked out for me and cared about me. In so many ways she was like a second mother. She was there to pat me on the back when I did well and cheered and rooted for me every step of the way. She always made me believe I was the best and that I'd be something. Finally, before I reached the point where I could no longer speak and before I started to cry, I just boarded the plane and never looked back. If I had, I would have turned around and gone home with them.

My flight connected in—appropriately enough—Atlanta, and there I met Eddie Matthews. Not THE Eddie Mathews. But this Eddie Matthews turned out to be one of my best friends on the team that year. He was a higher-round draft pick out of a college in Illinois, and we wound up sitting together on the short flight to the Sarasota airport, which is no more than twenty minutes south of Bradenton.

We had a lot of the same concerns and apprehensions, things like how grueling the camp would be physically and mentally and the demands on us to perform well right away. It was nice to be able to vent those thoughts with someone in the same boat, especially after the emotional scene at the airport, which was still fresh in my mind.

Upon landing, I was greeted by a smaller, forty-something Hispanic fellow (he reminded me a little bit of Rafael Belliard) named Pedro Gonzalez, who turned out to be my manager. He is currently the general manager of the Braves' Dominican Summer League team in San Pedro de Marcoris, a town that has produced some of the greatest Dominican talent.

He drove us to the spring training complex, Pirate City, which the Pittsburgh Pirates loaned to the Braves for the Gulf Coast League season. Along the way, Pedro, who spoke with an accent, explained the daily schedule to us and stressed being punctual. Tardiness would not be tolerated, he said. It was all interesting and new, and much of the remainder of the time was spent in small talk about where we were from.

When we got there and were brought to the dorm and mingled with the rest of the players, I was a little surprised to not hear too many speaking English and I discovered that most of the young players were Latin American. The Gulf Coast League, it turned out, was standard for high-school-aged draftees and younger players coming from Latin America. "What am I getting myself into?" I wondered.

I'd never been exposed to players from different cultures, and for a moment it was a little scary, but I got to know everybody and came to find out they were in the same boat. In many ways it was harder for them because many of them couldn't speak English and Pedro had the task of having to teach them a new language as well as how to play.

The dormitory room was fifteen by twenty with a bathroom and two bunk beds. One of my roommates was Mark Lemke. Mark and I hit it off right away and to this day we're the best of friends. Drafted in the twenty-fifth round in the June 1983 draft, Mark was from Utica, New York, so I was relieved to find someone from almost the same neck of the woods who could relate to even the simplest things like cold weather. He had played in Bradenton for fifty-three games in '83, then started the 1984 season at Anderson, South Carolina. But he hit .149 and was sent back to Bradenton. That wasn't so great for Mark, but it was great for me because I gained a friend who'd already played at Bradenton and could show me the ropes such as where to eat and where to go for entertainment, and just how things were done around the organization.

Mark is quiet, which could be misinterpreted as being unfriendly, but once you get to know him he's a terrific guy. He might not have the most talent in the world, but he busts his butt for you every night. As a pitcher, you want someone like him behind you, someone who's extremely competitive and hard on himself, someone who expects to hit .300 every year and doesn't tolerate errors. When we won it all eleven years later, we didn't have to say anything to each other. I knew exactly what he was feeling and vice versa.

When I finally settled in, I actually didn't have too bad of a time. I was making $600 a month and got breakfast and dinner free at Morrison's Cafeteria, a chain restaurant the team had worked out a meal deal with. The rooms were equipped with air-conditioning and a little TV, but no phone. Somehow I'd envisioned something a little more elaborate. Maybe like a lot people, I had misconceptions about how glamorous professional baseball is supposed to be—I thought we'd be staying at a fancy hotel and that everyone would be doing stuff for you. But it was nothing like that. You had to do things for yourself. I still felt the stress that stemmed from being away from home for the first time, but the combination of getting to know Mark and Eddie and getting into the routine of practices and game preparation put me more at ease.

Curfew was 11:00 P.M. and Pedro made bed checks, which wasn't that onerous as it gave you the sense that someone was looking out after you.

Another player I met was Drew Denson, the Braves' number one pick. From everything I saw he deserved to be the first guy taken, particularly with the great start to his career, and he had great tools. An awesome hitter with strength, it certainly looked to me like he was going to be a major league player, but whether because of injuries or a lack of opportunity, Drew never got his chance. He hit .277 with eighteen homers and sixty-nine RBIs for Indianapolis of the Cincinnati chain in 1995. Drew wasn't the first or last prospect to fall into a trap like that. Being the second-round pick, I felt pressure—mostly from myself—to perform right away. I had received one of the highest bonuses given for a second-round pick, so I wanted to show everyone I was worth it. And maybe I wanted to prove to myself that I could make it, that I belonged.

The season had already begun by the time I got there, so I didn't have much time to practice—maybe a week—before they threw me out there for my first start. I held my own over the two innings I worked, even though I was a nervous wreck and trying to throw the ball through the catcher to impress people. My curveball was a little off, but my fastball was decent and I spotted it well. It was a relief to get over that hump, to pass the test.

It took me a little longer to adapt to the intense heat down there. Midsummer, for instance, I was pitching in a game against the Clear-water Phillies, and as I walked off the mound someone kept yelling, "Tommy! Tommy!" But I looked through him and kept walking. He called me again, "Tommy! Tommy!" I looked up and saw the person and kept walking. Well, the person I was ignoring was my brother Mike! And beside him was my whole family, who had come down from Billerica to surprise me, as they would now and then throughout my minor league career. It was a weird experience looking at someone I knew and loved yet being unable to recognize him.

I was annoyed at myself for letting the heat get to me like that. I didn't see myself as a Hulk Hogan or something, but thought I was strong enough not to let the weather get the best of me, not a kid who grew up in New England used to dealing with subzero temperatures. My thinking had been if I could deal with that I could deal with any weather conditions. While the weather was a big downside initially, it gradually increased my endurance and ultimately prepared me for Atlanta, where it can get pretty hot and humid in the summer.

But something else was going on with me, too. I'd never had a sore arm like this before. It wasn't normal soreness, which was worrying. The trainer diagnosed it as tendinitis and prescribed ten days of rest. Ten days is a long time not to be able to do what you do best while just sitting there and watching your teammates play. I was going crazy waiting for the soreness to go away, but after the ten days, my shoulder didn't feel any better. I told Pedro I had to see a doctor. All this and my family's visit—which thrilled me at first, then made me miss them more—made me homesick. I was having thoughts about quitting and going back to the University of Lowell to play hockey. That was a life I was comfortable and familiar with and I longed for it. Then came Johnny Sain.

Everyone was telling me not to throw, to rest my arm. Johnny listened to my problem and said, "We're going to throw every day and get your arm strong." I was shocked, but took his advice to heart. After all, this man, the roving minor league pitching instructor at the time, was a legendary pitching coach of the New York Yankees staff in the 1960s as well as a favorite pitcher of Dad's in the Boston Braves' "Spahn and Sain and Pray for Rain" days. This was a man who knew his business.

Before I knew it, my arm felt great! It turned out to be a typical case of a kid coming out of high school—a New England high school—where he didn't throw a lot of innings and played first base and center field in between pitching. I wound up pitching pretty well my last couple of times out and finished the year with a 2–3 record and a 3.34 ERA. I started seven games and I accomplished something I would match one other time (and that was the following year at Sumter): I struck out more batters—thirty-four—than innings pitched—thirty-two.

Finally, I felt good about the season and my arm. The Braves wanted me to go instructional ball, which was central to Johnny's philosophy (which is what Leo, his student, preaches to the Braves pitchers today).

People thought Johnny was crazy for making pitchers throw every day. But I feel he was just a little ahead of his time and now Leo has perfected it. If you look at our pitching staff today, we don't have many people with arm problems. We're not throwing all-out every day, but at a pace where we gradually build up strength toward our next starts. The traditional philosophy has always been that you throw only once off a mound between starts for twenty minutes at 75 percent effort. For me that method takes more out of me than if I go out there every day like we do at 50 percent.

What bugs me is I still hear how people criticize Leo for making us throw so much. It blows my mind when you look at the success of Leo's pitching staffs that anyone would question his methods.

Another key to Leo's throwing program is that he's always there watching you. He spends the same amount of time with each pitcher. You watch other pitching coaches around the league and they're out shagging or throwing batting practice. Not Leo.

It's been a great success formula for the Braves—a throwback to the old days—and it's worked for us.

For the first time in my life I was getting instruction on mechanics, and I started to really understand pitching. Johnny didn't try to change too much that first year, mainly focusing on having me throw my curveball and slider better. We didn't spend too much time on a change-up. I mean, I had one, but it was a joke. I think continuity in the Braves organization really started at this time—Bobby Cox was the general manager and he seemed to get everyone instructing younger players the same way. I had Johnny and then Leo, an Instructional League coach, after my first year, and that philosophy has really carried me right through the years. This sharing of a single vision is one of the reasons the Braves are a successful franchise.

For me it has meant getting the very best instruction in baseball. There are pitching coaches who have great reputations, like Ray Miller in Pittsburgh, but Leo has to be ranked right up there. I don't know how I'd react if I ever got traded or if Bobby and Leo weren't around anymore. I've come up and played my whole career with a particular way of approaching the game, and if someone new ever came in with a new philosophy, I'd be lost.

A good pitching coach is both strong on mechanics and capable of detecting flaws in the delivery. Not everyone has both of those abilities, but I'm lucky enough to have Leo. He also has a pretty good idea of how to set hitters up because of his experience as a minor league pitcher. And he knows what every pitcher's strengths are and he accentuates those things. John Smoltz, for instance, pitches nothing like me and I pitch nothing like John Smoltz. So Leo will emphasize different mechanical things to each of us. For instance, with a power pitcher like John, Leo keeps an eye on his tendency to fly open, meaning he's coming out of his delivery because of the force at which he drives to the plate, or he tries to overthrow the ball and finds himself throwing out of the strike zone.

To do this effectively, a coach needs to know the personalities of his players, which Leo does. He knows who needs a kick in the butt, who needs a pat on the back. I never needed either. In fact, over the years I've become Leo's sounding board—when somebody else is screwing up he'll yell at me. There have been times when I'm throwing on the side and Leo starts yelling at me because the guy who threw before me didn't have a very good session.

"We're giving up too many runs as a pitching staff!" "We're getting behind on the count too much!"

He'll yell that stuff at me because he knows I can take it and it's not going to bother me. I'll say, "Leo, who are you mad at today?"

Leo has always been a true-blue Braves organizational man. He spent eighteen years in the minors, pitching for about eight years, then coaching in the Braves organization before he got his break as the co-pitching coach under Eddie Haas in 1985. He returned to the minors to coach at Sumter and Greenville in 1986 and 1987 and triple-A Richmond from 1988 to June 1990. That's when he joined Bobby as the pitching guru in Atlanta.

After two Instructional League seasons we spent together in Bradenton, I wouldn't see Leo again until he arrived at the Braves in June 1990.

By the summer of 1985 I was toiling for the Sumter, South Carolina, Braves, having moved up a classification from the rookie league in Bradenton to A ball. I was kind of skinny to begin with, but playing in Sumter was like playing in an oven. It would drop down to about a hundred by game time and we played most of our games at night. The pounds were dripping off my body. You've heard of "Sweating to the Oldies"? Well, I was sweatin' to the grueling "Sumter Blues."

The best thing about Sumter was the air force base. Not that I'm a plane buff, it's just that the folks there were nice enough to let the players use the golf course on the grounds, always a welcome change of pace for us. It was also the place where I started the fierce regimen of golf that I'm now faithful to (more on that later). Otherwise, Sumter wasn't overly exciting. There were two bars that some of the older players went to, but I was still too young, so I couldn't get into any trouble that way, and I'm sure there was a story or two about a barroom brawl where one guy was looking the wrong way at someone else's girlfriend. Never anything major, but things I was happy to avoid.

Most of us ate at Sizzler's Steak House, where we'd devour the all-you-can-eat buffet, stretching the $10-a-day meal money we received. By then I was actually making $700 a month, a slight raise from Bradenton.

Buddy Bailey, who is now the triple-A manager of the Red Sox, managed us that year. We had a heck of a team with Mark Lemke and Ronnie Gant kind of sharing second base, Jeff Blauser at short-stop, and Denson at first base. We went on to win the first half of the Southern Division of the South Atlantic League that year.

We all lived over at the same apartment complex and we had a lot of fun with pool parties, cookouts, and the like. I roomed with a couple of pitchers from Ohio—John Kilner and Rick Seibert. We had a good friendly competition going with each other, and I remember the highlight of that season was sweeping the Blue Jays. The three of us had awesome games and each night one of us would come home and say, try and top that! Rick and John were both a little older than I was, so their experience kind of rubbed off on me. John and I were pretty similar—finesse-type guys, Rick was a power pitcher.

The first half of the season, Rube Walker was our pitching coach, the second half, Larry Jaster. Larry was helpful to me because he was a left-hander whose style was similar to mine, so he understood all my little quirks. I finished the year 9–6 with a 2.35 ERA and 174 strikeouts in 169 innings. I was succeeding with a pretty good fast-ball and curve and my location was good. But I knew as I moved up the ladder my success wouldn't continue unless I started throwing a change-up, so I started tinkering with a circle change-up that is thrown with your thumb on the bottom of the ball and index finger over the ball and the rest of the fingers around the ball in the form of a circle. That worked. It was just the beginning, though.

At Sumter, I also made my first pro All-Star game, though it didn't turn out as I'd hoped. I went down to Charleston, South Carolina, with Buddy, who was named the manager of the Southern Division of the Southern League. We hit in the top of the first, and when I stepped out to the mound in the bottom of the inning, it was getting dark and time to turn the lights on.

Somewhere down the street, a transformer blew, preventing the lights from operating. It took them an hour and a half to get every-thing in order, and by that time, I'd gotten cold and Buddy wasn't about to let me go out there after warming up a second time. He knew I could come up with a sore shoulder or something. Buddy did the right thing, the cautious thing, by not allowing me to go out there. It was my first All-Star game and I couldn't pitch!

I was really pissed that day. I had pitched really well the first half of the year to earn this honor, and then something I couldn't control ruined the whole experience.

But that entire year gave me a sense that I was on the right track. I was facing decent hitters and while not necessarily dominating them, I was getting them out with my stuff. A particularly good game was a 3–0 one-hitter against Spartanburg on June 25 of that year.

Spartanburg was an older ballpark with a short left field fence, which wasn't very conducive to a left-handed pitcher. But that night I owned the ballpark. It may have been the first time in my professional career that I really put together a great outing from start to finish.

It was also a good test because of the weather, the temperature always hovering in the nineties to the low one hundreds with high humidity. Pitching after spending six or seven hours in a hot, sweltering bus was about as true a test of endurance as any I'd ever meet. On some of those days, it inevitably again made me long for the coolness of a hockey game. Though feeling that I was hitting my stride as a pitcher now and climbing up the ladder, I still missed hockey a little. That fall I went home to play in a street hockey league in Billerica. But that was the last time hockey would enter into my life. Afterward, I realized that I had to say good-bye to my first love once and for all and devote my off-seasons to conditioning and getting ready for my baseball career.

Even though I was far away from being a major league pitcher, it appeared the Braves liked me. Buddy gave me a good recommendation after that season and wrote on his report that he thought I was a prospect. Buddy was a tough manager, but a fair one. If you did your job, he respected you, and I respected him. He was a man who wanted to win. He was then a young manager—in his late twenties at the time—and was trying to impress the organization. There's a fine balance between trying to win and developing and instructing players, but I think Buddy succeeded at doing both.

He learned a lot as a manager that year about how to handle pitchers, too. I remember there was a game when he tried to go a little longer with me than he should have. He was trying to force the issue. I just wasn't effective anymore and got us into a jam. Like any young pitcher, I never wanted to come out of a game. I always wanted to work out of every jam to prove my ability to squeeze out of tight situations. While deep inside you want someone to rescue you, you never show that. Well, by the time he brought in the relievers, the damage had been done and we lost the game. From then on, Buddy knew that every pitcher had a limit. He went on to be a very successful manager and he could wind up being a big league manager soon.

I was moving up. Twenty years old, I was heading to double-A ball, a pivotal stage of the farm system where they start separating out the guys who had the best potential to succeed in The Show. In double-A the hitters start to mature and pitchers start developing fuller repertoires, perfecting their deliveries and starting to understand about mechanics and how to correct little flaws on their own.

The team was in Greenville, South Carolina, which was geographically and symbolically closer to Atlanta. The proximity meant you were more plugged in to the grapevine and the media and you tended to hear a lot more about how the prospects were doing and what the front office thought about the prospects, because the talk shows and the Atlanta newspapers were easy to come by. It was also where I started seeing players who would make it to the major leagues. The hitters had more power and were faster and they understood the strike zone better so you couldn't get away with the mistakes you got away with in A ball.

The three guys that I had good battles with that year were Mark McGwire and Terry Steinbach from the Huntsville, Alabama, A's and Bo Jackson with the Memphis Chicks (the Kansas City Royals' double-A affiliate). I'll never forget one of the first times I'd seen Bo, watching him not long after he'd signed to play baseball and had joined Memphis. He was taking infield practice and the last ball hit to him was a pop-up into short right field. For some reason—and he may have been trying to put on a show for the fans—he took the ball and threw a missile into the left field bullpen! I don't really know how far that was, but I know if I tried it, I'd probably have surgery the next day. My jaw literally dropped and I said out loud, "Oh, my God!"

Bo struggled the first week at Memphis—in the game I pitched against him, I struck him out three times. Talk about a little confidence rush! About a month later we saw him and I couldn't believe the progress he'd made. He wasn't the same man. I struck him out in his first at bat in that game. Four strikeouts in a row against Bo Jackson! I was feeling like Roger Clemens, but then on the next at bat, I came down to earth. He didn't get all of it, but it was one of those long, high fly balls that easily got over the left center field fence. I had seen him in batting practice hit some absolute bombs, which is why I say he didn't get all of it. But from then on, I knew he was something special and would have a great career in baseball and football.

It made me wonder whether I could have been a two-sport star like Bo. I don't think I had the physical ability to be able to endure the rigors of both baseball and hockey, and that's why I so marveled at what Bo and, later, Deion Sanders did.

Steinie (whom I later had the pleasure of spending many hours with during the labor talks in the winter of 1995—one of the few pleasures of that whole mess) had an unbelievable year: He hit .325 with twenty-four homers and knocked in 132 runs! Once the season was over in Huntsville he went right up to the A's in September and was in the majors for good. McGwire, who was the second player drafted that year by the A's after the Mets took outfielder Shawn Abner, had been a big slugger at USC and was the most highly touted guy in the country. He was only in double-A until June before he got sent to triple-A Tacoma, but he hit his share of homers and batted over .300 for Huntsville that year. With both of those guys and Bo, I was especially alert on the mound because they could scorch a line drive right back at me. When those guys connected, they really connected.

Because the Braves had been so bad for so long they were getting good draft position and able to select better talent. It was also a tribute to their scouting staff that many of their picks made it. In 1984, they had taken Drew first, me second, and Jeff Blauser first in the secondary phase of the draft, which still existed back then. Ronnie Gant was taken in the 1983 draft, David Justice in the sixth round in 1985, Kent Mercker number one in 1986. Back then they were just names, but Paul Snyder and his scouting staff were putting together the core of the future.

Bill Slack was my double-A pitching coach, and he was one of the most positive people I ever pitched for. Slacky, who will probably retire from our organization after the 1996 season, was always pumping me up and telling me I was going to make it if I kept up the good work. He was also probably the most demanding pitching coach I ever had, as we were constantly working on pitches I was having trouble with and location and you name it. I pitched very well that year—11–6, 3.41 ERA (through July 31)—and I was again voted to the Southern League All-Star team. I was starting to hear comparisons to Braves starter Zane Smith, but I was trying to not take that stuff to heart because I was still so far from the big leagues.

I couldn't help but hear rumors about making the jump from

double-A to the big leagues. There were new rumors every day in the papers about the lefty phenom coming up. The Braves were 72–89 under Chuck Tanner that year, after going 66–96 in 1985. These were not the best of times in Braves World and the feeling was since we're going nowhere anyway, why not bring on some of the young prospects?

By late July all I would hear was that any day I would be heading to the big leagues. It was doing a number on me mentally. I would take the pressure of that speculation to the mound and then I'd lose and I'd say, "Geez, what's going on here?" Finally, I sat down with Slacky and I said, "Look, tell me what's going on because all I'm doing when I go out there to pitch is think about going to the big leagues. And if I go out there and pitch a bad game or two it sets me back a couple of weeks and maybe they'll go with someone else."

"You're not going anywhere," Bill said. "You're having a good year right here and we're going to keep this team together. We're going to go through the play-offs with you on our pitching staff."

That was a relief in a way. Sure, everyone wants to go to the big leagues and skip a classification, but I didn't feel I was ready for that. Having confronted that and dealing with it pretty well, a week later I then got the word from my manager, Jim Beauchamp, "You're going to triple-A."

"I don't want to go," I said. "We have a month left in the season and I'm comfortable with everything here. Why do I have to change things now?" It seems strange now because most guys would have been jumping for joy at the chance to get to the next level—the final level—but for some reason I wasn't happy. Fortunately, Jim ignored my protest. Once I got to Richmond and settled in I realized it wasn't so bad. The guys at triple-A were great and made me feel welcome.

I wound up rooming with Brad Komminsk, who had been a big prospect in the Braves system but never really made an impact in the majors. He was nice enough to let me live in his apartment and he showed me the way of life around triple-A baseball—little things like where to eat and shop—and he also took care of me with equipment when I needed it because guys like Brad, who had already been in the big leagues, had much more extensive contracts with the athletic companies. To this day, I send a box of a lot of shoes, shirts, gloves, and so on to the minor league complex so guys can have the best equipment. Sometimes I earmark it for someone in particular and sometimes I just send it down for anyone.

My triple-A debut was at McCoy Stadium in Pawtucket, Rhode Island. For the first time since I'd been drafted in 1984, I was playing close to home. This was nerve-racking because my family and friends—my old coaches from Billerica—were going to watch me play for the first time as a professional.

McCoy Stadium is a great old ballpark nestled in the industrial area in Pawtucket. It's a very small stadium—a hitter's paradise—and really was the triple-A equivalent of Fenway Park. It was definitely one of minor league baseball's jewels—owned by a nice man named Ben Mondor—who just ran a first-class organization along with Mike Tamburro, Lou Schwechheimer, and Bill Wanless. They took care of me with a lot of passes on that day, July 31. There were 2,084 fans at the game that day, and I'll bet over a hundred of them were from Billerica. Mom and Dad, my brothers, sister, friends—everyone was there to watch my triple-A debut.

What a stinker.

Fooling around with a forkball that just was not working, I lasted two and a third innings and allowed four hits, eight runs, walked four, and struck out one. I gave up a grand slam in the third inning to Dave Sax, Steve Sax's brother. Sax drove in six runs in that game and just wore me out. We used five pitchers and lost 18–0! It was one of the most humiliating games I'd ever been involved with.

After I gave up the grand slam, I loaded the bases again with a couple of walks and a single by Todd Benzinger, and left the game with one out and handed the ball to Ed Hodge. What a nice spot to put Eddie in! He served up a grand slam to catcher Danny Sheaffer, who's still playing in the big leagues. They scored nine runs in the third inning. The *Providence Journal* wrote the next morning that it was the first time in the 102-year history of the International League that two grand slams had been hit in the same inning.

Part of a record I didn't want anything to do with, but there it was right in my lap and part of me for the rest of my life until some-one gave up three in one inning.

The one consolation was that it was great to see my family and friends after a game like that and after a long year. I felt lousy because Richmond was in a pennant race and I was struggling with my control and adjusting to the fiercer hitters. We had a veteran pitching staff—guys like Charlie Puleo and Steve Shields—who had already been in the big leagues, so this meant a lot to them. And here I was going out every fifth day getting my butt kicked.

These guys were so much better than me, and they all rallied around me. Brad and infielder Paul Runge and pitcher Mike Jones tried to loosen me up and make me feel a part of things. Bruce Del Canton, the pitching coach at Richmond, kept telling me that everyone had to go through this. They had all made the jump to triple-A before, too, and they knew how tough it was. The more I struggled, the more I wanted to keep to myself and not say anything to anybody. But they wouldn't let me go off in the corner and drown in my sorrow.

After seven starts I was 1–5 with a 5.63 ERA. I walked twenty-seven batters in forty innings and struck out only twelve. No thanks to me we made the play-offs and won the Governor's Cup, which is the International League championship. My streak of dominating at every level was ending with a thud. Well, at least another year was over. I'd gone to another level and hopefully I'd learned from my mistakes and knew what I had to do to get better.

The Braves wanted me to go to winter ball, but I told them no thanks. It had been a long year and I'd thrown about 185 innings, the most in my career. I wanted to avoid winter ball anyway, because I'd always heard such horror stories players had and luckily I was able to avoid it. Some got sick drinking the water in the Dominican Republic or Mexico, or they'd get held up and robbed of their money. I didn't want to risk my well-being. I just told the Braves that I'd do everything I could to work on my mechanics, so I volunteered to go to Instructional League. That helped me a lot mentally as I started the next year and was invited to my first major league camp.

Even though I'd failed in my first triple-A experience, I knew I had the stuff and the confidence that I was going to get better and conquer it.

I could smell the big leagues now and I wasn't going to let anything stop me.

5

Welcome to The Show, Tom Glavine

MANY MAJOR LEAGUERS KNEW EXACTLY WHEN THEY WERE going to be called up to the big leagues by either reading about it in the paper or being tipped off by someone in the organization that it's going to happen on a certain day. Not the case with me.

I had pitched in a 7–2 loss to the Toledo Mud Hens on August 12, 1987, a game in which I went seven and a third innings and allowed just two runs on five hits and wasn't around to get a decision. I returned to the hotel after the game feeling a little down as usual after a tough loss.

My whole season at Richmond had been a study in frustration—one tough loss after another. I was 6–12, but my ERA was 3.35. I had pitched 150⅓ innings and allowed 142 hits. My walks were up higher than I wanted—fifty-six—and I struck out ninety-one, which is okay because I wasn't a strikeout pitcher then, either, but I'd come a long way from the previous year in that triple-A hitters no longer awed me. My confidence level was high because I had the knack of being able to outthink the hitters and rarely did anyone get a good swing at me.

The phone rang. It was Roy Majtyka, our manager.

"Tom, this is Roy, you're going to the big leagues. They want you up there tomorrow—they're going to Houston—so get some sleep and we'll get you out there first thing in the morning."

I asked him, "How did this happen? Why do they want me now?"

"They traded Doyle Alexander to the Detroit Tigers for a kid named John Smoltz. They have a spot in the rotation for you. Go get 'em!"

I hung up the phone stunned. I was overcome yet so peaceful at the same time. I had achieved what I'd always wanted—a shot at proving myself in the majors. I was twenty years old, and sure, I was more of a man now than that day when my family dropped me off at the airport, but I didn't know what to do next. This was a dream come true!

I knew it would mean a lot to my parents, so I didn't have to think very long about who to call. After all, they'd been through this long haul with me, taking trips to Bradenton, Sumter, and Greenville. Countless times Mom had cooked hot meals for my teammates and me. Mom answered the phone, and when I told her she was ecstatic and she yelled the news out to Dad.

Dad, bursting with happiness, shouted and applauded.

I tried to phone friends, but it seemed like nobody else was around. Roy told me I had a 5:00 A.M. flight back to Richmond so I should gather up all of my stuff and head for Atlanta, but I didn't sleep at all.

A thousand things were going through my mind. I was reflecting back on all the minor league years and how long it had taken me to get to this point. I thought about how I'd fit in with the big league club and how I'd get along with veterans, coaches, and the manager. I thought about what I could do to make a good impression, how to act, how to talk. I knew some of the guys because I'd gone to my first major league camp that spring. I was one of the first players sent back to the minors and I was used sparingly, carried along as the extra pitcher in games and rarely getting to pitch. But I got to meet Dale Murphy and Ken Griffey Sr. and Bruce Benedict, three people I really respected. Bruce, who was the starting catcher, always gave me good pitching tips, and Murph was the guy everyone watched to see how a player should go about his work and act. Griffey was also a classy man, who smiled and always had something nice to say. But that was spring training, and this was the real thing.

By the time I got to Houston with the team, I was exhausted, but I was too excited to feel it. Pitchers Rick Mahler and Zane Smith made me feel welcome by offering their help and wisdom. Murph was one of the first veterans who welcomed me and offered the same encouragement and spoke to me about the psychology of major league hitters and how they think and react at the plate, what they're looking for on a certain count, and so on. I've continued those talks with hitters throughout my career, constantly trying to learn a new perspective on how the hitter thinks when he's at the plate.

This was a veteran team, but veterans who were playing out the end of their careers—Graig Nettles, Ken Griffey, Gary Roenicke, Ken Oberkfell. Murph was still hitting pretty well, but I figured by the time some of the young talent the Braves had drafted was ready, Murph would be on the downside. There was no upside that I could see at the time.

But it was my first time in the big leagues and I vowed to myself that I would listen and learn and make the most of it. The first couple of days were weird. Chuck Tanner didn't say too much to me, other than I'd be getting the ball every five days and that I was part of his starting rotation, but I'll always be grateful that he's the guy who wanted me up here. And thankfully, Bobby, the general manager at that time, had wanted to start bringing up the younger guys.

Chuck didn't put any pressure on me to be a star right from the beginning, which was a good way to break into major league baseball with a bad team. I've known so many guys over the years who come up and there's immediate pressure on them to win and turn the fortunes of the franchise around almost like Larry Bird did with the Celtics. Bobby Horner was in that position early in his career with the Braves. It ruins some guys to the point where they're sent back down and never return to the majors. I think that happened to some degree with Komminsk, who had this big buildup and was never able to deliver on the expectations. I guess I was viewed as something of a "savior," but I didn't feel that way. I was trying to blend in, just be one of the guys, though that's not easy to do as a rookie. Luckily, Blauser had gotten the call (for the second time that year) just prior to my arrival, so it was nice to have someone else in the same boat.

The day before my first start, I just charted the pitches and tried to get an idea of some of the Astros hitters. On August 17, the date of my major league debut, I went over the hitters with Ozzie Virgil, our catcher, and then we met in Chuck's office for the usual pregame meeting, where we reviewed scouting reports, analyzing the strengths and weaknesses of their decent-hitting lineup. They weren't the best hitting team in the league, but it didn't matter—I was nervous.

I had never pitched in a dome before, either. If there was a silver lining it was that very little pressure was on me. I mean, this was a pretty lousy team going absolutely nowhere. The veterans were playing for pride more than anything.

There were only 18,810 at the Astrodome, and in that place it looked practically empty. That was fine with me.

Like my triple-A debut, my major league coming-out was nothing to write home about. And very much like that game, all hell broke out. In fact they were about the worst seventy-six pitches I've ever thrown.

I stepped out there and like most young pitchers, I wanted to throw the ball hard. The adrenaline was rushing and I thought if I could throw a fastball in there at ninety miles per hour, nobody was going to hit it. But, I found out, everyone can hit it.

I allowed two runs in my first-ever first inning. Gerald Young was out on a line drive to center field. But then Billy Hatcher singled up the middle and Billy Doran reached on an infield single to third base. With runners at first and second, catcher Alan Ashby singled to left, scoring the first run. I retired Kevin Bass on a fielder's choice. But with Doran on third base, I allowed a single to left to Glenn Davis for the second run. I loaded the bases when I walked Ken Caminiti, but then I wiggled out of a bases-loaded jam when I retired Dale Berra on a liner to center. Whew!

I lasted only three and two-thirds innings, allowed ten hits and six earned runs, walked five, and struck out only one. My ERA at the end of the day was 14.73. Welcome to The Show, Tom Glavine.

There was a huge brawl during the game. Rick Mahler hit Bass and Davis with consecutive pitches in the bottom of the sixth and the benches emptied, and I dutifully ran out there, too, but as is generally the case with these spats, nothing serious happened. The most vivid memory of the game was having to come to the plate and hit against Mike Scott. Mike had won the Cy Young Award in 1986 and he was throwing hard. The first pitch I saw came in at ninety-five miles per hour! When it hit the catcher's mitt—and I let it go by because you can't hit what you can't see—it made a noise so loud you could probably have heard it back in Billerica. I'd never heard the mitt pop that much, and for his sake I hoped the catcher had extra padding in his glove. I had never heard the sound of busted leather like that in the minors.

Things had to improve from there, and they did. Five days later at home in my first start at Atlanta–Fulton County Stadium against the Pittsburgh Pirates, I won my first major league game by pitching seven and a third strong innings, allowing seven hits and three runs, and we won 10–3. Another first was a home run to Mike Diaz, and I remember thinking, "All right, that's out of the way."

When the game was over, Willie Stargell, our hitting coach, came up to me in the clubhouse and handed me the ball. It's a tradition to give the player a ball to commemorate his first anything.

"I got the ball for you, kid," Willie said.

I said thanks and then looked at it. There was some writing on it that read, "Hey, Mom, it's my first major league f——g win." I just looked at it and my chin dropped. He just didn't mess up the ball in my first win, did he? How could he do this? This wasn't funny. This was cruel. Now I'd have the ball to my first major league win with this stuff on it.

He just burst out laughing. He pulled the real ball out of his pocket that our assistant trainer, Jeff Porter, had retrieved.

"Here's the real one, kid. You pitched good. Congratulations," said Willie.

I was not too impressed with Fulton County Stadium when I first saw it. It was, of course, a hitter's ballpark because the ball carried so well in the hot, humid air. It was called the Launching Pad, which is like a pitcher's worst nightmare. But in time I got used to it and I didn't let the place intimidate me. After all, I'd grown up watching games at Fenway Park, and you couldn't get much smaller than the place they called the "lyrical little bandbox."

I think in a lot of ways it was good for me to have spent my career in such a place because it made me concentrate that much more on keeping the ball down and away from hitters' power zones. After a while, it really didn't matter where I pitched, and the ballparks became secondary. Your success or failure as a pitcher has little to do with the ballpark. There were some I certainly felt more comfortable at than others and particular mounds I liked more than others, but everybody has to deal with whatever elements or conditions are presented to them and you have to adjust to them. Adjusting for pitchers or hitters is what keeps them in the big leagues and becomes, oftentimes, the difference between the guy who wins twenty games and the guy who has the talent to win twenty, but wins ten.

Five days after breaking into the win column, I also broke into the hit column. I loved hitting when I was in high school, and I've always prided myself on my ability to at least get the job done with the bat and help myself as a pitcher. But we didn't hit that much in the minors because the rule was if you played American League–affiliated teams, the DH would be used and it turned out that most of the teams in our leagues were American League–affiliated.

But on August 28 at Busch Stadium in St. Louis, I stroked a single up the middle off right-hander Danny Cox. When I hit it, my initial reaction was, "Man, of all the places to hit it, you hit it toward Ozzie Smith!" But Ozzie was playing me way in the hole and not even the greatest shortstop to ever play the game could have come close to fielding it.

I hadn't worked on hitting too much my first couple of years because I was too busy trying to master pitching. But as the years went by I spent quality time working on my bunting. Our third base coach, Jimy (this is the correct spelling) Williams, always takes the pitchers out to work on situational-type stuff, like how to lay down the perfect bunt and execute a hit-and-run. It's important for a pitcher to be able to do it because it could make a difference on how long the manager will go with you in a game. A manager already has enough reasons to take a pitcher out of a game, so I didn't want him to yank me in a crucial situation because I couldn't bunt. I vowed early on that I was not going to be the type of pitcher who just brought his bat up to the plate and kept it on his shoulder as he took strike three. I wasn't going to be an automatic out.

In 1992, in fact, I hit .247 with seven RBIs, and I'll guarantee you that some of those RBIs helped win games. I came really close to being one of the few pitchers in major league history to have a higher batting average than ERA. On July 1 of that year, I was hitting .313 and my ERA was 2.18. But because of a rib injury, I didn't pitch or hit well at the end of the year.

All of our pitchers in Atlanta understand the value of battling as a hitter just like you battle as a pitcher. You want to make the opposing pitcher work for that out, and if you can get a hit once in a while, you're going to give the team an unexpected boost. For a pitcher it can mean the difference in three or four wins a year if he can hit. I'm convinced of that.

And it's all worth it for the times when Bobby has said to me, "If this guy gets on, let's try a hit-and-run." That's showing me quite a bit of respect, because he's not saying, "Sacrifice the guy over to second." And that's the way I like it. I like being as aggressive at the plate as I am on the mound.

As a team we pay close attention to pitchers on the opposing teams who hit well. In our meetings we'll say, "Don't take this guy for granted." Some of the better-hitting pitchers that come to mind are Allen Watson of the San Francisco Giants, Mark Portugal with the Cincinnati Reds, and Billy Swift of the Colorado Rockies. The Phillies have a couple of good ones in Tyler Green and Tommy Greene. It's another thing for the opposing team to worry about, and you can never have enough of those.

We ended the season in last place, 69–92. I couldn't believe how bad we were, and it was kind of depressing to think I'd be spending the next few years with more of the same before we had a chance to get better.

Chuck and my pitching coach, Bruce Del Canton, did break me in well. My highest pitch count was 109, in my final start, September 30 at Houston, and that was probably my best start, allowing only four hits and one unearned run in seven innings. At least I had been able to return to the Astrodome and get my revenge. I had another good start versus Cincinnati when I allowed only one run and four hits in seven innings to earn my second major league win. So, there was a lot of hope on my part. I think I showed Chuck and Bruce I could pitch in the big leagues.

I also had a chance to pitch to the best hitters in the league—guys like Mike Schmidt, Darryl Strawberry, and Eric Davis. I was nervous the first time I faced them but relaxed the times following.

I took a step backward in '88, though. At twenty-one years old, I should have been getting myself established, but instead I had a 7–17 year. That was tough to deal with. I pitched better than my record showed, but we had a bad team that didn't score runs and our defense wasn't very good. From June 15 to August 7, I had twenty-two unearned runs scored against me while the offense averaged only 2.6 runs per game.

But while our defense was poor, a lot of the blame was my own. The foshball change-up I was using just wasn't a consistent enough pitch for me, so I wound up using my fastball and breaking pitch more. I needed more than that.

At the All-Star break I was 3–9 with a 5.38 ERA. I called my parents a lot that year and leaned on them more and more. I'd tell them, "I stink. I can't do it." And they would just emphasize the positive and try to keep me upbeat. It was a difficult time.

I had four games in May where I didn't make it out of the fourth inning. I allowed twenty-one earned runs and twenty-two hits in seven and a third innings over that stretch. It was the first and probably the last time in my career that I was looking over my shoulder. I really believed I was going to be sent back to Richmond, which I wouldn't have blamed them one bit for doing.

It was right around this time that Chuck got fired and Russ Nixon, our third base coach, took over. We had started the year 12–27, and even though it was obvious it was the players who had the deficiency, as always the manager gets fired.

Russ called a team meeting when he took over and gave us a pep talk about playing hard every day and keeping our heads up even though we were so hopelessly behind.

After his talk, he looked over to me and waved me into his office. I thought, "Oh, no, this is it. This is where he tells me I'm going back down." But instead, Russ sat me down and said, "I know you're struggling a bit, but look, we don't have anyone at triple-A that's ready to pitch in the big leagues right now or anybody who's better than you that I want pitching up here. So, you're going to get the ball every five days. Forget about everything else you're thinking."

That certainly eased my mind. I worked hard between starts with Bruce trying to correct some problems in my delivery. In my next start at Wrigley Field, I felt my fortunes were turning. I pitched a pretty good game, lasting six and a third innings and allowing only four hits and one run and walking only one batter (this after walking eleven in my previous two starts).

I had a really nice run for four starts and then lapsed into another slump, not as bad as the first one but a tough one to deal with. We went 54–106 that year, our largest number of losses since 1935 when the Boston Braves went 35–115. Only 848,089 came to Fulton County Stadium that year. I was actually surprised it was that many. Honestly, there was nothing to watch.

Easing the pain a little for me during this stretch was Pete Smith. We were roommates and both of us were having the same horrible, bad-luck year. Pete was from Burlington, Massachusetts, and we had pitched against each other in high school.

He was a first-round pick of the Phillies, but was traded to us in the Steve Bedrosian deal in 1986 along with Ozzie Virgil. "Bedrock," another Massachusetts pitcher who had been hugely popular with the Braves, went on to win the Cy Young Award for the Phillies in '87, when he recorded forty saves. The Atlanta media made a big deal of that at the time, but really, we were rebuilding with young pitchers, and Steve, who had been a starter for us, was really perfectly suited to be a reliever, as he proved in subsequent years.

When we were in high school, the media in Massachusetts was always trying to create a big rivalry between Pete Smith and me. There really was none. We were two pretty good pitchers from the same area, who did well. That helped bring us together when Pete got to the Braves and became my best friend in baseball.

Pete also helped end my basketball career. In the off-season, I always liked to fool around and shoot a few hoops. Since I'd always played hockey, I'd never had the chance to play basketball except for intramurals. So to stay in shape in the winter of 1988, Pete and I played full-court basketball games.

In one game he threw a crosscourt bounce pass to his teammate. I was backing up, playing defense, and somehow I stepped right on the ball and severely sprained my ankle. It got big and ugly. Here I am trying to make the team again the next spring and I almost have to miss the start of spring training because of the ankle. Luckily, it cleared up before camp started. To think I could've blown it because of a stupid pick-up game.

Pete finished 7–15 in 1988 with a decent 3.69 ERA. He allowed only 183 hits in 195 innings pitched, which was a sign that he pitched well enough to have turned that record right around with a better team. Pete would always say, "Forget about our record. Look at our innings pitched and the number of hits we're allowing. We're not that bad. It's not our fault."

Smoltzie had also come up on July 23 of that year, and Russ put him right into the starting rotation. Pete and I were just in awe of Smoltzie's stuff. He threw in the nineties with great movement. Even though he struggled with a 2–7 record and a 5.46 ERA that year, you just had a feeling he was going to be a fixture around here for a long time. Smoltzie grew up in Lansing, Michigan, and was quite a baseball and basketball star. He was really struggling at Glens Falls—4–10 with a 5.68 ERA—when the Tigers made a huge mistake and dealt him for Doyle Alexander. Their mistake was our gain.

Bobby was working his magic in the front office, drafting Steve Avery with the first pick in the June draft that year.

By the end of 1988 we had Lemke, Blauser, and myself up. David Justice was going to make his debut in 1989 along with Kent Mercker and Mike Stanton. Now there was some young blood taking over the spots of the veterans. Tommy Greene would arrive in 1989 with Derek Lilliquist. Along with Smoltzie and Pete, we were known as "the Young Guns."

In spring training of 1989, I invented the wheel, sliced bread, and electricity all in one. Maybe it's not that dramatic in the big scheme of things, but in terms of what this invention did for me? It transformed me from a struggling young pitcher to a successful young pitcher and allowed me to become the pitcher I am today.

I was shagging in the outfield at West Palm Beach, our spring training facility, when I bent over to pick up a ball and I gripped it funny. I didn't get it right, the way you would normally grip a ball with your middle finger and index finger.

It kind of settled more on my middle finger and my ring finger. I looked at it and thought to myself that it would be awfully hard to throw the ball hard and sure that way. I tried throwing it and it just didn't come out of my hand the way a normal pitch would, but, I thought, this might be pretty good for me. The question was, "How am I gonna control it?"

I thought I might be onto something, but I told myself not to get too excited. The next day I was scheduled to throw and I grabbed my catcher, Bruce Benedict, and my pitching coach, Bruce Del Canton, and I said, "There's something I want to show you." I showed him the grip, but he didn't say much. I started throwing and it worked really well.

This didn't happen totally by accident. I'd been thinking, racking my brain, trying to come up with something that would come out of my hand with the same look as a fastball, but throw it, grip it, or do something that would slow down the ball.

I started using the new grip in spring training games that year and I was having success with it. It actually had a little more sink to it, and it was just a lot more consistent than my change-up [foshball], which I used following my brief experiment with the circle change. If I threw the foshball absolutely perfect it had some sink to it and the speed was good. But if I threw it a little too hard, which I did a lot, it straightened out and it didn't look much different from my fastball. The foshball has become a popular pitch—used a lot by Red Sox pitchers. It's an easy pitch to throw where the fingers are spread wider than a fastball grip, but less severe than a forkball and thrown with the same arm action as a fastball.

The key with my new pitch was I didn't have to slow down my

arm speed or change anything with my delivery. Everything was the same. You want to be able to stand on the mound and say to the hitter, "I'm throwing a change-up!" but when it comes out of my hand it looks just like a fastball to the hitter.

The hardest thing for a hitter to do is stay back on a change-up even if they know it's coming because there might be that slightest difference in speed that will throw him off. Mechanically speaking, the hitter has to be perfect in order to take that pitch and hit it the other way. Most hitters can't have perfect mechanics going every at bat or every swing, so as a pitcher you take advantage of that.

In spring training I was throwing it on 2–0 and 3–2 counts, normal fastball counts, and getting it over for strikes or getting hitters to fish for it. In the past I'd thrown fastballs on those counts and I was getting hit.

The second benefit of the change-up is that the hitter knows it's coming, but every once in a while you hold it back and throw something different and that really screws him up.

For instance, I can have a hitter go up there the first time in a change-up situation and I get him out with a slider. He'll remember that and then the next time he's going up there looking for a slider, and I'll get him with a change-up. As long as you plant some seed of doubt with him and then can back it up by getting him out with any of your pitches, you're going to have success.

In the years after my discovery, I tried to teach it to other guys on the staff, but the grip was just too difficult for most guys to grasp. Kent Mercker tried it for a while, but he just couldn't get it. Ave fooled with it, but it wasn't good for him either. To my knowledge there isn't another pitcher in baseball who uses the same grip. Maybe I've just got a unique hand or something.

The discovery of the grip was the turning point of my career.

In 1989, I went 14–8 with a 3.68 ERA. I struck out ninety and walked forty in 186 innings and I stuck with the change-up all year, even though there were times it didn't work like I wanted it to. I tied Mark Langston, who was pitching for the Expos, with four shutouts. I got off to a 5–0 start, kicking it off with a four-hit complete-game win over the Dodgers on April 7, after they'd come off a World Championship year in 1988. Left-handed hitters hit only .204 against me, and overall, just .243. This is the year that my first-inning problems became a trademark for the rest of my career. I allowed a .299 batting average in the first, but then it would go down to .246 in innings two through six and .227 in the late innings. And I earned my first major league shutout April 12 at San Diego in a 5–0 win.

For some reason, I owned the Dodgers that year—4–0, two shutouts, and three complete games against them, and I didn't allow an earned run in thirty-four and two-thirds innings after going 0–5 against them in 1987 and 1988.

I'm not sure I ever really pitched all that well against them again (I was 7–6 against them the next five seasons—11–11 with a 4.10 ERA overall), and by the luck of the draw, I didn't face them in 1995.

But as great as things were going, I sprained my left ankle on May 16 at Wrigley Field after throwing just seven pitches. I missed two starts and pitched a little erratically after that until I got smoked by Houston at the Astrodome on June 11, when I allowed seven hits and seven runs.

It turned out I had bone chips in the ankle and I had surgery on September 25 of that year to remove them. I missed three or four starts after my last start on September 14 at San Diego, and if you figure I would have won two or three of them, I probably would have had seventeen wins. But the ankle had reached the point where it was bothering me and we all felt it might alter my delivery and I'd wind up hurting my shoulder. To bolster our offense we acquired Lonnie Smith that year, and he fulfilled his promise, hitting .315, third in the National League, with twenty-one homers and seventy-nine RBIs.

Murph was struggling again. For the second straight year, he hit below .230 and his power was diminishing. It was too bad. When I got to the big leagues in '87, Murph was crushing the ball. If a pitcher made the slightest mistake, he'd hit the ball out of the park, and his stats showed it: He hit a career-high forty-four homers, knocked in 105 runs, and hit .295. After that it was just a gradual decline.

Off the field, Murph was not only one of the classiest players I'd ever been around but he was a team leader and in Atlanta he was beloved and cherished. He was the perfect role model for kids, polite and considerate of others, though intensely private; the kind of guy you'd want your son to be like. He wasn't flashy and never showed anyone up, and he respected the game and its players.

He was one of the older guys I really felt badly for because after the great numbers he'd put up, he had to endure long, losing seasons in Atlanta. In parts of fifteen seasons with the Braves, Murph was involved in just one divisional winner, in 1982, and finished second in 1983 and 1984. But since he first joined the Braves in 1976, eight of those teams finished last in the National League West division and three others finished fifth!

For a guy who gave so much to the game and so much to the fans here, that just wasn't fair. I wished the Braves could have accelerated the clock for him and made him a part of our success. In a lot of ways, Murph is a part of us. Anyone who has worn the Braves uniform since has had to live up to being the person Murph was. It's something I think about a lot.

Should he be in the Hall of Fame? I don't know. He's probably one of those guys who's on the bubble. I guess it all depends on what the individual writer's criteria for the whole team player are. That seems to be up to interpretation these days. It seems like character has become a bigger issue with the voters, and if that's the case, then Murph should get in because he was one of the greatest human beings that ever played the game and hit 398 home runs.

The Hall of Fame is certainly a sensitive subject in Atlanta. It just seems like the writers have gotten away from looking at the numbers, and are factoring in all kinds of stuff that, quite frankly, is puzzling to me.

Like with Phil Niekro and Don Sutton. I don't care how they won three hundred games, the fact is they did, and that should be a lock. To have that type of consistency for all those years is absolutely amazing to me. I mean, somewhere along the way, you come up with a sore arm or you're going to get hurt and it's going to set you back. The injury factor probably doesn't enter into it with Phil because he threw a knuckleball, but with Don? Look at his year-to-year. Maybe he didn't win twenty games often enough for the voters' liking, but all of those years of winning fifteen, seventeen, nineteen games. He had a .559 winning percentage and his ERA was 3.26. How much different was Sutton's record from Steve Carlton's? Carlton won 329 games and he's a unanimous selection, which he should be. He had an ERA of 3.22 and his winning percentage was .574. Steve spent twenty-four years in the big leagues. Don spent twenty-three. So don't give me the argument that Steve performed his feat in shorter time.

And Knucksie won 318 games in twenty-four years. He had a lower winning percentage, .537, but he was playing for some brutal teams. Add to that the fact that he was a knuckleball pitcher who had a lifetime ERA of 3.35 and that he ended his career with almost a 2–1 ratio in strikeouts to walks—3,342 strikeouts to 1,809 walks. For a knuckleball pitcher to have that type of ratio is incredible to me.

My feelings on the subject might not mean much, but there's something wrong with the process and I hope it can be improved. It's not just an Atlanta thing, either. People will say that, because I'm going to bat for guys who pitched for the Braves and, in Don's case, a guy who broadcasts our games. But that has nothing to do with it. It's a matter of what's right and who's deserving.

But the Hall of Fame was not the first thing on my mind back then. Neither was the possibility that I would be traded. That would soon change.

6

Things Change

IT SEEMS THAT ALL PLAYERS GO THROUGH A PERIOD OF TRADE talks at one time or another, but I never thought any of what I went through made much sense.

It was my impression that the Braves were building their organization with pitching, and I thought after going 14–8 in 1989 that I probably was a big part of that. Well, that winter the Red Sox signed Jeff Reardon, a free agent who'd had a nice career with the New York Mets, Montreal Expos, and a championship season in Minnesota. He was a local boy—from Dalton, Massachusetts—so the Red Sox figured it was a great public relations move to pick him up.

The one flaw in their thinking was that they also had Lee Smith. Though Lee had twenty-five saves in 1989, the Red Sox were looking to move him. Part of it may have been that cloud that followed Lee around everywhere—that at some point he was going to break down because of his supposedly bad knees. Of course, Lee never broke down and is still one of the best closers in the game today.

With two closers, Boston's GM, Lou Gorman, thought he could deal Smith for a young starting pitcher. He knew where to come—to the Braves.

I was home in Boston that off-season and I got an earful of rumors there, but I was more concerned about what was being said in Atlanta. The rumors, of course, were just as strong there, too.

Among them was talk of a deal involving Mike Greenwell or Wade Boggs for me.

But none of that made a whole lot of sense to me. Why would they trade a young pitcher for Boggsie, who was getting older and who had just had some off-field problems (Okay, the guy's still hitting over .300 today), or for Greenwell when we had some young hitters like David coming up?

After all those weeks of speculation and worry, what happened? Nothing. Not that Lou Gorman didn't try.

"I don't think I ever tried any harder to pry away one of their young pitchers than I did that winter," said Gorman. "I asked for Glavine. Bobby said absolutely not. I asked for Mercker and Bobby turned me down. I asked for Avery and Bobby thought I was crazy. When I knew he wouldn't give me Glavine, I pressed on Mercker."

Lou wound up trading Smith to St. Louis for outfielder Tom Brunansky, but not until early May 1990.

Earlier in my career, around 1988, rumors surfaced that the Pirates were looking for young pitching and willing to trade Barry Bonds for it. They were bankrolled pretty high with Barry and Bobby Bonilla and Andy Van Slyke, one of the best all-around players in the game. Add to the mix some tough pitchers who were starting to demand high salaries and it was easy to see why the Pirates needed to do something.

My name was certainly bandied about quite a bit, but nothing ever happened. Syd Thrift, who was then with the Pirates, had four different conversations with Bobby about me.

"I asked and I asked and I asked," said Thrift. "Bobby didn't even flinch when he said no. I tried every package imaginable and I just couldn't get it done. He never even gave me an 'I'll think about it.' At the time I recognized Tommy as a young pitcher who knew how to pitch and that's pretty rare. But I guess Bobby knew that, too. And as for the rumors I tried to trade Barry Bonds, that's not true. I would never have traded Barry. I was trying to make a deal for a lesser package, but Barry was never in it."

It was gratifying to later find out that Bobby fought so hard to keep me in Atlanta. We never really talked about it personally, because it wasn't my business to pry into what the front office was doing; it was a confidential matter that Bobby had to deal with when he was the GM. I know at many press conferences, especially during the postseason in 1991, Bobby was often asked how close he came to trading me and he'd always say that he never thought about it.

"It wasn't just Boston or Pittsburgh," Bobby admitted. "It was just about every team in baseball at one point made an attempt to acquire Tom Glavine, and that is no exaggeration. They would offer a package of four or five players and they'd tell you they were doing you a big favor because if a last-place team like us made a big deal like that it would draw attention to the team and I would look good. Well, I didn't buy any of that and I'd been through that in my years in Toronto with Dave Stieb. I knew if I held on to Tommy and if I could build a team around him, we'd eventually win down the road and that's what happened."

I have to admit, if I had to be traded anywhere, Boston would be the place I'd want to go because it's home. On the flip side, I'm not sure I would have completely enjoyed it. There are rabid fans there and the media is tough. If I wasn't perfect, being the local boy, they'd probably get on me pretty good and I wouldn't have wanted to deal with that. If I went there later in my career I could handle it and probably enjoy it.

But, really, I didn't want to go anywhere. I could see we were finally about to build something. Eventually, the rumors just went away and I didn't have to worry about that sort of thing again, especially after 1991 when I won the Cy Young Award.

By the start of 1990, we had a lot of our key people up. Ronnie Gant was emerging. David Justice had gotten his feet wet at the end of the 1989 season, then had a breakthrough 1990. Jeff and Lemke were really coming into their own. And our pitching staff was starting to blend together pretty well with Smoltzie, Merck, Stanton, and myself, and Mark Wohlers was coming up from the minors getting his feet wet.

When you looked around the clubhouse, you couldn't help but feel we were building something. Unfortunately, that feeling didn't immediately translate into winning: in 1990 we had another miserable year—last place at 65–97.

During that season I got caught up in the fact we were losing, and I was losing, too. I had a setback developmentally that year, but it was more mental than anything else. The great change-up I'd discovered in 1989 was now driving me crazy, so much so that I practically stopped using it at all.

This was a dumb thing to do. I should have stuck with it until it came around for me, but I got impatient. I went 10–12 that season and people on the outside looking in were saying maybe he's not as good as he showed in 1989, maybe this is the real Tom Glavine.

Well, I knew that wasn't the case. Looking back, I did pitch pretty well at times. What I learned was that as a pitcher, I can only control so much of what happens out there. You stand on the mound, you've got the ball in your hands, you get the sign from the catcher. You know what pitch you want to make and you know where you want to locate it. After that, you don't have a lot of control over what happens.

You can throw it right down the middle of the plate and the hitter misses it and sometimes you make a pitch that you think is just the greatest and it's hit hard somewhere.

There were frustrating times when I'd sit there on the bench during the game and I'd wonder, "Gosh, when are we going to score some runs and when are we going to make some plays?" It was then that I quit worrying about that stuff. Sometimes people don't understand that it's not only the pitcher's fault when the other team scores. Pitchers and quarterbacks get too much credit when a team wins and too much blame when the team loses. I made thirty-three starts, nineteen of which were considered quality starts (when you allow three runs or less in six-plus innings). From April 22 to May 25, I had seven in a row, yet my record was only 2–2 with a 2.56 ERA. I was the only pitcher in the National League who threw complete games in my first two starts and who didn't allow an earned run. But after that good start with very little to show for it, I started to struggle.

After my fifteenth start, a pretty good eight-inning effort against Montreal at home, I was 4–5 with a 3.95 ERA. But from that point through the end of August, I hit a real tough patch, going 2–6 with a 5.12 ERA. In August alone I was 0–5 with a 6.30 ERA.

On June 23 the inevitable happened. Russ Nixon was fired. All winter long the papers were speculating that if Russ got off to a bad start, he'd be gone. Well, we were 25–40, so Bobby made the decision. Looking back, it wasn't his fault we weren't playing well. After all, we were a team in transition, trying to get our younger guys to believe in themselves and trying to improve team confidence.

I liked Russ for the way he treated me. I know a lot of people on the team didn't like him, particularly for his reputation for not dealing with players one-on-one, blasting guys in the newspapers before he actually spoke to them. I don't know if there's a bigger cardinal sin among managers in baseball because the player eventually feels like it's him against the manager *and* the media, and that's not conducive to creating team spirit. The fact that we spend more time together as a team than with our families means the relationships are just as important, and certain things should be dealt with internally and not in public.

Russ was also put in a tough situation because the year before he was our third base coach. Coaches have different relationships with their players than managers do. They can be friendly and goof around, something a manager rarely does. The transition had to be difficult for Russ because he had to change the way he interacted with us. Our current third base coach, Jimy Williams, couldn't be the same guy he is now if he were put in a position to manage the Braves.

I'll say this for Russ, though, he gave me the ball every five days and showed incredible patience with me. I can't thank him enough for that. He could have sent me back to Richmond when I was struggling in 1988, but he kept with me and I'm sorry it didn't work out for him.

When Russ was fired the speculation was that Pat Corrales or Jimy Williams was going to get the job because they were so close to Bobby. As it turned out, Bobby took the job himself and hired them as coaches. I think he was at the end of his rope in that capacity because he hated being in an office and wanted to get back in uniform.

When Bobby took over, there was a renewed sense in the clubhouse that things were going to turn around for us. Some guys were a little worried he would evaluate the team up close and then make changes. But as it turned out, it was Bobby all along who was calling the shots and giving the younger guys a chance to develop.

Bobby reassigned some of the existing coaches and brought in a whole new staff rich in experience. Pat, who had managed the Philadelphia Phillies in 1982 and 1983 and then the Cleveland Indians from 1984 through 1987, came in to coach first base after being the team's advance scout. Clarence Jones, who had been our first base coach, became our hitting coach. Jimy Williams, who had been Bobby's third base coach in Toronto, came over to be our third base coach after managing the Blue Jays for parts of four years.

And Leo, Richmond's pitching coach, was elevated to major league pitching coach.

The following year, Bobby added Jim Beauchamp, my double-A manager, as the bench coach, and Ned Yost was hired to be the bull pen coach. The staff has been together ever since, and it's really been a great group of coaches to be associated with because their knowledge and experience really helps, especially with the young players.

The most important change for me personally was reuniting with Leo. It was strange to go back to throwing every day and all the stuff Leo preaches because even though our organization had, like I said, a single vision, Bruce Del Canton didn't share all of Leo's theories. But I knew this was going to be the best thing for all of us.

We needed to get on the same page and head toward a common goal. With a new staff, there was new hope. Changing managers didn't help our win-loss record, but it created a new attitude around the clubhouse. We knew we were going to finish last, but now we were emphasizing the positives, looking at the makings of a good young team. Ronnie Gant had a breakthrough year, hitting .303 with thirty-two homers, eighty-four RBIs, and thirty-three stolen bases. He had come up with me in 1987 and gradually started building. He had a relapse year in 1989 when it was obvious he wasn't going to be a major league infielder, and that's when the Braves really got smart and converted him to the outfield. He was basically replacing Murph as the power source from the right side and a guy who could steal a base. We hadn't had that type of all-around superstar in our lineup before.

In a sad development, Bobby traded Murph to the Phillies on August 4. Bobby was always criticized in the media for not dealing Murph sooner when he could have gotten a better package, but I understood why he waited so long. Murph was just the type of guy who you hoped would retire an Atlanta Brave. He should have been a one-team player. Believe me, this was tough to take for a lot of us who had known Murph. It sent a shock through the city, and while Bobby took some heat for not dealing him sooner, he took some from the those fans loyal to Murph as well. Looking back it was really the right thing to do for everybody at the time.

David Justice had come along and had been playing all over for us. But his natural position is right. So when Murph was traded, David took his spot and flowered, hitting .282 with twenty-eight homers and seventy-eight RBIs. Now we had the potent bat from the right and left sides. Ronnie was twenty-five years old, David was twenty-four.

Ave also came up, on June 13, and went 3–11 with a 5.64 ERA, getting his feet wet in the majors. Blauser and Lemke started to come

on to make up a good, young middle infield, and Blauser was showing that he was going to be a very good hitting shortstop. Smoltzie
had a very good year—14–11 with a 3.85 ERA and named to the All-
Star team—and threw over 230 innings, his bulldog mentality beginning to show.

Now, we all knew that if the front office could sign a few guys
through free agency to complement our young team, we were going
to start to creep up from the basement.

In September, not only was my pitching improving rapidly, but my
entire life was about to change. I met Carri.

A golf friend of mine, Rick Moore, owned a tanning salon in
Atlanta and Carri worked there. She had just terminated a relationship and wasn't really looking to get involved. I had been dating my
high school sweetheart, but that had ended. I was at the point in my
life where I needed to find someone and settle down. I was going
out more than I should and enjoying all of the things that a young,
single big league ballplayer enjoys. And I was getting tired of that
whole scene.

Not that I was a wild man. I'm not Dennis Rodman or Albert
Belle or people who tend to bring attention to themselves off the
field. I was a young kid in his twenties who liked to have fun. But I
was raised to do the right thing and treat people with respect. And
ultimately I know the things I do outside of baseball or even on the
field reflect not only on me but on my parents and the Atlanta
Braves organization. I would never do anything that would embarrass me or my family or the Braves. And that means a lot to me.

I'm not going to say I haven't made mistakes, because I have.
I've driven a car after I'd had a couple of beers and I'm smart
enough now to know the consequences of that and the consequences to my family if I ever do something like that again. But
that's probably the worst thing I've ever done. For the most part I've
conducted my life in a proper manner that I'm comfortable and
happy with. I don't have to look back on something and say, "I
really regret doing that." Or, "Because of my actions, I hurt somebody." And I hope it stays that way. Marriage has also taught me that
I can't be selfish anymore and think that a particular situation is
affecting only me. If I do something harmful to myself, I'm harming
my baby and my wife, so I think twice about taking risks.

During that year I really decided to get serious about baseball and stop staying out late. I'd invested a lot of time and effort in becoming a big league pitcher and I knew I had to push myself to the next level if I was going to stick around a long time.

I was back in Atlanta in September and Rick knew where I liked to hang out. On this particular weekend I had some people down from home and was entertaining them at a restaurant.

After grabbing a bite to eat after work one night, Rick invited Carri to meet me. She wasn't interested at first, but her curiosity got the best of her. She didn't know who I was because she wasn't a baseball fan, but when he introduced us that night we hit it off really well, talking for the longest time. Right after, I left for a seven-day West Coast trip, but we decided we'd get together when I got back.

I called her twice on the road trip and everything was cool. We went out when I returned and we've been together ever since. We got married on November 7, 1992. I had proposed to her on Christmas Day 1991, though up to that point whenever we talked marriage I'd always say I didn't think I was ready. So I kept her in the dark.

On Christmas Day, I told her to sit on the couch and close her eyes because I had a big gift I wanted to get for her. I came out and I got down on one knee, put the ring on her finger, and asked her to marry me. She said yes!

When I met Carri everything else fell into place. I got more serious about baseball. I got more rest. I ate better. I think if you're comfortable with your home life it makes it really easy to concentrate on things at your job. I think that applies to everybody. And it showed in my stats: since September 1990, I've been a very successful pitcher—95–42 (.693) with a 2.49 ERA through the 1995 season, and that doesn't include postseason.

We all have little personal dilemmas going on that we bring to the workplace. That's natural. But when it comes to marital problems or problems with your children, that's the type of stuff that can affect your performance. Believe me, I've seen it happen.

I haven't had too many down times since 1991. But when I do, I know I can go home to Carri and Amber at the end of the day, and that makes everything better. Carri is good to talk to about problems and she offers me support and positive reinforcement, which are two things any person needs from a spouse.

In a lot of ways, I'm happy I met Carri when I did. She didn't have to endure those rocky times with the Braves. She got there just at the right moment, when everything splendidly fit together.

I made my home in Atlanta for the first time in the winter of 1990. I took with me the positives of the final month. I won four of my last five starts. Except for some of the trade rumors, I had a restful, peaceful winter. And I thought, finally, in 1991, the Atlanta Braves were going to stop being the laughingstock of baseball and start making progress. Little did I know how much.

Good Things Happen
Outside the White Lines

FROM 1987 TO 1990, THE ATLANTA BRAVES WERE A COMBINED 251–392, a .390 winning percentage. To sum it up, we stunk. That's a lot of losing, a lot of frustration, and a lot of angry moments. Things were so bad that it was a little tough to get a tee-time at any of the local country clubs. I'd call and say, "I'm Tom Glavine with the Atlanta Braves. Is it possible to come over and play a round today?"

The guy on the other end would often just laugh and hang up. Some would say, "Sorry, we have nothing available today." Or, "You can't play at our course."

More important, our attendance figures were an indication of how poor and unpopular we had become. From 1988 to 1990, we failed to draw a million fans each year. Do you know how humiliating it is to go out and play before just a few thousand fans a night when you're a big league club? It's not easy, and makes you feel like nobody cares about you or how well you do. Sometimes staying motivated is a challenge. You ask, "Who am I playing for?"

There was no doubt we were the dregs of baseball. Nobody liked us and certainly nobody respected us. After the 1990 season, though, because of our nucleus and our potential for betterment, we spent time talking about goals for 1991.

I once sat down with Smoltzie and said, "What do you think, can we get to middle of the pack this year?"

"I know we can. We're all getting better. We've been around the league a few years and we're ready to make a move," Smoltzie said.

The preseason prognosticators didn't give us a chance. Many of them did pick us to exit the basement, one publication picking us fifth instead of last. The *Boston Globe* picked us first, but to this day I don't know if that was a serious pick or if they were just having a little fun. Maybe it was a stab in the dark, an "I'll make an outrageous pick and if it happens I'll look good." If they were serious, they knew something a lot of people didn't.

It was easy to talk and read about it, but after playing .390 ball for most of four years, it's hard to imagine winning. I hadn't been on a winning team since Richmond. We had to face it—until we knew how to win, we weren't going to win. Someone had to come in and start making us feel as if we were winners.

Bobby did that to a large degree, and Leo was really great with the pitching staff, constantly reinforcing the fact that we had the ability to be among the best.

And someone else impressed me right off the bat in spring training camp with his attitude—our new general manager, John Schuerholz. He was a classy guy who always carried himself in a very professional way, very businesslike, and he always dressed well.

Hired by Stan Kasten, our team president, after the two ran into each other at an owner's meeting in New York, John came on board in October 1990. John had served as the general manager of the Kansas City Royals from 1981 to 1990, winning a championship in 1985 and six divisional titles.

Bobby really didn't want the headaches associated with being both a GM and the manager. He just wanted to manage, and having accomplished a lot as a GM in terms of acquiring strong talent in the draft, he handed the reins over the John.

I really thought the way he accepted John Schuerholz was cool. I mean, it could have been a tough situation with a guy coming in from the outside taking over the job that Bobby once held. But Bobby didn't care about that as long as John was going to improve the team and as long as the two of them could sit down and make a decision. And as long as John listened to what Bobby needed to properly manage the team.

John handled the whole situation with so much class. I remember that when the press asked whether there'd be a problem with

Bobby, he said something like, "If I were hiring a manager, I would have hired Bobby Cox." Perfect. And it's not like it was just a line. He meant it. It was genuine. If there was any falsehood about that it would have come out or Bobby would have spotted it. But the two felt totally comfortable with each other and all was splendid.

"Bobby had sat in my chair for five years before me," John said, "and I knew right away I had to make this work. I'd known Bobby from the conversations we'd had when we were GMs. And even when he was sitting in my chair, I knew he was one of the best field managers in the game. We created a very decent working relationship. It was obvious we shared the same vision for this team and how to go about making it better, and because of that, Bobby and I got along wonderfully and it worked right away."

There was no reason not to give John our undivided attention and respect. So I listened when, on the first day the full squad worked out at West Palm Beach, John, who was in his early fifties with jet-black hair and quite fit, came down from his office and introduced himself to the team and made an eloquent and inspirational speech that really has stuck with me.

He vowed he was going to change things from the front office all the way down to the field. He talked about simple things big and small. He didn't miss a detail.

John recalled: "In the most heartfelt manner I told the players they were no longer going to be embarrassed about wearing the Braves name across their chests. That from this moment on we were going to be a proud organization and that I was going to expect more from the players in terms of commitment and in turn I was going to make some changes and acquire some players to help turn it around. I told them we needed to work together toward a common goal and together we were going to deliver. It was the first time I'd ever addressed a team like that."

The speech was similar to the chat he had with Ronnie Gant and myself that winter. We were on a winter caravan, traveling to the outskirts of our fan base—all the way up to Chattanooga, Tennessee, where we were trying to drum up some support for our team in advance of the 1991 season.

John told us then that he thought we had a good enough nucleus. If he could bring in players from winning organizations and traditions who could show us how to win, and at the same time improve our defense, then we'd be on our way to being a winning organization. He had a similar powwow with the front office staff, telling them, "I don't want to ever see one of you walking down the hall with your head down. We're going to build self-esteem and create a professional environment. We're going to feel like we're part of a winning organization." He even instituted a dress code. Of course, fancy suits with suspenders doesn't make you a winner. John certainly could have talked a good game and not backed it up. There are a lot of those people out there. But I started seeing action and it was fun to watch him piece it all together. From the moment I met him I felt he was genuine and determined to get the Braves to the next level. He had a way of making everyone feel confident just by the positive talk.

He went out and signed key free agents. First Sid Bream and Rafael Belliard, whom the Pirates decided not to retain. Then Terry Pendleton, who had been on winning teams in St. Louis, and later Deion Sanders after the Yankees had let him go.

I don't know if John envisioned the impact they would make on our team, but if he did he's a genius.

"The one criteria I had for anyone I brought in here," he said, "they had to have come from a winning organization."

Raffy gave us great defense in the middle infield. Heck, we led the league in errors in 1990 with 158 and we needed someone who could come in there and stabilize things. Now we had a pretty decent infield with Terry, a former Gold Glove winner, at third; Jeff, an excellent offensive shortstop, with Raffy coming in late in the game for defense; Mark Lemke and Jeff Treadway at second; Sid, also a very good fielder, at first; and Greg Olson behind the plate.

From the moment they arrived at camp, Sid and Terry instilled the attitude John was seeking in the clubhouse.

"It couldn't have worked out better," John said. "We didn't envision it would work that quickly, but we thought we'd be able to build on something that first year."

I'll say! Terry was the NL MVP, leading the league in hitting with a .319 average, twenty-two homers, eighty-six runs batted in, and a great year at third base to boot. How could anyone envision that after Terry came off one of his worst years with the Cardinals?

All Sid did was get off to a great start, hitting .288 with nine homers and thirty-four RBIs in our first fifty-nine games before he underwent knee surgery on June 18 and then didn't return to us until August 1. And then the guy came back and just picked up where he left off with leadership.

Because Terry went on to have an MVP season, he emerged as

more of the leader than Sid, but both had the respect and ear of everybody in that clubhouse. There was no acceptance of losing, no writing off a loss as we had in the past.

Terry and Sid didn't have many meetings with us, but the ones they had were very effective. They never let us get too happy when things were going well. They kept a real even keel with everyone in the clubhouse. We would just watch them go about their jobs and see their work habits day in and day out, amazed at the commitment these guys made. It was no secret why they'd been winners in Pittsburgh and St. Louis.

They didn't lead in a loud kind of way, either. Sid was such a quiet guy and Terry kidded around a lot, but I can only remember one or two times all year when after a tough loss they stormed into the clubhouse and started throwing things around.

We weren't just a trashy team from Atlanta anymore. We were a team that had immense pride. For the first time, we were a unit.

Bobby was the perfect leader of this team because he really had the same kind of personality as Terry and Sid. He is a quiet guy who expects you to play the game the right way. He doesn't tolerate mental mistakes more than a couple of times before he gets upset and calls you into his office to let you know. Nor did he call many team meetings, either. He just had the knack of pushing the right buttons on people, and now he had veteran leadership in the clubhouse to help him.

But John wasn't done wheeling and dealing. Right at the end of spring training, he made a huge trade, acquiring Otis Nixon from the Montreal Expos for a couple of minor leaguers. We share a spring training complex with the Expos, so we were quite familiar with Otis's ability.

Being part of the pitcher clique, we always talked about stuff like this amongst ourselves and felt unanimously that this was going to be a big move for us. We finally had the ideal leadoff hitter—and I was thrilled to death that I didn't have to face him again. I'm telling you, he was one of the biggest pests in the league. He'd get on base by laying down a bunt or he'd hit a ground ball into the hole and beat it out, or he'd tap a slow roller somewhere and an infielder would have no chance. It wasn't easy pitching to him.

When he's on base, he makes life a living hell for the pitcher. He's so fast and so quick that he gets the pitcher thinking about him all the time, ruining his concentration on the batter, causing him to throw a mistake pitch.

Well, now other teams had to worry about him. One brilliant performance was against his former team on June 16. It was a game we lost, but what a job: He stole six bases. We were all sitting in the dugout just marveling at how well he could read a pitcher's moves and he was driving them to practically throw up their hands and say, "Go ahead and steal."

To this day I regret one incident involving Otis. We were playing the Phillies in Philadelphia on June 19 and Otis was facing Roger McDowell. There was some bad blood between the two teams. In fact, Otis had been suspended for an incident with pitcher Wally Ritchie back on June 4, another game I started. Ritchie threw at Otis and Otis charged the mound and put a flying dropkick into Ritchie's chest, cleats first.

Otis had appealed the suspension and was still playing by the time the 19th rolled around. He didn't start that game, but came into it in the seventh inning. I thought the whole thing was behind us because it was so late in the game and nothing had happened. But I guess that was only because Otis hadn't stepped to the plate yet.

McDowell drilled him in the top of the ninth. There were runners at first and second with one out. We were way ahead, 9–2, and I was pitching pretty well, with a career-high twelve strikeouts.

So now I have to hit the first guy up the next inning because it's an unwritten rule in baseball—and it's been this way ever since I can remember, even in amateur baseball—that when your teammate is hit with a pitch you feel was intentional (and we all know about "purpose pitches"), you retaliate to protect your teammates from further harm. But the next guy up was Dale Murphy!

Like I said before, I really admired Murph. He was the major star on the Braves when I first got to the big leagues and I even had my locker next to his for a couple of years. He took me under his wing and showed me the ropes in the big leagues, and now I gotta hit him?

He stepped up to the plate in the bottom of the ninth and everyone in our dugout was waiting for the big confrontation. I stood nervously on the mound and Murph just dug in there, probably knowing I had to throw at him. I threw a couple of pitches close and the umpire, Tom Hallion, warned me that if I didn't knock it off I'd be gone. I threw the third one fine. Then I threw one behind Murph and got tossed! I didn't even wait for Tom to give me the heave-ho, I just headed for the dugout and the Philly fans booed me as loud as I've ever been booed.

I wasn't happy with myself. Throwing it behind him is not the same as hitting him. A pitcher who can't bring himself to hit the opposing player after his teammate has been beaned is, well, gutless. And that's exactly how I felt as I walked off the mound.

I should have hit Murph. Ex-teammate, friend, idol, whatever he meant to me shouldn't have mattered. And now how was I going to face Otis? I mean I was caught between a rock and a hard place. There's Murph, who I loved, and Otis, who I think is a great guy and is my teammate.

Otis recalled: "I chewed Tom out in the elevator in our hotel after the game. I told him how weak that was. I said, 'You threw him a change-up? I can't believe you did that.' Tommy was just listening and he agreed with me. He said he was sorry and that what he did wasn't right."

Otis did admit that he could relate to my dilemma.

"When I was in Montreal," he said, "I had someone who watched over me. That was Tim Raines. I don't know what I would do if I was in your shoes and Timmy came up. Would I have the balls to throw at him? Probably not. Don't worry about it. I understand."

That was a great thing for Otis to say to me. The fact that he understood meant so much to me because I didn't want to lose him as a friend and I certainly didn't want him to think I wouldn't fight for him.

After the game, Murph saw me in the runway and yelled, "Hey Tommy, come here." We shook hands outside the Phillies clubhouse and he slapped me on the back and said there were no hard feelings, that he understood the situation. While he appreciated that I hadn't hit him, it would have been okay with him if I had. "We'll always be friends," said Murph. "Nothing that happens between the white lines will affect that." That was just like Murph—class all the way.

I learned a valuable lesson that day: You always protect your teammates and you do the right thing no matter who's standing in the batter's box. You have to separate your personal feelings from business. And at that point, my business should have been protecting Otis. I should have dealt with the consequences later. I was lucky to have such an understanding teammate like Otis who didn't hold a grudge.

Another thing I learned was how wildly popular Murph was—I received hundreds of letters, 98 percent of them negative, with a "How could you do that to Dale Murphy?" tone.

I haven't had too many scrapes with players, and I would never throw at someone's head and risk ending someone's career. And it's not "automatic" that you have to retaliate. Like I said, if you know the pitch had a purpose you retaliate. How do you know it? You can tell by the situation in the inning, the count, if the pitcher has good control, and sometimes it's obvious. There are fewer "beanball" incidents in the National League because the pitcher has to bat, and he is held accountable for his actions.

Because I pitch away from the plate, I avoid problems. Several years ago I came in tight on Mookie Wilson and he started yelling at me and we got into a shouting match, but that's the only time I had a problem, because I wasn't trying to hit him.

One of the most shocking stories of the year also involved Otis. On September 16 we lost Otis when he tested positive for cocaine, a violation of his drug program. He was suspended for sixty days, which meant he was lost to us for not only the season, but also the play-offs and the World Series. It couldn't have come at a worst time. We were leading the Dodgers by a half-game, playing a tough series with San Francisco, and heading into a tough series with the Dodgers. It was down to the nitty-gritty and now we'd lost our lead-off hitter, center fielder, and a guy who'd stolen seventy-two bases and hit .297!

But when I first heard about Otis's relapse, I felt bad for him, not the team. We had Lonnie Smith and Deion to turn to so the team would survive. Otis, though, was such a class act that it was hard to imagine that he had ever had those problems, and if he had, they had to be long behind him.

It was heartbreaking that he had come so far—he originally tested positive for drug use while a player with the Cleveland Indians but had turned his life around and had become a model citizen in the community, speaking to kids and adults about staying away from drugs. Now he'd relapsed and he had to go through the whole process over again. The Players' Association filed a grievance on his behalf, trying to reduce the sixty-day suspension. But the rules were pretty clear. Major League Baseball had to make it a tough penalty in order to deter that type of behavior.

Later in the month, Otis stopped in and stood up before the team and apologized for letting it happen. He said, "I'm sorry I let you guys down. I'm going to work at it and come back stronger than ever. I'll be rooting for you in the play-offs." He didn't have to do that. Nobody on our team ever said to him or behind his back, "How could you let this happen at a time like this?" I remember saying to him after he spoke to us, "Go and get yourself right again and then come back to us." We were all concerned.

Bobby tried to downplay the incident in the media. Everybody was saying that Otis's departure would mean that our chariot would soon turn into a pumpkin. How untrue. Actually, Otis's departure was a way for all of us to come together and prove them wrong.

The Otis incident was my first experience with a player involved with drugs. Maybe I'm naive, but I honestly never saw it in the minors or in the majors and I never saw this one coming either. If it was being done around me, it was kept away from me, and while some fans think drug policies are too harsh, especially when it involves a hometown player, it's a serious problem that requires a serious penalty and a thoughtful rehabilitation that hopefully will prevent relapse.

And then there was Deion.

We'd certainly heard a wide range of opinions about him over the years. In '91 he didn't spend a great deal of time with us. He was our opening-day left fielder, but Deion struggled at the plate, hitting .197 before he was optioned back to Richmond on May 23. He became the first man ever to play two professional sports at the same time—with the NFL Atlanta Falcons and the Braves.

Deion was an entertainer, no question about it. He was distracting in a good kind of way because the attention of the media and the fans would inevitably shift his way, often providing a break for the rest of us who could then walk around rather anonymously for a while and just focus on playing baseball.

At first, I didn't know if signing Deion was a good move. I was hearing some unflattering things about him through the media or from other players—the universal things about him being self-absorbed, too showy for his own good, and that he fancied himself as the star—but I always reserve judgment until I meet someone personally and watch how he interacts with teammates and watch his work habits.

So when Deion came in I gave him the benefit of the doubt. And I'm glad I did. What I ultimately found is that when you cut through all the glitter, he's a good guy and a good teammate.

The attention he received certainly created a circus atmosphere, but did that affect the way we played as a team during that time? I don't think so. He returned to us briefly after Otis's suspension in late September in typical Deion fashion. We were taking batting practice when a helicopter landed in the parking lot. At first we thought it was one of those radio traffic copters, but it was Deion arriving in his very own chopper. That was bizarre and showy and all that, but in the big scheme of things, so what? That was Deion. He made grand entrances and grand exits. Heck, in the last game he played for us before departing for the Falcons training camp on June 28, he hit a three-run homer to help us win the game. If he did that all the time, he could have come to the ballpark on a fly-ing pig.

When Deion came to bat, he brought excitement to the game. He had great athletic ability and tremendous speed. Otis was fast, Ronnie was fast, but Deion? He was in a class by himself. And when he ran out to the field or stepped to the plate, he would either get a rousing ovation or get booed. Only a special athlete can create that type of emotion from the crowd.

He took some heat for not sticking to one sport and bailing out on us because he had to play football. But I think it's great that he was able to play two sports. As someone who was very good at two sports and who might have had a professional hockey career, I understand his desire and congratulate him for it. And if he hadn't tried football, he wouldn't have the two Super Bowl rings he has now.

It seemed to me that baseball was a real challenge to him. He was already an established football star, a complete natural in that sport, the best cover man in the NFL. But I know from talking to him, he wanted to be regarded as good in baseball as he was in football, and that really made him work very hard.

And that's a side of him the public doesn't seem to know. I think the public has the wrong idea of who the real Deion Sanders is. They see the flashy Deion on screen and don't see the preparation—he doesn't just show up and perform like an all-star. Certainly, if he had played baseball full-time, he would have been among the best.

We had a great clubhouse that was loose and free-spirited, and we were enjoying winning. For some of us that was so refreshing. We certainly had our ups and downs, and at the All-Star break we were nine and a half games out, but we sensed that the deficit wasn't a huge one to overcome. Heck, in the past we'd been behind by a lot more games.

The final piece to the puzzle was founded by Bobby and developed by Leo: our young, maturing pitching staff. Part of the turnaround was due to Smoltzie's great second half. He was 2–11 at the All-Star break with a 5.16 ERA, and it seemed like he felt personally responsible for our position in the standings, which wasn't true. He'd often say to the media, "I think everybody is sick and tired of seeing me lose." And he vowed to do something about it. Over the second half he went 12–2 with a 2.62 ERA, and it was evident that his work with Jack Llewelyn, the Braves' sports psychologist, whom we will discuss later, helped him focus and concentrate during crucial times in the game, especially with men on base. Smoltzie was also completely fed up with himself and he vowed he was going to turn it around because he has so much pride.

Ave was just having an incredible year—18–8, a 2.54 ERA, and he was a twenty-one-year-old kid. To watch someone that young with his sheer dominance, poise, and confidence was the stuff of legends. He threw hard, overpowering NL hitters. What was more impressive, as I struggled the last month, was that he won huge games against the hated Los Angeles Dodgers with masterful performances.

A guy who didn't get enough credit as the leader of our starting rotation that year was Charlie Leibrandt. He came in and won fifteen games and was a stabilizer throughout the year. As a young pitching staff we all learned a lot from Charlie about the value of work habits, strategy, how to take a loss, and how to act after a win. He was to our pitching staff what Terry was to the rest of the team—the go-to guy when things weren't quite right and you needed to talk to someone.

Ave, Charlie, and I gave the Braves three lefties with fifteen or more wins, which was the first time that had happened in the National League since the 1917 New York Giants. We also had nice contributions in the number five spot from Pete Smith and from Kent Mercker, who had a great year in the bull pen.

We were often criticized because we didn't have the traditional closer, but I'll tell you, not one of us ever felt we had to pitch a complete game and we never shuddered to think we had to hand it over to the pen. Those guys did a terrific job. Juan Berenguer converted seventeen of eighteen save opportunities until we lost him for the season when he went down with a stress fracture in his elbow. Hard-throwing lefty Mike Stanton was seven for ten. To replace Juan, Schuerholz went out and got Alejandro Peña from the Mets. Alejandro, who would become a frequent visitor to our team over the next few years, was just lights out the rest of the season, recording ten saves in eleven opportunities. Mark Wohlers, who was just coming up to the big leagues, also contributed.

And I can't talk about our pitching staff's success without mentioning Greg Olson. He did a great job handling us. His fiery, competitive nature kept us on our toes all year and he never allowed us to get complacent. He caught a stretch of thirty-two straight games toward the end of the year. I think that tells it all about his competitive fire.

The wonderful thing about the '91 team is that we always seemed to rise to the occasion when the odds were against us.

And that was the first time I was able to say that.

8

Mr. Potential No More

QUITE FRANKLY I WAS SICK OF HEARING THE "P" WORD. TOM Glavine: Mr. Potential. I was the survivor of trade rumors because of the P word, but I wasn't exactly conjuring up images of Warren Spahn in the eyes of Braves fans.

That was about to change.

When I hit spring training in '91, I felt possessed to become the pitcher that Leo, Bobby, John, and everyone else envisioned I'd be. All I ever heard was, "He's a young pitcher who understands how to pitch. That's a rare quality."

If that was the case, then why in four seasons did I have only one winning season? After a 14–8 season in 1989, when I really felt good about myself, I lapsed into a 10–12 season in '90 when I couldn't find consistency with my funky-grip change-up and foolishly decided to de-emphasize it.

But now my senses were returning. I knew if I was going to be successful in the National League, I had to find consistency with it, go with it even when it wasn't my best because eventually it would come around. More than that, I had to have more faith in my ability, and that meant not giving in to hitters anymore, but forcing them to adjust to me, make them beat my best stuff. It all came down to taking control of my career.

In spring training I kept a sign on my locker that said, "It's payback time," a phrase that truly summed up how I felt about what I was trying to accomplish.

For inspiration, I always studied the way other pitchers worked the hitters, particularly Hershiser and the way he baffles them. Jimmy Key was another favorite because he was a left-hander who worked the outside part of the plate much like I did. I kept saying to myself, "You can do that!" And then there was Tom Browning.

On April 20, 1991, I was sitting in the dugout looking out and watching a masterful performance against us by the Cincinnati Reds' Browning. I had pitched pretty dreadfully the night before—three and a third innings, three hits, four runs. Tom had been a very successful pitcher since I'd come up to the big leagues. He was 18–5 in '88, 15–12 in '89, and 15–9 in '90. He won twenty games back in 1985. He had also pitched a perfect game.

At one point, I turned to someone sitting beside me and said, "I have better stuff than he does. Why can't I pitch a consistent game like him?" I'd go up to different pitchers and coaches and I'd ask, "What does he do that makes him so successful?"

I was watching a guy that I wanted to be like and emulate in the way he showed complete confidence, no fear, knowing exactly what he wanted to throw in every possible situation, and not being afraid to challenge the hitter with his best pitch. This was all stuff that I knew, but I wasn't bringing those basics to the mound, whether it was due to a mental block, lack of confidence, whatever. But like I said, I thought I had better stuff.

Three days later, we faced the Dodgers, an excellent team, the guys to beat in our division. My approach and execution paid off big with a complete-game shutout, four hits, no walks, and ten strikeouts. It was the first time I can remember watching, learning (after watching Browning), and then applying it almost to perfection on the mound. There was no better feeling for a young pitcher than doing that and knowing that maybe I can keep going out there and doing it. I had tapped into a certain mind-set, a developing rhythm, that made pitching fun. And it was showing in my stats.

From April 23 to June 9, I went 8–0 with a 2.34 ERA, earning National League Pitcher of the Month honors after going undefeated in six starts. Finally, yes, it was payback time. I was living out the dream that I'd had since I'd come up to the big leagues—to be a consistent winning pitcher his team could depend on every time he got the ball.

By the All-Star break, I was 12–4 with a 1.98 ERA in seventeen starts—quite a difference from my 5–5, 3.79 numbers at the break in '90. Cincinnati Reds manager Lou Piniella, who managed the

National League team that year, selected me as the starting pitcher for the All-Star game at Toronto's Skydome.

It was an honor, yes, but it was a sense of accomplishment, somewhat similar to the first time I got called up to the big leagues. For the first time in my career I was now considered among the elite pitchers in the National League. I had fulfilled one dream of playing in the big leagues; now I was fulfilling another of being among the best. I couldn't believe I had gotten on track so quickly.

I was the only Brave selected to the All-Star team that year. Thrilled, but a little nervous, I sought Smoltzie's advice (he had been picked for the '90 All-Star game). He told me how fun it would be, just soak everything in, hang out at the All-Star game party, and also do a little learning by listening to the other pitchers because you can always pick up some knowledge from them.

His advice didn't calm me completely. After all, I was twenty-five years old, this was my first real national exposure, and I was going up against a tough AL lineup. The American League had won three games in a row, so there was pressure on us to do well and break the streak. As much as some players and the media say the All-Star game is just a showcase and nobody takes it seriously, that's not so. They had guys like Rickey Henderson, Roberto Alomar, Wade Boggs, Ken Griffey Jr., Joe Carter, Carlton Fisk, Cecil Fielder, Kirby Puckett, Rafael Palmeiro, Cal Ripken Jr., Ruben Sierra, Danny Tartabull, Mark McGwire, Paul Molitor, Dave Henderson, and Harold Baines. These are men of pride and fierce competitiveness. If you don't take them seriously they'll make you look like an amateur.

Obviously, I didn't want to embarrass myself against them. I just told myself to apply the principles that I'd used to accumulate twelve first-half wins to this game. I was going two innings tops, so it wasn't a matter of staying out there for seven or nine. The unnerving part was that as the starter, I'd have to contend with a crowd going crazy for the American League guys.

At the same time I was really motivated to perform well right off the bat, thanks especially to Rickey Henderson. When reporters asked him about facing me the day before the game he said, "Who?" I don't know if he didn't follow the game and didn't know anything about the National League or if he was showing me disrespect.

The more I thought about it, though, the more I felt that he had intended it as an insult. It bothered me more because it was Rickey Henderson, and I've never been much of a fan of hot dogs in the game. Obviously I know that Rickey will probably be in the Hall of

Fame someday because of his base-stealing records, but it bothers me to see guys make a big deal about doing something ordinary. You're paid to strike out a batter, to hit a home run, or to steal a base. Why parade around like you've done something amazing when all you've done is what you're paid to do?

You see it more in football with everyone having to do a little dance after they score or after they've sacked the quarterback, as if to say, "Look at how great I am!" Deion does it in football after an interception or a great kickoff or punt return, and I hate to see him do it, but he never did that stuff in baseball. I think it's a bad thing for kids to see. I'm not saying that at one point in my life I haven't pumped my fist after I've gotten a key out to end a game. That's just my emotion coming through. But to rub it in the face of your opponent, that's not good sportsmanship and it taints the game.

Still, Rickey's comment served as a motivational tool for me. I was going to go out there and say, "You don't know who I am? Well, you're gonna know by the end of the game!" It turned out I pitched well. I got Rickey out on a weak foul pop-up to start the first inning, and hopefully by the end of the year he knew who I was. If he still doesn't, or if he's forgotten me, maybe we can become reacquainted sometime.

I struck out three and allowed only a single and a walk. After two innings we led 1–0 and that was it for me. We ended up losing, though, because Ripken came up in the third and ripped a three-run homer against Dennis Martinez.

We were 39–40 at the break, certainly reason to be satisfied after losing ninety-seven games in 1990. But we knew we were not playing up to our potential as a team. In that first half we often lapsed into bad spells. June 14–18 was the lowest point in our season, when we lost a season-high five straight games.

We lost seven of our last nine games and five of the last seven to the Dodgers before the break. Already, the papers pretty much had us buried like we were going to retreat and become the Braves of the previous few years. But we proved them wrong. We just busted out, winning four in a row and seven out of eight coming out of the gate.

In one of those games, against the Cardinals, the conditions at Busch Stadium might have been the hottest I've ever pitched in. It was 114 degrees on the stifling turf, and I remember having to change my uniform a couple of times. I weighed myself after the game and I'd lost eight pounds! That was certainly a far cry from that day in Bradenton, when under similar conditions the heat overtook me.

I made sure to drink plenty of fluids between innings and got out of the sun when I could. I knew how important the game was to us, so after Geronimo Peña hit a home run in the first inning I just vowed to myself that it was all they were going to get. Bearing down, I went the distance, allowing six hits for a victory.

With a 4–0 start and the Dodgers in the midst of what was an 0–7 start after the break, the nine-and-a-half-game deficit dropped to five and we just kept chipping away. The big difference for us was Smoltzie, who won six of his first seven starts after the break and really became our hottest starter.

By this time the crowds at Fulton County Stadium were beginning to increase and the level of excitement was really mounting. And the tomahawk chop started in earnest.

The chop didn't just appear spontaneously. Fittingly, it started with Neon himself, Deion Sanders, during spring training. A follower of his from Florida State University, where the tomahawk chop was born, introduced it at the games, and before you knew it, other fans followed suit. It caught on like wildfire. Braves fans started doing a chant with it. And there were times when the fans got so into it, I'd be sitting on the bench with goose bumps.

The tomahawk chop and the excitement it created really put the bad years behind us quickly. Our ballpark became known as the "Chop Shop," and a local entrepreneur made up thousands of Styrofoam tomahawks and began selling them in the city and around the ballpark. Unfortunately, it became controversial when Native American groups protested that our "Braves" name was offensive and demeaning.

I can sympathize with their concerns. And if I put myself in their position I could understand why it's offensive. Yet, having thought about it a lot, I believe in the end it's a very innocent thing and it's not meant as disrespect to Native Americans. In fact, I always thought of it as a tribute. "Braves" to me calls up images of honorable and courageous warriors. Why would we depict ourselves as something derogatory?

I know that opposing players have been totally intimidated by the chant and the chopping action. You've always heard how athletes try to block out distractions when they're playing and focus only on the field of play. But I think that's almost impossible to do in our stadium. When fifty thousand people are doing the chop in unison and chanting, it's like fielding a tenth man. You couldn't help but be inspired when the rhythm got into your head. It was truly an adrenaline rush for all of us.

This was the first time I could remember a Braves crowd really caring about whether we won or lost. It was so much fun to watch.

That's why I say the excitement of the crowds the second half of the season and into the postseason was so new that it could never be duplicated again. I know the Twins felt that their World Championship in 1987 was more exciting than the one in 1991 because it was virgin territory to the fans.

And I'm not sure I could have appreciated what was happening as much I did if I hadn't gone through the humiliation of the losing seasons and the paltry crowds of five thousand at some of those late-season games.

We proceeded with our incredible season—and yes, you will hear the cliché once in this book—one game at a time. By July 16 we were in second place, four and a half games behind the Dodgers. On July 31, the end of a four-game sweep against the Pirates, we were 53–46. We were beginning to frustrate teams who thought they'd be the ones to put this upstart team in their place. But they couldn't make us vanish.

The Pirates were running away with the East Division at the time and they were surely the team we'd have to face in the play-offs. Smoltzie and I won games, and our bull pen was superb in that series as Merck picked up a couple of key saves. As much as our bull pen came under scrutiny, a great statistic that year was that we were 81–1 when we led after eight innings. That's only one time we failed to win a game we led very late, which was a tribute to the guys out in the bull pen.

By August 27, we were tied for first place! This wasn't like being in first in mid-May, because the division isn't won that early in the season. This was the end of the so-called dog days and we were sitting pretty.

We were also getting some of our key personnel back. Sid returned on August 29 after a long struggle with a knee injury; David had returned to the lineup on August 20 after being out since

June 28 with a back injury. Their return proved to be unbelievable for our offense, for Sid was a leader and David was our left-handed home run threat and run producer.

I was 17–8 by the end of August. I just marveled at Ave, a twenty-one-year-old kid who was as cool as can be. He had a great stretch of six straight wins from July 3 to August 9. And Smoltzie was perfect. You could have done a video right then and there on perfect pitching mechanics. We were starting to feel as if on any given night, the opponent had to be almost perfect to beat us.

It was a nice feeling heading into September.

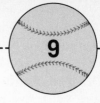

9

Finally, a Brave September in Atlanta

OVER THE YEARS, SEPTEMBER IN ATLANTA HADN'T EXACTLY been April in Paris. But this September was different. The fans did not forsake us for the NFL Falcons or Georgia and Georgia Tech football.

Typically, September signified the Braves were well out of the race, the kids were going back to school, and there was usually no reason to give us a second thought until the following spring.

But Braves fever was catching. School-age kids, white- and blue-collar workers, people from every occupation had the Braves on their mind. If you visited Atlanta you'd see people sporting Braves T-shirts and caps, and the rage was foam rubber tomahawks. There were demands on our time for local appearances at schools and malls, requests for clinics and speaking engagements.

The whole situation was reminiscent of 1967 in Boston. Though I was only a year old at the time, I'd heard about the "Impossible Dream Red Sox" throughout my childhood and how they forever changed baseball in Boston.

I guess this was shaping up as a similar situation. We had finished last and now we were vying for first. We were winning exciting baseball games. Our team had a special character to it that kept overcoming injuries and teams with supposedly better ability. We had a young and emerging pitching staff that was finally backing up its potential. We had two young sluggers named Gant and Justice, the speed of Otis and Deion, the leadership of Pendleton, and a front office that wanted to win.

While everything around was moving fast and furious, we had one mellowing influence throughout the year: Bobby Cox.

Our team took on his personality. He rarely got excited or pissed off, always keeping everything in perspective.

I think that was one of the reasons why our rivalry with the Dodgers became so interesting. Bobby and Tommy Lasorda are very different. Tommy would come to town talking a mile a minute and trash-talking about the race between the Braves and the Dodgers. Bobby would just keep his mouth shut and speak softly to reporters and never say any more than what they asked.

There wasn't tremendous emotion in his voice or manner when we'd run off five straight wins. And there was little panic in his eyes when we lost five straight. There weren't many of those inspiring "Gipper" speeches in the clubhouse. But there was no mistaking who was in charge. I often sit in the dugout and watch how he handles different situations, always amazed at how sure he is of himself and how prepared he is to instantly handle whatever pops up. Bobby had been there before. He'd seen it. Done it. He knew what worked and what didn't.

That said, Bobby is a very emotional manager while the game is going on. He reacts to everything. On a close pitch that's called a ball, he'll yell something out at the umpire like "Where was it?" If one of our pitchers is having trouble with control, it's "What's going on out there!" If someone misses a bunt sign, he'll kick something. Things like that. I've often wondered if he reacts as strongly when I'm on the mound. Maybe I'm better off not knowing.

Yet, he's not the type of manager who will air out a player right after a mistake is made, knowing the player feels bad enough. He'll wait until after the game or the next day to address it.

He spends quite a while in meetings with the coaches to go over strategy and get their input about situations—how to get the most out of this guy or that guy or future matchups against certain pitchers. He's not a tremendously technical manager—not like a Tony LaRussa, who will always go by the percentages, righty pitcher versus righty hitter and vice versa. Bobby uses a lot of instinct mixed in with some statistical data and scouting reports. He doesn't go by the book all the time, sometimes basing a certain matchup on how the particular pitcher is throwing and how well the hitter is swinging. This makes him more susceptible to criticism, but Bobby can take it.

He was cool the day we heard about Otis's suspension. Some managers might have reacted by saying what a huge loss it was and how it would be difficult to overcome. Using it as an excuse just in case they didn't win.

Bobby kept telling reporters, "This isn't a big loss. We'll get over this and keep going strong." He meant no disrespect to Otis. But his feeling was always that someone else would get an opportunity to help us win, and I guess in a way, he was curious to see how we handled it as a team. Also, isn't it good to stay positive?

He loved the fact that he had two guys like Terry and Sid, who could act as his player lieutenants, and he was always a manager who delegated responsibility to his coaches. Leo knew what strings to pull with Smoltzie, Ave, and me, and Charlie was such a solid veteran that his leadership was invaluable to us. It was almost like having another coach out there.

Bobby just wanted to be the guy who, if something big happened and he needed to step in, would weigh in as the final authority. That's exactly how we viewed him.

And over the years he's seen me as more of a leader on the team, someone he can ask to speak to a certain pitcher or player in an effort to motivate that player or to warn him about what might lie ahead.

Bobby has always been secure enough in himself to hire guys like Pat and Jimy who had managed in the big leagues before. He knows he has experienced, quality people and he uses them to relay messages and to make sure we're doing our work. He treats us like professional men, and we in turn respect him for that and play our hearts out for him.

So while a lot of players and media and fans were caught up in what was going on, Bobby wanted us to focus on our jobs on the field.

Maybe complete respect still wasn't coming our way around the league, though the national media had definitely adopted us. Reporters from all over the country were starting to write about this improbable year. Some were openly rooting for us because the media loves an underdog. And some questioned whether we could maintain this pace throughout the entire baseball season.

It took a while to get used to the sudden media blitz, but it was a problem we hoped we would have to overcome every year. We actually enjoyed it, not like the Cleveland Indians, who despise the media and one of whose executives actually said last winter that the large throng of media was interfering with the Indians' work. With baseball still recovering from the bad publicity of the baseball strike, baseball needs all of the press attention it can get.

We were becoming "America's Team," thanks, in part, to TBS, because our games were broadcast to more than sixty million households, which made it easy for fans from Portland, Maine, to Portland, Oregon, to adopt us. All of the mail coming in from all over the country was overwhelming. I used to get a few cards and letters from folks in the Atlanta area and that was it. Now the Braves' New World was all over the South, Midsouth, and the Deep South, and places we often considered the outskirts of our fan base were suddenly shifting closer to the center.

But the media attention and growing number of fans didn't pressure us—just being contenders for the first time in most of our careers was enough motivation. We knew every game from September on was going to be huge. We didn't think we were going to run away with the West Division race, but we believed the Dodgers weren't going to bury us, either.

I'm not sure the Dodger players fully respected us until the very end, when we held on to win it from under them. After all, until we took them three out of four in mid-September, they'd beaten us eight out of twelve. Overall, they won the season series, 11–7.

Darryl Strawberry helped us keep the competitive fire burning. He did a lot of trash-talking about us that summer, saying, "I never gave the Braves a second thought" and predicting we wouldn't be around at the end. That was a mistake.

We had proud players on our team. Guys like Terry and Sid and Charlie took those words to heart. Inevitably, anything that Darryl said would wind up on the clubhouse bulletin board. Greg Olson was always fuming about Darryl's comments. He'd often read a comment or see a sound bite on TV about Darryl and say, "You aren't going to be saying that stuff when this is over and we've won the division."

Just like I wanted to shut Rickey up at the All-Star game, this gave me a similar feeling but with more at stake.

The Braves and Dodgers were now a heated rivalry. Maybe this wasn't quite New York versus Boston or Chicago versus St. Louis or even L.A. versus San Francisco. But for us it was a war. The Dodgers were a team both we and our fans hated.

When they came to town on September 13, Darryl and Tommy took the heat from our fans. They ragged on Darryl when he was in the outfield and taunted him when he came to the plate. Every time Tommy stepped to the mound to talk to a pitcher or take one out of the game he was met with a chorus of boos. It seemed fans poured their heart and soul into this as if it were personal—like every rivalry should feel.

Dodger fans are certainly behind their team, but with forty-five thousand fans doing the tomahawk chop and singing their war cry, signs all over the ballpark—a lot of them unflattering to Darryl and Tommy—the Dodgers had not experienced this type of hostility anywhere.

We were 80–60 when the series began. I was really pumped up that day because I was scheduled to start the first game. Maybe I was too pumped or something because I wasn't as sharp as I could have been. Darryl just wore me out. He went four-for-five and hit a home run against me. I gave up ten hits and five runs in seven and a third innings, and it was one of those games where Mike Morgan just kept our offense at bay. I battled and we battled as a team. We tried everything but the kitchen sink against Darryl, including a shift where we put four infielders on the right side because Darryl is such a notorious pull hitter.

In the first inning he solved the shift with an RBI single to center. Then he grounded out to third, hit a leadoff homer to right on a 1–1 pitch in the sixth, and singled to left field in the seventh.

The worst part was we were knocked out of first place.

At that point I was frustrated because head-to-head they were proving that they were better. Through thirteen games, they had outscored us, 60–47.

In a hard-fought game the next night, we took it to eleven innings before Ronnie broke it up with an RBI single to give us a 3–2 win, and we were back in first. We solidified that when Ave pitched a great game, a four-hitter, in a 9–1 complete-game win that was highlighted by Sid's first-inning grand slam off Ramon Martinez, a tough pitcher with a great fastball who had won twenty in 1990 and was on his way to a seventeen-win season.

I don't know if we let down or what after that, but we dropped a couple of games to the Giants and again dropped a half-game out of the standings. After Otis's suspension came down, Terry and Sid decided we needed to close the locker room doors— no media, no coaches, and no Bobby—and just talk about things. We needed to reassure ourselves that this was no time to get tight and panic and no time to throw in the towel.

Losing our leadoff hitter and center fielder who is such a catalyst was a potentially damaging situation. Sid and Terry went around that room and looked everyone in the eye and stressed that our talent and heart and determination were what got us here and we needed to go out and display all of that day in and day out on a consistent basis.

We went out to San Diego and before only 10,551, we smoked the Padres in two games. I won the first game of the series 6–4. I didn't pitch especially well, but good enough to keep us close and for Alejandro to come in and preserve the win. We went to L.A., down a half-game to the Dodgers, and immediately got the lead back when Ave shut them out, 3–0. The next night we lost a tough one when Juan Samuel tripled in the winning run off Mike Stanton in the bottom of the ninth to win it 2–1.

In that game, a rarity occurred: Our two best infielders, Raffy and Terry, both made errors in the ninth to set up the winning hit. Terry felt bad but he didn't flinch. He just said to forget about it and go get them and keep our heads up. He said errors are going to happen sometimes and there's nothing you can do.

Unfortunately, I wasn't able to pick us up the next day. I got tired pretty quickly and left the game after four innings. Not that it mattered, as Ramon Martinez was throwing smoke and McDowell just closed us out.

My shoulder was fatigued, but I wasn't worried about it, knowing the difference between a tired shoulder that will rebound and a shoulder that was sore and needed long-term rest and likely land me on the disabled list, and this was the former.

We flew home from the West Coast with a 3–4 record on the trip and one and a half games back of the Dodgers. The schedule was tough—home against Cincinnati for three, to Houston for three, to Cincy for three, before finishing off the season with three against the Astros at home. If it was going to come down to the wire, at least we knew that we'd be playing at home before our enthusiastic fans, while the Dodgers had to play in unfriendly Candlestick Park, which has to be the toughest park for a road team to play in because you never quite get used to the wind conditions there.

We had twelve games left, the Dodgers eleven. Everyone was speculating on how we had to do to win: 8–4? 9–3?

After we lost two out of three to the Reds, we found ourselves two games back. From there, we just decided to put destiny in our own hands. We started the final road trip in Houston. We needed to get tough and forget about what the Dodgers were doing.

We won some huge close games in that stretch, putting together a season-high winning streak of eight games. I pitched the first game of the series against Houston and was able to give them six good innings, allowing two runs with ten strikeouts before I tired. We battled the Astros for thirteen innings on September 29 before we beat them, 6–5. Smoltzie threw zeroes against the Reds in the first game of that series at Riverfront Stadium. We were a game out and we knew everything was important every time out.

On October 1 we were getting blown away by the Reds, down six runs against José Rijo. We chipped away when Lou Piniella brought in Dibble to secure a one-run lead. Dibble was the hardest thrower in baseball at the time. He was throwing then like Mark Wohlers throws now—a fastball that would consistently come into the hitter at a hundred miles an hour. In 99 percent of the cases, the hitter knew what was coming, but even if he did, he would end up swinging and missing or popping it up. That's a testimony to David Justice's bat speed. He took Rob deep—a two-run homer—and gave us a 7–6 lead and an eventual win when Alejandro threw smoke in the bottom of the ninth.

Alejandro came up huge for us at the end. He saved five of the last nine games. His arrival came at a perfect time, and the fact that he was able to get into sync with the rest of us toward the common goal of winning the division was a tribute to his professionalism. He knew what this meant to us. He had been on great teams with the Dodgers, so when John acquired him, he did so with the knowledge that Alejandro would fit right in and understand the scope of the situation.

The next night, we pulled even for first! The Padres beat the Dodgers 9–4, and I was going out there with the thought that I could put us in first with a good performance if the Dodgers lost.

I finally got my twentieth win. It had taken fifteen days to get number twenty, and I knew it was my last attempt. For the first time since September 8, I was able to get eight full innings in. I allowed five hits, and only one of the three runs off me was earned. Once again, Alejandro took care of the save in the ninth and preserved the 6–3 victory.

With three games left, the horses of our starting rotation emerged. We were a rotation that had finally lived up to its potential all season. But if we were to truly prove how good we were we had to finish it off. Tied with the Dodgers with three games to go, I'm sure the betting was heavy on the Dodgers. But Ave went out and won 5–2 while the Dodgers were losing!

The next day, Smoltzie threw a complete game and we took a 5–2 win over Houston. More than forty-five thousand at the stadium were going completely whacko. And who could blame them? The scoreboard gave indications that we were on our way to clinching the National League West Division. The Giants were beating the Dodgers 4–0 in what was really a great series because it pitted Tommy against Dusty Baker, a former Dodger who had played for Tommy.

We stood around the pitcher's mound and watched with the fans a feed of the game on the scoreboard screen. With two outs in the ninth, Eddie Murray came up and grounded to second base. Robby Thompson fielded it and threw to Will Clark for the out.

Total euphoria! We had won it! We defied all the odds. We were a hundred-to-one shot at the start of the year and we beat that. We were hugging and dancing around the mound and waving to our fans, who were going nuts.

We had done the unthinkable. I remember going around to guys like Blauser and Lemke and Smoltzie and yelling, "Can you believe we did it!" I think the feeling was that nothing could beat this moment. I mean, we wanted to go into the play-offs against Pittsburgh and beat them and then go to the World Series and beat whoever we would meet. But if we didn't, it wasn't the end of the world. The fact of the matter was that baseball was back in Atlanta.

A lot of careers turned the corner. Including mine.

I finished the regular season 20–11 with a 2.55 ERA, but I was only 8–7 after my 12–4 start and I was concerned about my late-season struggles.

But the play-offs were a whole new season. Though many of us might have had aches and pains we forgot about them. The adrenaline season was really upon us. If you can't get up for the postseason, you can't get up for anything.

10

The Adrenaline Season

AS I SAT IN MEETINGS AND SCOURED SCOUTING REPORTS ON the Pittsburgh Pirates, one thing was clear: This wasn't the easiest team in the world. Barry Bonds, Bobby Bonilla, Andy Van Slyke, and rookie Orlando Merced posed obvious problems.

Bonds was one of the most feared hitters in our league. He had driven in 116 runs, his .419 on-base percentage was the best in the league, and he also had a .514 slugging percentage. He hit .292 with twenty-five homers to boot. He stole forty-three bases.

Bonilla hit forty-four doubles to lead the National League. He was a powerful switch-hitter who also knocked in 100 runs. Van Slyke was one of the best defensive center fielders in the game, who also pounded seventeen homers and drove in eighty-three runs. Merced's first full year in the majors produced ten homers and fifty RBIs.

Chico Lind was one of the best second basemen in the game; Jay Bell, who hit sixteen homers, was considered an excellent shortstop. Steve Buechele had come over from the Texas Rangers in a deal late in the season, he'd hit eighteen homers in Texas and four more for the Pirates.

Their pitching rotation was led by veteran righty Doug Drabek, a twenty-two-game winner and Cy Young Award winner in 1990 who went 15–14 in the regular season in '91. They had two tough-to-hit lefties in Zane Smith, who won sixteen games, and John Smiley,

20–8 and my biggest competitor for Cy Young honors that season. Randy Tomlin and Bob Walk combined for seventeen wins, and they had a very good bull pen with Stan Belinda, Roger Mason, Bill Landrum, Bob Kipper, and Bob Patterson.

They led all of baseball with ninety-eight regular-season wins and led the National League in runs with 768, in batting average at .263, and in doubles with 259. They tied us with eighteen complete games and tied the Cardinals with fifty-one saves.

They had been in the play-offs in 1990 and lost to the Reds, four games to two. They certainly had every motivation to want to win in 1991. Their big three—Bonilla, Bonds, and Van Slyke—had an awful play-off series in '90 and were looking to vindicate themselves.

They were led by one of the best managers in the game, Jim Leyland, and one of the finest pitching coaches, Ray Miller. This was a solid organization, offensively, defensively, management, coaching, and overall talent.

And when breaking it down, maybe the Pirates should have been the favorites. Maybe they were better on paper. We were, after all, the miracle team, and they were the established veteran team. They had soaked in all of the NL West pennant race and waited patiently to see whom they were playing. After all, they had locked up the NL East very early and won the division by fourteen games over the second-place Cards.

Bobby picked his rotation and I got the nod to pitch Game 1 against Drabek at Three Rivers Stadium. The way Bobby and Leo lined it up was Ave against Zane Smith in Game 2; back in Atlanta, Smoltzie against Smiley in Game 3 and Charlie Leibrandt against Randy Tomlin in Game 4. He wanted to go four deep, feeling all of us had earned a chance to start in the play-offs, and we all appreciated the opportunity.

The media seemed to think that Pittsburgh had the advantage, but we were glad to assume the underdog role. Whether the press clippings made us angry or simply motivated us to prove everyone wrong, I'm not sure. In the end we would prevail, but, boy, were we nervous to start the game.

I stepped out to the Three Rivers Stadium mound for my warm-ups and I probably wasn't as steady on my feet as I should have been. Having never been in this spot before, I had a thousand things racing through my head. But the biggest theme was, hold them down and give your team a chance to get ahead. I think I pressed so much that the opposite happened. I was throwing my fastball too hard, aiming every pitch, trying to be too fine with every pitch I threw.

I was trying to pitch a nine-inning shutout in the first inning, and what I would end up doing was getting myself in a hole with Van Slyke, who took me deep in the first inning, giving the Pirates a 1–0 lead right off the bat.

They scored a couple more off me in the third, and we just never got off the ground offensively against Drabek. Our hitters admitted afterward they were a little nervous, but we started to loosen up when David hit a solo homer in the ninth. But it was too late, as Drabek and Walk pitched well and we took a 5–1 loss.

I certainly didn't feel great about losing the first game and putting our twenty-one-year-old pitcher in a spot where he needed to win. But that's what I did. Ave, though, wasn't pitching like a twenty-one-year-old kid. He was throwing like Sandy Koufax. He had been one of the most dominating pitchers in the National League the second half of the year, and his grit and poise were huge for us in September. So, why should that stop now? Thankfully for all of us, Ave pitched a masterpiece, a 1–0 shutout. He went eight and a third innings, allowed six hits, and struck out nine. He was matched pitch for pitch, it seemed, by Smith, more of a finesse pitcher, while Ave was just humming it by people.

"I was having fun," said Ave. "But then, how can you not have fun with a hundred million people watching you?"

That's called having pure ice water in your veins.

Ave probably had his finest moment in the ninth when Bonds popped out with Bonilla at second base. Ave just tied him up the entire game, and Barry was extremely frustrated he couldn't get the tying run in at that point. That seemed to be a sign of things to come for Barry. His postseason woes continued throughout the series and he was getting quite angry about comments from the media that he was choking in the big games. As usual, Alejandro came on and got the next two outs to preserve the win.

With the series tied 1–1, we were all feeling a lot better about our chances. In one great performance by Ave, we reassured ourselves we belonged on the same field. While we had no preconceived goals of going 1–1 or 2–0 in Pittsburgh, it was comforting to know we were returning to Atlanta for the next three games with the Pirates having to deal with the enthusiasm in our ballpark. And it was reassuring that we had Smoltzie on the mound.

Much was made of Smoltzie seeing Dr. Llewelyn, to deal with his concentration. It almost made it sound like it was Jack who was throwing the ball and getting the hitters out.

The team had suggested Smoltzie see Jack after his 2–11 start. I don't know what the two of them talked about, but it worked. Jack has even helped me out at times. I always heard guys saying, What do you need to speak to a sports psychologist for? How could you be having problems so bad that you need to talk to a guy like that?

Jack is just a good person to talk to. He listens well and he always seems to say the right thing.

There were times when I had games when I'd be breezing along and everything would be wonderful, and then all of a sudden, the next thing I knew I'd be giving up three or four runs and a great game would turn brutal. I always wondered why stuff like that would happen.

Is it me? Is it a concentration problem? Are there things I could do to prevent it? When you're doing well, you never stop to think about why you're performing well. It just happens naturally. It's when you're failing that you're trying to analyze every little detail about what you're doing wrong. Then, it's great to have a guy like Jack around, who leads you through the right process of solving the problem.

Jack basically asks you, What do you think about when things are going well? Compare that to what you're doing when you're struggling. Sometimes it's something very simple: You throw one bad pitch that gnaws at you for the next five and now you've thrown six bad pitches. Jack helps get rid of the thoughts going through your head about the one bad pitch and concentrate on making good pitches.

He also helps in visualization. He says, "Stand behind the plate. Stand behind the pitcher's mound. Visualize the pitch you want to make for a minute. Now get on the mound and throw the pitch and forget about it. Do the same for each pitch that follows."

It's all commonsense stuff, but sometimes to hear someone else say it makes everything fall into place. Jack's a nice person and a big fan of the team, so we know as pitchers his heart is in the right place and he's there to help.

I never really spoke to Smoltzie about it too much. He kept it quiet until the media found out, and then he was asked questions about it every day. It became a major story. And it seemed every time John pitched, the camera would focus on Jack in the stands. They'd show a close-up of Jack's face and a close-up of Smoltzie's face, making a mountain out of a molehill.

Smoltzie came out and pitched an excellent Game 3. He spotted the Pirates a 1–0 lead, but then our bats just broke out against Smiley. Smiley was gone after two innings, which was a huge boost to us on the bench. When you can knock a twenty-game winner out of a game, the confidence of the hitters grows. In the end we had an eleven-hit outburst and beat the Pirates 10–3.

Our fans were incessant throughout the game, tomahawking and chanting at often extremely high decibels. If we could stay hot with the bats we'd be able to win this thing, especially if our pitching staff could continue to hold down the middle of the Pirates' lineup. Smoltzie held Van Slyke, Bonds, and Bonilla to a combined two-for-thirteen in that game with no RBIs!

The Pirates were really down. Bonds was getting a little short with reporters. Van Slyke was wondering aloud whether the Pirates "were a bunch of gaggers."

The rest of the series depended on their character—they either put the tail between their legs and run or come back with everything they had. It was definitely the latter.

In a wonderfully pitched game, two left-handers, Charlie Leibrandt and Randy Tomlin, really battled each other. We had taken a 2–0 lead off Randy in the first inning, but the Pirates remained patient and Tomlin shut us down the rest of the way until he left the game in the seventh. In the tenth, after Merck walked Van Slyke to lead off the inning, who later stole second with two outs, he walked Steve Buechele intentionally, giving Bobby a big decision to make. Don Slaught was due up. Does he go with Alejandro to get the final out or does he take the chance and bring in Mark, who was very young and inexperienced at the time? I've got to admire Bobby's decision. He went with the kid. Hey, what a way to get Mark experience. I'm sure this helped down the line.

Leyland countered the move by bringing up left-handed hitter Mike "Spanky" Lavalliere. Good move on Jim's part because Slaught probably would have problems hitting a guy who throws ninety-five miles an hour, where Spanky was more apt to get his bat on the ball, being the slap hitter he is. The count ran to 0–2, which is right where Mark and the other four hundred pitchers in baseball would love to be in that situation.

The fastball came out of Mark's hands and Lavalliere just stayed with it and lined a base hit to right center, scoring Van Slyke with the winning run as the Pirates took Game 4, 3–2, to even the series at 2–2.

There was considerable speculation concerning Bobby's move that night and the day after. But Bobby was doing what any manager who understands how to run a pitching staff would do. Alejandro had thrown two innings the previous day after a heavy workload at the end of the season. At some point you have to go with somebody else. Heck, Mark did his job. He made good pitches. Sometimes you have to tip your cap to the hitter, and in this case Spanky did a great job.

Game 5 was mine. I knew I was going to be up against a tough pitcher in Smith, who as a fellow finesser works the outside part of the plate and is tough for the right-handed hitters to get to. It was the final game of the series at home, and we knew we needed to get it 3–2 in our favor upon returning to Pittsburgh.

I was definitely pitching well that night and matching Zane pitch for pitch, but it was a mistake when I was batting in the second inning that cost us dearly. With Brian Hunter on third and Greg Olson on first with one out, I looked down to Jimy to get the sign. For some reason, I didn't pick it up. It looked like a bunt sign, a suicide squeeze, but I wasn't totally sure and by walking down to Jimy and asking it would have made it obvious. So I just watched Brian from the corner of my eye, and as Zane delivered I could see Brian breaking for the plate. I tried to turn quickly and bunt, but I missed it and Brian was coming and was a dead duck at the plate. What a disaster! I felt awful, but I didn't let it affect me on the mound, and it was so early.

The problem was it was sizing up as one of those games where it seemed the first team that scored won. I gave up a fifth-inning run on a Chico Lind single and true to form, not another run was scored.

We'd come close in the bottom of the third when David reached on a two-base error by Redus at first. Mark came up and singled to left and David kept motoring. Jimy was waving his arms for David to score, which he did. But umpire Frank Pulli ruled that David had not touched third base with his right foot and the run was nullified.

To this day, I don't know. I was in the dugout and I didn't get a great look at it. David insisted afterward he touched the base. He said he had to touch the base with his right foot instead of his left as he would normally do because he couldn't take the normally wide turn with Buechele in his way.

"I felt my spikes hit the bag and I stumbled," David told reporters. "I know if I'd missed it, I'd have come back and touched it. The reason I didn't argue is that I knew they wouldn't change it.

But I did touch it. I wasn't worried. I figured I had a couple more times at bat to help my team."

Reporters sought everyone to get the truth behind the story. One telling comment came from Jimy, who when asked said, "I can't tell you for sure. If he [David] says so, I believe him. But if you're asking me if I'm sure the answer is no."

I kept telling reporters after the game, "This series isn't over yet. There's a long way to go. If you think this is over, you're wrong." I was questioned over and over about my bunting mistake, and understandably lost in the mess was that I'd pitched pretty well. Still, no excuses.

Back to Three Rivers we went. We were down 3–2 and our tomahawks were dormant although if our fans could have followed us they would have. Once again we were asking Ave to bail us out. How much more could we ask of this kid?

The pressure was on because our offense was certainly held off by the Pirates' pitching staff. We were going to draw Drabek, who had been held back because of stiffness. Well, our offense didn't do much until it absolutely had to. After a play-off-record twenty-six straight scoreless innings, we pushed across a run in the ninth inning and held on for a 1–0 victory.

Jimmy Leyland said afterward, "We could have played six more innings and not scored against him." Ray Miller: "I've seen a lot of pitchers—Gibson and Koufax . . . if he's not up with them now, he'll be there soon." Bobby: "He's as good as I've ever seen."

The series was tied, 3–3.

"It doesn't surprise me Avery pitched a heck of a game," said Bobby. "If we didn't win tonight, there is no tomorrow. He knew that. Steve's unflappable. He will not bend."

As loud as Fulton County Stadium had been, the Three Rivers Stadium crowd was stone silent. The 54,504 absolutely astonished fans who were making their way out of the stadium that night had witnessed this seldom seen domination by a kid lefty. Ave extended his scoreless string to sixteen and a third innings with eight shutout innings, and Alejandro did the rest in the ninth.

Bobby said one thing to us that really hit home: "There won't be any more pressure on us in Game 7 than there was on us tonight."

The Pirates had a perfect record in seventh games before they met us. I'm not sure what all of these facts and statistics mean sometimes, but they'd won five other times in Game 7—in the World Series of 1909 (versus Detroit), 1925 (versus Washington), 1960 (versus the Yankees), 1971 (versus Baltimore), and 1979 (versus Baltimore). Like I said, what 1925 has to do with 1991 I don't know, but it was great that we were able to hold them off.

Smoltzie went out and took care of business. He got three runs of first-inning support, two of them on Brian Hunter's two-run homer off John Smiley. John lasted only two-thirds of an inning. Smoltzie went the distance, allowing just six hits and one walk and striking out eight batters.

We had won the first pennant for the Braves since 1958! Ave was named the series MVP with two dominating wins. Our staff compiled a 1.57 ERA in the series against the league's best offensive team, which we held scoreless for the final twenty-two innings of the playoffs.

The numbers weren't pretty for the Pirates: Bonds was four-for-twenty-seven for a .148 average and no RBIs. Van Slyke was four-for-twenty-five with one homer and two RBIs for a .160 average. And while Bobby Bonilla hit .304, he was held to one RBI. With that type of domination of the middle of a potent lineup, it wasn't hard to see how we'd won it.

The next day Bobby got the news that he'd been named the Associated Press manager of the year.

Bobby said about the award, "You don't get these honors without good players and good coaches. So I share it with everybody. Somebody asked me if I managed better this year than any other time. I manage good all the time. Managers are geniuses when they have a good bull pen."

11

The Importance of the Tenth Man

WE'D BEATEN INCREDIBLE ODDS TO NOT ONLY HAVE WON OUR division but also the NL title. Now we were plunging into incredibly deep waters. We were facing the Minnesota Twins in the World Series.

Don't think we hadn't been paying attention to the other league. The Twins' story was the same worst-to-first as ours. Our version, at least in my opinion, was a little more exciting because only four years earlier the Twins had been champs. The Braves, meanwhile, hadn't even been to the World Series since 1954, much less won it.

But heading in there the pressure on us wasn't that great. Maybe it was an odd way to think, but for me winning the play-offs and getting into the World Series alleviated all of the pressures. I think if we hadn't at least made it to the World Series, the Cinderella story would have lost some of its sparkle.

One thing was certain: The fans of both cities would not be cheated. If you could hear perfectly fine before this series, you had to have experienced some hearing loss after it. That's how incredibly loud it was at both Fulton County Stadium and indoors at the Hubert H. Humphrey Metrodome.

We spent the day before the series began just trying to get

used to the surroundings at the Metrodome. It's a place that has caused visiting teams countless problems in the American League. People would say that by the time they left after a four-game series here, they had just gotten used to playing in the place. In '91, the Twins were 51–30 in their home ballpark, the best home record in the American League. We weren't much worse at 48–33 at home. You had two teams who loved to play in their home ball-parks, but the Metrodome was different. Here, singles can easily become doubles. Fielders have to be ready and pitchers can't make mistakes.

After our workout we understood all of that.

In what was a controversial decision, Bobby chose Charlie to pitch Game 1 and elected to go with me, Ave, and Smoltzie in Games 2, 3, and 4. The reason Coxie gave was that he thought Charlie had pitched here before and he wanted to give the rest of us a chance to adjust to the new surroundings. It made sense.

There were rumors I was tired and feeling the effects of the post-season. Sure, I don't deny I was fatigued, but so what? Everybody else was tired, too. Bobby lined up the rotation so I was scheduled to come back in Game 5 on three days' rest. My reaction was: Whatever it takes.

We faced Jack Morris right out of the chute and we couldn't do much against him. The big hit was a three-run homer by Greg Gagne, who had hit eight homers all season, in the fifth inning that gave the Twins a 4–0 lead. After the game, Charlie and Bobby were asked questions about the decision ad nauseam.

Charlie defended Bobby and himself, saying to reporters, "Bobby knows what he's doing. All year long, Bobby has stuck to a rotation, and it just so happened it was my turn to start. Sure, it must be tough to pass up a twenty-game winner who may win the Cy Young Award, but you have to understand Bobby's thinking of why change things now? We've been so successful with what we've done."

We had more important things to worry about—we found out firsthand during that game what the crowd noise stories were all about. The place was deafening. Our players were having problems just speaking to one another on the field, and it could do a number on your concentration. We knew right then and there we needed to silence the crowd to have a chance.

Also, maybe we were tired after having to stretch the Pirates to seven games while the Twins only needed five games to eliminate the Toronto Blue Jays. Our performance gave some credence to that because we just didn't seem to have it. But fatigue wasn't going to be the answer every time we lost.

It was my job to pull us even in the series. Going over the reports and the charts, I certainly had a good handle on their team. It was tough to pinpoint Kirby Puckett's tendencies because he swings at just about anything in and out of the strike zone. I knew I just had to pitch my game and not back down from anyone.

As usual, I had first-inning problems. Chili Davis took me out of the park for a two-run homer. Great! We wanted to eliminate the crowd from the game and now they were in it beyond belief. But our offense came back against Kevin Tapani and pulled to within one. Then, one of the most controversial plays of the series occurred right before our eyes. What we couldn't believe is that first base umpire Drew Coble didn't see what the rest of us saw—that on Ronnie Gant's single in the third, Ronnie made too wide of a turn and Scott Leius, the Twins' third baseman, threw back to Kent Hrbek, who made a sweeping tag of Ronnie. In the process, he lifted Ronnie off the bag and tagged him. Coble called him out!

Hrbek was something like six four, 260, and Ronnie is about fifty pounds lighter. Ronnie said later that he could feel Hrbek just lifting him off the bag. And the replays we saw later certainly showed that. It was a tough situation for us because instead of having runners at first and third, it took us out of a potentially big inning.

We came back to tie it 2–2, but I surrendered a solo homer to Leius in the eighth and the Twins went ahead for good, 3–2, to take a 2–0 lead in the series. I felt awful, but I hadn't pitched that badly. I guess when you win twenty games and you're the Cy Young favorite you're supposed to go out and pitch masterpieces every game. This was hardly a masterpiece, but it was a good solid outing and one we might have won had we got a break here and there.

This isn't the type of performance I'd get down on myself for. I'm not afraid to look in the mirror and place blame on myself for a loss, but I had allowed only three runs and there were good things I did out there, and if I'd pitched that way when our team was able to score runs, we would have won.

Yet the results were damaging. This was obviously our worst fear. We're down 2–0. The only redeeming aspect of it all was that we were returning home, where we hoped our fans would make a difference for us.

Of course, by now, another theme had begun: People were saying I wasn't a money pitcher because I was 0–3 in the postseason. I'd pitched two complete games and I lost a 1–0 game in the play-offs and a 3–2 game in which only one of the runs is earned and now I'm hearing this stuff. If the critics had looked at what happened in the game rather than look at the won-lost record, they would have seen that I was doing well enough to win— if we had gotten some breaks. But no excuses. In the World Series everyone turns it up a notch—every mistake is a costly one and at times nothing short of perfection will win a game.

We had our backs to the wall. But at least we knew we had the best guy out there for that situation in Ave.

We were taking the Twins out of their element, and I think that was huge in Game 3, another incredible game that went twelve innings before we won it, 5–4. The drama in that game! We could have easily lost it and taken a quick exit in the series. Instead the win rejuvenated us. Ave couldn't go all the way again, but he pitched seven innings and left the game in the eighth leading 4–2. David and Lonnie hit homers for us. But Minnesota came back and Chili took Alejandro deep to tie it in the eighth.

That created a sinking feeling in the dugout. Sinking, but not defeating. We knew the Twins had an excellent bull pen. After Scott Erickson was taken out after four and two-thirds innings, the Twins' bull pen kept us scoreless through the eleventh.

In the twelfth we were facing Rick Aguilera, who might have the nastiest split-fingered pitch in baseball. But Rick had to hit in the top of the twelfth because Twins manager Tom Kelly ran out of players. For a guy not used to digging into the batter's box, it can take something out of you. And he readily admitted after the game that it was a distraction for him, though he sent the final out of the top of the twelfth to deep center field.

"It was a little strange coming in to pitch after an at bat," Aggie said later. "It's different entering a game trying to get focused and try to pitch. I gave up the base hit to [David] Justice with one out and wound up walking [Greg] Olson with two out. I thought I had him on a 2–2 pitch. But that happens. Then Lemke got the big hit and the game was over."

It was huge beating Aggie because he had saved forty-two games for the Twins during the regular season.

The next night we tied the series at 2–2. Again we were starting to get breaks, calls that went against us in Minnesota. Smoltz matched up against Jack Morris and both pitched well. Smoltzie lasted seven innings and Morris six. It was a 2–2 game after seven innings and once again it came down to a fantastic finish. I've got to believe people watching this series had to be on the edge of their seats wondering what was next. It really did have it all, and there was so much more to come.

Our winning run was scored by Lemke on a sacrifice fly by Jerry Willard, our backup catcher. Lemke had tripled off left-hander Mark Guthrie with one out in the ninth. But Jerry's fly ball was caught in right by Shane Mack, who heaved a pea that beat Lemke to the plate, but the throw was up the first base line a little and Brian Harper, catching for the Twins that night, went over to retrieve it and then dove back toward Lemke who was sliding into home.

Terry Tata, the home plate umpire, called Lemke safe, but Harper argued for quite some time and had to be restrained. Harper claimed he had made contact with Lemke, but Tata ruled that the contact was elbow to elbow and that his glove never touched the runner.

Replays showed that Harper didn't tag Lemke out with the glove. Even Tom Kelly couldn't argue the call. So it was Brian against the world in that case and we wound up winning the game!

Game 5 was really the only laugher of the series and thankfully I was pitching. We won it 14–5, our third straight win, and now we were leading 3–2 in the best-of-seven series. I pitched as well as I had to and I was out of the game in the sixth after allowing three runs and four hits. We smacked three homers—David, Lonnie, and Brian Hunter all went deep.

The win provided a chance for us to catch our breath and really show the Twins that we're capable of scoring at any moment. But while we felt good about being ahead, we knew we had to go back to Minnesota. I really believe our fans made a difference over three games and had a role in deciding some of the close games. A lot of the Twins players denied that they noticed the hypnotizing toma-hawk chop and chant.

Our Game 5 win put Ave in position to win the World Series for us. If anyone deserved to be out there for it, he did. After an 18–8 season, he had been dominating in the postseason.

As games go, Saturday's Game 6 will rank among the most mem-orable. Kirby Puckett led off the eleventh with a homer, crushing a hanging change-up from Leibrandt, helping this series rival the 1975 Boston-Cincinnati seven-game classic.

This was Kirby's shining moment. In addition to his double in the first scoring Mack in a two-run Twins inning, he robbed Ronnie

Gant of a probable triple in the third with one of the great catches in World Series history, a perfectly timed leap against the center field wall.

Bobby was heavily criticized in the media for bringing Charlie into the game in the eleventh. Alejandro had already gone two innings and Bobby couldn't ask him to go three innings when he hadn't done it all year. You still have to prepare a little bit for the next day because you don't know what's going to happen.

The critics said Puckett kills lefties, and he did to a tune of .406. But Coxie just thought that Leibrandt had experience facing Kirby in the American League; he went with his instincts and it just didn't work out.

As a pitcher I didn't have any problem with that, especially as someone who knows Charlie. Charlie had good success against Kirby to that point in his career. So it was a gamble, but not much of a gamble.

Kirby just rose to the occasion, and he made good on his boast to Kelly before the game, "I'll take care of things." When he can say something like that and then go out and back it up, that's the sign of a great player.

Now came Game 7.

"It seems every game we've played since the last week of the season was the seventh game of the World Series," said Lemke. "Might as well play in the seventh game of the World Series."

Johnny Bench, who played in the 1975 World Series for the Cincinnati Reds against the Red Sox, said when asked to compare the '75 series to the '91 series, "I have no complaints. I've enjoyed every minute. It's perfect. A great series between two great teams."

October 27, 1991, the date of a game that is on the top five list of greatest games I've been involved with. I wasn't pitching, but I watched every pitch and every strike. John Smoltz and Jack Morris fought like two warriors to the death.

You have to understand that by the time you get to Game 7, you've thrown a lot of innings and a lot of pitches. Yet these two guys were nothing short of magnificent.

Smoltz got into the eighth, no runs, six hits. It was 0–0 after seven, and in the eighth we squandered an incredible opportunity to win the World Series. We had runners at second and third after Lonnie singled and executed a perfect hit-and-run with Terry, who doubled to the gap in left center and probably should have scored Lonnie. But Chuck Knoblauch pulled a little decoy, a fake throw, and

Lonnie held up at third base. Still, we had runners at second and third and nobody out, and we never got the run in.

Morris threw a 3–2–3 double-play ball after Sid Bream hit a roller to Hrbek. Morris came off the mound pumping his fist.

In the bottom of the tenth, Danny Gladden doubled off Alejandro, was advanced to third, and scored on Gene Larkin's fly ball over Brian Hunter's head to end the game.

Tommy Lasorda, who was at the game, called it "the greatest pitching performance in the history of the World Series."

It was hard to deny that. The irony of it is that Kelly had told Morris that he was coming out after nine innings, but Jack, knowing he was involved in such a great game, told Kelly he still had something left, and he sure did as he retired us in the tenth.

When I looked around the locker room that night I almost stopped to wonder whether this ride had been worth it. There were so many dejected faces. I tried to go over and console Charlie because he had meant so much to us, won fifteen games, and got us here. I wanted to tell Lonnie, "Hey, it's not your fault." And it really wasn't. We had the bases loaded and nobody out and couldn't score a damn run. But then again, you have to congratulate Jack for getting out of those situations. He was like a magician.

Even though we felt like losers for a while, we slowly started to talk it out. We went around that room and we dwelled on the positive things. We knew, for one, that we had been involved in the greatest World Series in recent memory. To be a part of that was very exciting. And when we looked at each other, all we had to say was "1990." We understood how far we'd come and what we'd accomplished.

All of us could see the positives, and the comments I received from fans, the media, and friends were all the same—the Braves had given major league baseball all they had in 1991 and created attention for the sport because everyone loves an underdog.

The city threw a parade downtown that was out of this world. An estimated 750,000 fans lined the streets downtown. There were so many people it was scary. Who could have imagined this? We all got up and said a few words, mostly looking ahead to 1992 when we vowed to return to the World Series and win it. Fans couldn't get enough of us that winter, fueled by all the anticipation about next year. It was just remarkable.

After the parade, Ted Turner treated us to a great luncheon in one of the tents set up at the ballpark for postgame hospitality. It was a wonderful day. Afterward, a lot of us went back to the locker room and said good-bye for the last time that fall. In a way we knew we might never experience this again. Oh, sure, we probably had a great chance to get back and maybe someday win it. But the 1991 season will always hold a special meaning for everyone who became involved, from the fans to the front office to the players, coaches, Bobby, the trainers, the clubhouse staff—everybody.

And I doubt to this day that anyone has ever forgotten that year.

On November 12 I received a phone call from Jack Lang of the Baseball Writers' Association of America, informing me I'd won the National League Cy Young Award.

I received 110 total points, besting St. Louis closer Lee Smith, who had 60. Smiley from the Pirates had twenty-six votes and I was happy to see Ave get in the top ten with one vote. He deserved to be up there.

I remember being nervous about getting the call because while I thought I would probably get it, you never know about these things until they're official. I gave a press conference before the Atlanta writers that night, and I remember being asked what I knew about Cy Young. I responded, "He must have been pretty good to have an award named after him." I was kidding of course and know a lot about Cy Young.

I was thrilled. If anything made losing the World Series slightly bearable it was winning the Cy Young Award. I would have given it up for a World Series trophy, though. An individual award can never feel the same as a championship. And I would realize that even more in 1995.

I became only the second Braves pitcher in their history to win the award. The first guy was Warren Spahn in 1957. I actually got to meet and sit with Warren at a Boston Baseball Writers' dinner that winter, which was a thrill for me and Dad, who was in the audience and couldn't believe I was sitting with the legendary pitcher.

I was also the first twenty-game winner since Phil Niekro in 1979.

I said at the press conference, "Twenty-five years from now I can tell my grandson that one season I was the best pitcher in the National League."

I wanted to sign a longer-term deal that winter, but John Schuerholz preferred to take it a year at a time. I had earned $722,000 that season. But I was only eligible for arbitration and thus there was no urgency on the team's part to take it beyond one year. I was disappointed because all players like to have long-term security, but I had enough faith in my ability to know I'd have better years ahead. I knew it would give me more incentive to come out in '92 to prove that '91 wasn't a fluke and perhaps pitch even better and more consistently over a full year.

I've never gotten really angry about contracts, feeling that in the end I'll get what I deserve and fair market value for my services. I've always believed that.

I was very busy that winter. There seemed to be one banquet after another to go to. Several personal appearances and several endorsement opportunities came my way. I realized I could really get caught up in the lifestyle quickly. But I caught myself and found the time to work out and stay in shape and really just did my regular throwing and workout routine that winter, getting prepared for next season.

I had a lot of hopes and expectations for both myself and the team.

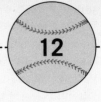

12

The Mysterious Rib

BY AUGUST 19, 1992, I WAS 19–3, PITCHING THE BEST BASEBALL of my career. The feel, the rhythm, the mechanics, the delivery— everything was perfect. My change-up was so consistent, I could stand on the mound and tell the hitter what was coming and I'd get him out.

At the time, we were up by six and a half games in the NL West standings.

With seven or eight starts to go and with my confidence at an all-time high, who knows how many wins I was looking at. Twenty-three, twenty-six? Maybe even another Cy Young Award. I also had a chance to win twenty games sooner than anyone in Braves history. But all this would soon become moot because of a bizarre series of events.

On August 21 after returning from Montreal, I got very sick, per- haps from something I'd eaten on the plane. I was wallowing in bed, getting up only to throw up every twenty minutes or so. I was sup- posed to play golf with some of the pitchers, but I had to cancel, which is something I never do.

By the end of the day, I'd been sick for so long that my back was killing me. The pain spread and seemed to focus on my left side. Naturally, I figured the discomfort was associated with heaving all day. The pain subsided in subsequent days, but it never went away altogether, and for a good two or three weeks, I had a dull pain back there, a knot that just wouldn't go away.

I received periodic treatment on it from our trainers. It helped, but I told myself not to think about it and hoped it would disappear. No chance. On August 25 I was warming up in the bull pen to pitch against the Expos that night. As usual, on my last ten pitches, I turned it up a notch, but this time about the fifth toss something grabbed me. Immediately I doubled over like I was kicked in the ribs.

"What the hell happened? What's the matter?" Leo asked frantically. "Did you hurt your shoulder?"

I told him there was some pain, but to reassure him I was okay, I started warming up again. Something wasn't right. But I went out there for less than five innings, and just faked my way through it. Every time I went to throw a pitch, I had this breathtaking pain that messed up my mechanics.

I finally had X rays that showed a hairline fracture of my left rib. Now that I knew what it was, I didn't want anyone else to know, especially the competition.

I've always believed you take every advantage you can out to the mound. If the opposition knows you're hurt, they'll have an edge as well as a little extra adrenaline. They'd bunt, hit-and-run, steal, maybe even brush me back off the plate when I came up to bat, forcing me to move around more than usual.

I and our medical staff felt it would improve and I'd be able to go out there and pitch well again. Even if I was 75 percent, I figured the way I'd pitched, that was a lot better than someone else's 100 percent.

People were definitely wondering what was the matter with me. I got the same questions like, "Do you have a sore arm? Are you tired again?"

I was starting to get criticized a little. Reporters were writing that I was tired and into my late-season swoon, just as they had said in '91. It was frustrating because I knew what was wrong, but nothing could be said. It opened my eyes on how quickly people can turn on you.

In my next start on August 30 at Philadelphia, I couldn't get out of the third inning.

I didn't want to take any time off—this was a pennant race and I wanted to be a part of it and I felt I could still help the team—so I made my next start against the Phillies at home and pitched seven strong innings. I thought I was turning the corner. Five days later, September 9, I pitched against Cincinnati and got my twentieth win. I pitched only five innings because in the first inning of that game, we rallied for seven runs and I came up to the plate to hit.

We had the bases loaded and two outs, and being someone who firmly believes a pitcher should always try to help himself with the bat, I got pretty pumped up. With a hit, I could break this game wide open! The rib injury was completely out of my mind. The first fastball I saw from Tim Belcher, I just swung out of my shoes, and suddenly I felt the familiar stab of pain on the left side again!

I did manage to single to center and drive in a run (contributing to my excellent hitting year—a career-high .247 with seven RBIs). But the pain kept me from enjoying my hitting exploits. Still, I wasn't about to give in to it, so I went back out to pitch. I battled my way through the fourth, when I loaded the bases for the second time in the game. I'm one hitter away from being out of this game. And who of all people do I have to face? Barry Larkin. Barry is one of the toughest outs in the National League, a sweet hitter, known for hitting in the clutch.

God must have been looking out for me here, because with what had to be divine intervention, Barry flied out to right field to get us out of the inning. In the fifth, I came out and I was completely out of it.

I don't know how I did it again, but I retired Chris Sabo, Glenn Braggs, and Joe Oliver. One-two-three. I walked off the mound, through the dugout, and into the trainers room. Writhing in pain I just threw up my hands and told Leo and Bobby, "Enough's enough. I can't do this anymore. I've reaggravated everything and I think it's time to miss a start."

That's pretty much when we fessed up to the media. I missed not one but three starts to let it heal.

I don't know if I would have handled the situation the same way the next time. I was a little pigheaded and headstrong about how I couldn't possibly succumb to this injury in the middle of a pennant race, risking the season and maybe even my career. It took me a long while to battle out of the bad habits I'd fallen into. And people often ask how the Braves allowed me to go out there when I was hurt. Because they respect me, they left it up to me. Everyone knew I was struggling with my mechanics and that something was wrong, but I couldn't have done more damage. The odd thing about that injury is to this day I don't know exactly how I got the hairline fracture. I don't know if it was from throwing up and coughing from the sickness or because I moved my body the wrong way.

John Schuerholz didn't tinker too much with our team in the winter of 1991. Why fix what's not broken? He did bring in Damon Berryhill, who became a big part of our team in '92 and proved to be a nice complement to Greg Olson; when Greg got hurt in September, Damon filled in nicely. Offensively, he was a pretty dangerous hitter with ten homers in 307 at bats and was terrific behind the plate.

Something just clicked between us. Damon and I seemed to share the same thoughts, so he was comfortable to throw to. The calls he made during a game I didn't have to spend time shaking off. So when Greg was out, we were lucky enough not to skip a beat. We never had to worry about who was catching.

Right before the play-off rosters were set, John traded a couple of minor leaguers to the Red Sox for Jeff Reardon. Jeff, being from Dalton, Massachusetts, was someone I'd looked up to. At the time it appeared to be the right move because Alejandro's elbow was shot due to tendinitis, which was a big blow for us. Jeff was a solid veteran reliever down the stretch and into the postseason. He pitched well in the play-offs but had a tough time in the World Series. Unfortunately, that's all everyone remembers.

We had every intention of picking up where we left off in '91 but couldn't find the right combinations in our lineup or in our bull pen. Bobby had to experiment a lot early in the season, especially with the leadoff hitter spot, because we had both Deion and Otis.

Otis had returned to the team on April 24 after being reinstated following his drug suspension. While it was a relief to have him back because of his talents, at first it was a little awkward. We all walked on eggshells because we didn't know what to say to him. But I think because he handled the suspension so well and talked to the team like he did, we welcomed him back with open arms. I think Deion learned a lot about base running, taking leads, and reading pitchers by being around him.

We also had other problems in our lineup. David Justice was struggling at the plate and also missed two weeks in April with a back problem. Lemke, who had been so crucial for us in the World Series in '91, was also slumping early. For some reason, we just weren't together yet.

And through it all, Bobby was taking some hits in the media. But true to his form, he ignored them and just waited for the ship to right itself.

My mission this season was to prove to everybody that I could repeat my 1991 season. I worked hard in spring training, where I had a 2.24 ERA in four starts, and Bobby named me the opening day starter. I pitched a two-hit complete-game shutout against Houston at the Astrodome.

While I was feeling strong as an ox, pitching at the top of my game, we were not doing it as a team. By May 26, we had the worst record in the East Division at 20–27. I wasn't feeling too good about our start. I did run into a first-inning rut around that time, even though I would usually recover and win the game. It lasted over five or six starts, and finally when I was pitching against San Diego, Leo had apparently had enough.

I'll let him set up the story: "I was talking around it with reporters who kept asking me about Tom's first-inning problems. I played it down. After all, he was winning just about every game. He's hearing this crap from everyone, so he doesn't need me to say anything. But then in the San Diego start it's the same thing. He gives up two runs in the first and finally, I had to say something."

Leo came out to the mound and said, "Tommy, does your arm hurt?"

"My f——ing arm doesn't hurt!" I said, exasperated.

"Well, if it doesn't then please throw the baseball like you can!" Then he marched straight back to the dugout.

I was fuming. What the hell was he doing coming out there talking to me like that for? Was he having a bad day? Was Bobby on him about something? I was pissed. When the inning ended after I got out of a jam, I walked clear down to the other end of the bench as far away from Leo as possible. Greg Olson went to him and said, "You were kind of rough on him, weren't you?"

"I'm sick of this first-inning bullshit!" Leo said loud enough so I could hear.

Well, I really settled down and pitched a good game and we won. Afterward, Leo walked by me and shook my hand. But we didn't say anything. The next day he said to me, "You really pitched a great game last night. Did I piss you off?"

I said, "Out of sheer respect for you Leo, you're lucky I didn't get right back in your face in front of everyone!"

After I had time to collect my emotions, I realized that it was just another one of Leo's motivational maneuvers that worked. He had gotten under my skin, knowing which buttons to push so I'd go to the next level. As it was happening I couldn't think clearly enough to know it was Leo's way of sending me a wake-up call. It was a slap in the face urging me to shape up. But he was absolutely right in doing what he did because we were all fed up with that first-inning nonsense.

Meanwhile, this was the year he started telling everyone I was the Whitey Ford—Leo's hero—of the nineties. To be compared to one of the greatest like that is a great compliment but also it means you have a lot to live up to. I've never deserved that comparison. Leo got to meet Whitey in spring training of 1993 through Bobby, who played with Whitey in New York. It was one of the great moments of Leo's life. He brought me along and said to Whitey, "Here's the Whitey Ford of the nineties."

When Leo said that, I felt awkward. Saying that in front of someone great like Whitey is a great compliment and ego boost, but I haven't yet achieved what Whitey Ford did, so I felt as if I was cheapening his accomplishments.

Whitey was quiet, but he did say, "You're a pretty darned good pitcher. I really enjoy watching you."

I always get tingles down my spine when I think of what that great man said.

I pitched back-to-back shutouts June 17 and June 23 against the Dodgers and Giants. I wound up throwing five shutouts that season. From May 27 to August 19, I went 13–0 in sixteen starts with a 2.13 ERA to set a Braves record. It was also the second longest streak in the National League since Doc Gooden's fourteen-gamer in 1985.

For the second straight year I was chosen to be the starting pitcher in the All-Star game in San Diego. I was 13–3 with a 2.57 ERA. And the rest was pretty bizarre. I got tagged for nine singles and five runs before Bobby, the National League manager, came out to end it.

It was one of the nights where they hit everything I threw. I don't think I was doing anything wrong mechanically. But every pitcher goes through a time when he has an awful time of it. It so happened it was during the All-Star game, and I felt pretty lousy about it. It was embarrassing to pitch like that in front of all those great players and on national television, but in many ways, I'm glad I got it out of my system in a game that didn't count in the standings for us.

And to reinforce to myself that nothing was wrong, I went out and pitched seven shutout innings, allowing six hits, against the Astros in my first start after the break.

At the break we were at 49–37, and in a hot streak. Even though we were in second place, trailing the Reds by two games, we had every confidence we could overtake them.

At the center of our success was Terry Pendleton. Now here's a guy coming off an MVP season and he goes right back out there and does it all over again. In a lot of ways, Terry had a better year. He drove in 105 runs with twenty-one homers and hit .311. His leadership was again a vital tool for us, though a year later we were a much more confident team thanks, in part, to the role Terry and Sid had played in 1991 when they taught us how to win.

Another unsung hero that season was my buddy Pete Smith, who went 7–0 down the stretch. Pete was my best friend in baseball during the time we played together, but we never knew each other in high school. For us to grow up in the same area and for both of us make it—that was storybook stuff. There was the made-up rivalry that the media there drummed up, which ironically made us aware of each other. Sometimes it's hard to make real good friends in this game, but he was one of them and he remains a friend to this day.

We'd lost Mike Bielecki, our number five starter, to a season-ending injury, and Pete was recalled from Richmond where he was 7–4 with a 2.14 ERA. He had pitched a seven-inning perfect game at Rochester, and then when he came back to us he pitched a lot of almost perfect ones.

He and Terry were a big part of the June 2 game against Philly, which many people saw as the turning point of the season. We hung in and overcame a 3–1 deficit late in the game. It was a 3–3 game in the ninth when Terry got hold of one of Mitch Williams's fastballs and lofted it over the left center field fence, giving us a 5–3 win. For the first time all year we won a game dramatically, championship style. And we also beat Williams, who was one of the best closers in the game that year.

The other dramatic part of the season came in our showdown versus Cincinnati, August 4–6. We swept them. I tapped off the series but didn't get a decision in our 7–5 win over the Reds. I wasn't sharp that night and trailed 5–2 in the eighth. If we had lost, the Reds would have retaken first place, but what transpired were three straight great at bats by Terry, Greg, and David, all of whom had 0–2 counts from lefty Norm Charlton, one of the "Nasty Boys" relievers, and all of whom knocked in runs to tie the game 5–5 in the bottom of the eighth.

Lou Piniella, whom I really enjoyed from the All-Star experience in 1991, decided to keep Charlton in for the ninth. Norm got the first two outs before Otis reached base with a walk and then promptly stole second. Terry was due up. Most of us in the dugout thought Charlton would walk Terry intentionally and take his chances with Ronnie, who was in a slump at the time. Terry is just murder against lefties. But Lou decided he wanted to challenge him. As usual, Terry got the best of it and launched a two-run homer to win the game for us. Lou took a lot of criticism for that one and had to answer questions about it for a couple of days.

For us, it was another inspiring win. Even though I didn't get the win, I think coming back like we did enabled us to go into the next two games with a lot more confidence than Cincinnati. We took those two, and after that we just took off and never looked back.

I think for a lot of people this wasn't as exciting as '91. But we became a very dominating team during the season. We went 98–64, the best record in baseball. We hit a league-high 138 home runs, and our pitching staff had a 3.14 ERA, by far the best in baseball.

I won twenty games for the second straight season, even with that damn rib injury, and Smoltzie continued to dominate as a power pitcher, leading the league with 215 strikeouts, a 15–12 record, and a 2.65 ERA. Ave had an 11–11 season, but that was deceiving when you considered his 3.35 ERA and the fact that only twenty-five runs were scored in his eleven losses. Charlie Leibrandt won fifteen games for the second straight year. There were unsung types like Marvin Freeman, who made fifty-eight appearances out of our bull pen, just ahead of Kent Mercker, who had fifty-three, and Jeff Blauser, who hit fourteen homers as a shortstop. There was also the blossoming of Deion, who hit .304 with eight homers and twenty-six stolen bases in ninety-seven games. Brian Hunter hit fourteen homers.

It was again a very solid team. And glancing to the East, Pittsburgh was at it again. Despite exits in the play-offs in '90 and '91, they got themselves together and won ninety-six games without Bobby Bonilla (who had defected to the Mets) in the middle of their order.

And so we were on the threshold of another tough play-off series with the Pirates and a chance to finish off a championship for our fans, who came out at a record 3,077,400, the first time more than three million fans came out to watch the Braves.

13

A Second Chance

MAYBE WE HAD TROUBLE WINNING THE WORLD SERIES IN '91 and '92, but you have to admit we won the Academy Award for best drama in a play-off series. As great as our 1991 play-offs were with Pittsburgh, '92 seemed to take the cake.

Having to play the same team for the second consecutive post-season is very tough. You know they're gunning for you because they want nothing more than to make amends for the previous year.

Because I was still recovering from the rib problem and my mechanics were way off by the end of the season, I was held back until the third game. This decision was fine with me because I needed the time to rest. Bobby went with Smoltzie and Ave in the first two games in Pittsburgh.

There was some talk-show chatter going on that really got to me. People were actually questioning why Bobby was pitching me at all in the postseason. I'd just come off my second twenty-win season, and sure, I struggled when I was trying to get through the injury and couldn't get my mechanics quite right. But it was coming along, and the play-offs are a whole new season anyway.

To counteract this, Leo pumped me up every day. He would tell me to ignore what people were saying and just concentrate on proving people wrong.

After we'd gone up two games, I really wanted to continue what Smoltzie and Ave had done. I was pitted against Tim Wakefield, the knuckleballer who was in his rookie year and pitching as well back then as he did for the Red Sox in 1995. His knuckleball was dancing to places that our hitters couldn't touch. We had lost to him once in August, and I remember hitters just shaking their heads after they faced him. That's the way he pitched that night.

We were tied 2–2 through seven innings. Ronnie and Sid had hit solo homers. But in the eighth I got tired and couldn't get my pitches where I wanted them. After Gary Redus singled with one out, Jay Bell doubled and they had runners at second and third when Bobby came out and called for Mike Stanton to pitch to Van Slyke. Mike threw a pretty decent pitch on the inside corner to Andy, but he drove it deep to center and Redus scored the winning run.

The killer for me was Game 6. I had a chance to win the play-offs. We were up 3–2 and we were back home. We lost Game 5, 7–1, as Ave finally had the outing of someone who's human and Bob Walk pitched a nice game. It also marked the revival of Barry Bonds, who had two hits and a stolen base, and also made an incredible diving catch to rob Ronnie Gant of at least a double in the fourth inning.

The last thing we wanted was for Barry to come out of his shell. He had met with Jimmy Leyland in his office for an hour after Game 2 in one of those pep-talk-type sessions where Jimmy told him to relax and have fun. It was obvious Barry was pressing and all of the added media coverage he was getting was distracting to him.

It was no secret that coming into this series and in '91, Barry was the guy we wanted to hold down. He's so talented that if you can keep him at bay you have a chance of winning the game.

I don't think there was a real personality problem with Barry. Sure, he's flamboyant, cocky, call it whatever you want. He talks a lot when he's out on the field. But unlike some guys, Barry plays hard. He backs up what he's saying. Sure, I don't act like Barry on the field and there's always that part of you that wants to shut him up and keep him out of the game. But the real reason you want to beat him and keep him from hurting you is because he's the big cheese in that lineup. Normally, you're very careful with a guy like that. You pitch around him. But it was obvious to us that he was struggling, so we decided, "Let's go after him and hope that he keeps struggling."

Then again, you can't just focus on Barry. The way the Pirates offense worked those two years is the top of their order tried to get on base, Jay would bunt the runner over, and Barry would drive him in.

So you're definitely focused as a pitcher on what leads up to Barry Bonds. At the very best, you're hoping to get a chance to face him one-on-one with nobody else on base.

I think what I did well against him in that series better than I've been able to do since is use the inside part of the plate effectively. That probably opened up my fastball away and a slider in. I had a good thing going against him, but since then he's worn me out, making adjustments while I haven't.

Up 3–2 in the series we headed back to Fulton County Stadium and all I had to do was pitch like I had in Game 3 and we probably would have won and given ourselves an extra day to prepare for the Blue Jays in the World Series. But I stunk out the place. I was starting to wonder whether all those people were right about me.

The Pirates destroyed me, 13–4. I allowed eight runs and six hits and never got an out in the second inning. In fact, I threw twenty pitches that inning and after the twentieth pitch the Pirates were up 8–0. As in the All-Star game, it seemed everything I threw up there they hit, but the stakes were so much higher.

Talk about depressed. I had a chance to wrap it up and I gave the Pirates more confidence and more life. There was no redeeming aspect of the rest of this game, though David did hit a couple of homers against Wakefield.

I could tell Bobby wasn't thrilled with me after that one, and why should he be? He was diplomatic to the press. "Tommy actually had good stuff, but there are two pitches he threw to Bell and Bonds that were in the middle part of the plate. We have to go out and play much better baseball than we did tonight and get better pitching."

That's for sure. I put Smoltzie in a very difficult situation to have to pitch a Game 7. He went out and pitched a solid game, but our offense couldn't muster much against Doug Drabek. We trailed 2–0.

But in the ninth, the Braves became the Braves. The greatest thing about our team has been our ability to pull off the sensational with our backs against the wall. At this point we were barely breathing—three outs away from that Pirates payback.

We were all a little jittery in the dugout. We were talking it up, saying all of the positive things you can in those situations, like "C'mon, we can win this thing!" Or "One hit at a time!"

Terry was scheduled to lead off the inning. And as big a player as Terry is, the fact remained that he hadn't been able to touch Drabek the last two years in the play-offs—zero-for-fifteen. But because he was the big-play player for us you just throw those stats out the window. He doubled to right field in what was an incredibly huge hit. Everyone was aware of Terry's troubles against Drabek and the feeling was, "Okay, if Terry can find a way, we can all find a way."

David then grounded routinely to Chico Lind at second, and amazingly the ball bounced off his glove! The man is a Gold Glove second baseman and anything hit remotely close to him is an automatic out.

Suddenly, there's hope. Our fans are overjoyed and the tomahawks are flying and the chant is going on and everyone's into it. After Doug walked Sid to load the bases, Jimmy Leyland brought in Stan Belinda, who is a guy with hard, nasty stuff.

Ronnie got the first run in with a sacrifice fly. With the score 2–1, there's a lot of emotion in the dugout. Even Bobby was clapping his hands trying to inspire Damon Berryhill, the next batter. In a nice, patient at bat, Berryhill walked, and then Belinda got Brian Hunter on a soft pop-up.

There's two outs, bases loaded. This is our last chance. Bobby looked up and down the bench and there weren't many hitters available in this situation. Finally he settled on Cabrera. Francisco hadn't been used all that often, but here was a guy who had a real quick bat. And what people didn't know at the time was he had hit a home run off Belinda in 1991.

So Francisco comes up and works the count to 2–1. Stan is coming right at him because that's the way he pitches. He also has that imposing look on his face when he pitches and that's often intimidating to the hitter. But on a 2–1 pitch, Francisco got a fastball and lined a single to left. David scored the tying run, but Jimy Williams, our third base coach, decided Sid's going to try to score the winning run. Barry made a nice play heading toward the corner to retrieve the ball and he threw a strike to Mike Lavalliere at the plate. But Sid, who often ran as if he had a piano on his back, shed the keyboard and slid in just slightly ahead of the throw!

My teammates and I sprinted out to home plate for the celebration and to congratulate the play-off hero, Mr. Cabrera.

The celebration continued in the clubhouse afterward and Deion got a little carried away and decided to pour a bucket of ice water over Tim McCarver, the color commentator for CBS. Tim had criticized Deion for playing both sports at such a crucial time. Deion had played in an Atlanta Falcons–Miami game and then helicoptered into Fulton County Stadium for our play-off game against Pittsburgh.

What Deion did wasn't necessary. As frustrating as things

reporters or commentators say might sometimes be, you should never retaliate like that. That's not the proper way for a professional to act. And that goes for Albert Belle with Hannah Storm and other media people he's been nasty to over the years.

Deion also went after John Schuerholz during the World Series when John said that Deion reneged on their agreement by continuing to play football. He told *New York Newsday,* "I don't like Schuerholz trying to damage my credibility. One thing I pride myself in is being real. If a man ain't got his word, he ain't got nothing." Schuerholz fired back, "There are some people I've known in my life I respect. I'd be hurt if they were critical of me. He's not one of them."

You hate to see that kind of bickering between player and management, especially in the postseason when everyone should be on the same page and where differences should be put aside for the time being. That's what bothered me about that spat. Sometimes strong words can motivate a player and other times it just creates chaos. I don't think John's words affected Deion's play one way or another, but at a time like this it's better to say nothing.

We had pushed ourselves into the World Series once again, by spilling every ounce of energy, sweat, and blood. We now understood the magnitude of the World Series, the media attention, the attention of people all over the world focused squarely on us.

This World Series was a little different in that it was being hailed as a "true" World Series because the participants represented the United States and Canada. I guess I've never thought about Montreal or Toronto being teams from another country since they play major league baseball and we routinely visit Canada during the season. I didn't really feel like I was in the Olympics or anything like that. I guess the hype and marketing for the series was certainly geared toward that, though.

There were other little side stories. Obviously, Bobby and Jimy had been with the Blue Jays, both having managed the team in the 1980s. Cito Gaston was the hitting coach and Jimy was a third base coach when Bobby managed there in 1985. But I never thought either of them got caught up in that at all other than all of them being happy they were in the World Series.

Otis was experiencing his first postseason, having missed the '91 series while serving the drug suspension. He truly appreciated being out there. He said, "It's the greatest feeling in the world being here and being able to play. I have to thank the man upstairs because there was a lot of doubt that I would be back, but I had a lot of support out there."

And, ah, Jack Morris was now pitching for Toronto. Jack said in a pregame press conference that pitching three games in the World Series this year shouldn't be as taxing as it was in 1991. "I'm physically stronger, and we're in the same time zone for all the games." Great. How could he be stronger than what we saw in 1991? They also had a great staff with David Cone, Jimmy Key, and Juan Guzman and a great lineup with Robbie Alomar, Dave Winfield, Joe Carter, and John Olerud. It wasn't going to be easy.

Meanwhile, I was going through another crisis because Bobby decided to go with me in Game 1 and was having his head taken off by the media. When Leo told me I was pitching Game 1, he gave me a sermon:

"I don't care what you've gone through. The fact of the matter is you've won twenty games for us each of the last two years and I wouldn't want anybody else out there than you!"

Those were words I needed to hear. Leo always knew how to get straight to my soul.

For that reason, and for the way I pitched, I have to list my Game 1 performance in the top five games I've been involved with. If there was ever a time when I wanted to stand up and tell reporters "I told you so and the hell with you!" that was it. It was a very gratifying game. Whenever you tell me I can't succeed at something or criticize my manager for a move like that, then I respond. I guess maybe sometimes you need a kick in the butt like that.

I was also pissed off that Bobby was suddenly getting this label that he was the manager "who couldn't win the big series." I just thought that was totally unfair. Look at all the games he won and how he worked behind the scenes at acquiring great young players when he was the GM. And look at what happened. He took a last place team to first place in a half a year.

It's always been that Bobby doesn't get a lot of credit when we win because our team is so damned good. But when we lose he takes on an awful lot of the blame. That came up even more later.

Damon and I had a good game plan, which we implemented pretty well. We wanted to establish the inside part of the plate against their big right-handed hitters. I also wanted to throw a lot more breaking pitches than normal to keep them off balance. Other than Carter's fourth-inning homer we succeeded.

I told myself I wasn't going to let a solo homer get the best of me. I settled back in and stuck to the game plan and got the next twelve batters out. Pat Borders stroked a leadoff single in the eighth, but we erased him on a double-play ball.

Jack was pretty tough. He had an excellent forkball going and we were chasing it for a while. But then in the sixth we started getting a little more patient with him. David walked and Sid stayed with a forkball and sent it to the opposite field for a single. Then Damon really rocked the place when he blasted a home run over the right field wall to give us a 3–1 lead.

The way I was pitching, I knew I could make the runs stand up. After all the crap I took before the game, there was no way I was going to give it back. We held on and won and finally we had beaten Jack!

It was all pretty frustrating for our team from there. Offensively we didn't take advantage of certain opportunities presented to us and we didn't make the pitches when we needed to. Jeff Reardon was right in the middle of losses in Game 2 and Game 3, and as a pitcher I can sympathize with what he went through. After Jeff's performances in those games our organization was heavily criticized for not going out and getting a big-name closer. All I can say is, the guys in the bull pen did a fine job all year for us. If they hadn't, we wouldn't have made the postseason and won ninety-eight games. People forget that.

In Game 2, we were up 4–3 as the game headed into the ninth, and they rallied off Jeff, topped off by an Ed Sprague homer that won it for them 5–4. In Game 3 we were tied 2–2 in the ninth but with the bases loaded and one out, Candy Maldonado pounced on one of Jeff's mistakes and singled in the winning run.

Down 2–1, I was coming back on three days' rest, I was up against Jimmy Key, who, as I've said, pitches a lot like me and is a guy I've always admired. He gave me a lot to admire in that game. He was virtually unhittable. At one stage he retired sixteen straight batters. Only one hit separated his performance from mine over six innings and it was a costly one—a sixth-inning homer by Pat Borders. It wasn't a bad pitch, he just went down in the strike zone and got it. Even Borders described it as "a high fly ball that scraped the back of the wall. It didn't go very far, but it counts."

Jimmy went into the eighth inning and that's when Duane Ward and Tom Henke took over and shut the door on our offense. Their bull pen definitely did the job.

They scored the winning run in the seventh when Devon singled up the middle, scoring Kelly Gruber with the second run. Terry cut off the throw to the plate and some debated whether we would have had Gruber, but I doubt it.

One of the most controversial plays of the game came in the eighth when we had runners at first and third and Damon decided to bunt to get on base. He popped it up. Bobby was mad. Damon certainly didn't mean to pop up, but Bobby wanted him swinging away. Lemke brought us to within a run on his tapper off Jimmy's glove, and then Otis made a heads-up play when he went to first on strike three.

And then Jeff Blauser followed with a groundout to end the inning. Bobby was questioned about why he didn't bring out a left-handed hitter to face Ward, who replaced Jimmy with two outs. He had Deion and Sid available, but what he said I agree with: Jeff is one of our best pure hitters and he can handle any pitcher. The fact is we squandered a great opportunity to score and tie the game.

Down three games to one, it was easy to point fingers. I thought we had pitched well enough to at least be even, but we were hitting .185 and the middle of our order had been held pretty easily by Toronto pitching. Deion was a shining star for us, five-for-seven in his first two games. Bobby was using him in left field over Ronnie Gant against right-handed pitching because Ronnie was mired in a slump. Ronnie didn't like it, but he understood that Bobby needed to do what was best for the club.

Before Game 5 we held a team meeting to clear the air on some stuff. David had gone on a radio show and referred to some problems that were hurting team morale. Sid came out before Game 5 and said, "I know all players were giving 110 percent. But there are two ways of going out there on the ball field. You can be excited about playing but you have to have the right kind of mind-set or focus. To some degree that's what we've been lacking. I don't believe we've been going out with the same intensity."

Bobby responded to the comments by saying he didn't agree.

Maybe we didn't have the same intensity. Maybe it was difficult to recapture it after '91. I saw a lot of guys busting out there. It was just breaks and it was Toronto's pitching. They were doing a great job.

We went out and played with that intensity in Game 5 and won 7–2, assuring ourselves we'd go back to Atlanta. Everyone thought Jack would destroy us in that game and Toronto would win at home in five. But Lonnie belted a fifth-inning grand slam, the type of big hit we hadn't had up to that point. Cito was second-guessed quite a bit for leaving Jack in too long, but how can you blame him? Jack is a tough guy to take out of a game based on his track record. Still, everyone thought Cito had made a tactical blunder because with the final two games in Atlanta, Jack might be called upon.

It was a pretty good matchup with Ave going against Cone. Both pitchers are absolutely intimidating. Cone has some of the best stuff in baseball for a right-hander and Ave for a lefty. Candy Maldonado homered and gave the Jays a 2–1 lead in the fourth and Bobby decided Ave would only go four innings on three days' rest. Pete Smith, who went 7–0 for us at the end of the regular season, threw three zeroes, keeping us alive.

With a 2–1 lead, the Jays brought in Tom Henke. Blauser singled, went to third on Damon's sacrifice bunt, and after Francisco came up to pinch-hit and lined out to left, Otis came through with a two-out single in the shortstop hole. We tied it!

The game remained tied into the eleventh with Charlie Leibrandt still on the mound. With his thirty wins over two seasons, Charlie was the heart of our pitching staff and we all had faith in him. But Charlie got into trouble when Devon White and Robbie Alomar singled. When Carter came to bat, some were wondering where Reardon was, but Bobby stuck with Charlie thinking that if we got out of the inning, Jeff would be there to go to. Charlie did get Carter to fly out, but then Winfield lined a two-run double, hitting a decent change-up.

Despite being down two runs, we still had a chance and nothing we did would have surprised me. We rallied against Jimmy Key, who had come into the game in relief in the tenth, with a Blauser single and eventually scored on Brian Hunter's grounder. We caught a break when Damon's grounder took a bad hop over Alfredo Griffin's head. Raffy moved the runners along with a bunt. Now there were two outs and it was in Otis's hands.

I can't remember a tenser moment as I sat on the bench. I said to myself, "God, one more big play and we're back in this thing again." Everyone had their eyes on Otis, almost willing him to hit. Otis, one of the best bunters I've ever seen, tried to drag one down the first base line, but it wasn't quite beyond the reach of Mike Timlin. He threw Otis out at first base. The game, the series, was over.

My emotions went from one extreme to the other. There was so much hope that we were going to pull it out again. When we didn't, and the Blue Jays were jumping all over the field, reality set in in a hurry.

I made my way back to the locker room where the pain and anguish in everyone's face were plain to see. We were all stunned into silence. Two years in a row we'd made it to the greatest event in baseball and lost. How many more times would it take before we won it all and how much did we have left in our hearts to get here again? It made us all wonder.

My personal life, at least, was looking up. On November 2, Carri and I were married at the Country Club of the South in Atlanta. We invited about 250 people and it was a joyous moment in my life. Knowing that Carri and I were starting a new life together made all the heartache bearable. Now there was more to worry about than just me. I had someone to answer to, someone to come home to, and someone else to think about every time I stepped out on the field.

Meanwhile, I had entered into contract talks with the Braves. My agent, Gregg Clifton, and John Schuerholz spoke off and on for about three weeks. The talks progressed smoothly and there were never many bumps along the way. I think the relationship I'd built with the Braves over the years really helped.

A lot of that stemmed from the philosophy of my first agent, the late Bob Woolf. He told me early on, "Look, I could sit here and argue with these guys and maybe get you an extra five or ten thousand dollars, but at this stage in your career, I'd rather not create an uproar, because somewhere down the road we're going to get into an argument and it's going to be over millions of dollars. I'd rather develop an amicable relationship with these guys so when it comes time to discuss a long-term deal, there's gonna be a lot friendlier atmosphere."

He hit the nail on the head. After he passed away and Gregg, who had taken over for Bob as the CEO, began long-term contract talks after the 1992 season, they couldn't have gone any smoother. And Gregg got me a great contract, which was consummated on December 17. It was a nice Christmas present. I received a $1 million signing bonus and salaries of $4.5 million for 1993, $4.5 million for 1994, $4.5 million in 1995, and $5 million in 1996. I also have an option year for $5 million in 1997.

The money was gratifying and I was happy to have Carri to share it with. More good news was on the way—a surprise addition to the team.

14

Here Comes Mad Dog

ON DECEMBER 9, 1992, EIGHT DAYS BEFORE I'D SIGNED MY long-term deal with the Braves, John Schuerholz shocked baseball and signed Greg Maddux to a five-year deal worth $28 million. I was completely surprised.

We already had what I thought was the best starting rotation in baseball, so that was the last aspect of our game that needed help, but Greg's contract certainly defined the market for my deal, which was about $3.5 million less than Greg's. Rumors were hot that we were going to get Barry Bonds, which would have been great for our offense and seemed to make more sense. But the more I thought about Mad Dog coming on board, the better I liked the idea. By adding a Cy Young Award winner to it, now we'd really have the best rotation in baseball. There was a downside, though; it meant that Charlie Leibrandt wouldn't be re-signed. Charlie had become a huge part of our staff, fit in perfectly, and he was one of the gang. I had learned a lot from him. Needless to say, I was disappointed.

Sooner or later there comes a point where the business drives team management to make tough decisions. With a chance to improve his pitching, which is the name of the game, there was no way Schuerholz could pass up one of the best available. Doggie had his share of suitors; in fact, he turned down something like $6 to $7 million more from the Yankees. He decided on Atlanta because he understood that he'd be part of a great staff with a team that had an excellent chance to win it all, not to mention that Atlanta is a great place to live with a superior quality of life.

It was also a great move by John because, while the reduction of TV revenues after the CBS-TV deal expired hit owners hard, forcing reductions in payroll across the board, Greg was a good investment, someone who would offer management, the fans, and Ted Turner peace of mind. In other words, money well spent.

Everything was about money.

It wasn't easy to say good-bye to Charlie, who eventually signed with the Texas Rangers. But one of the first days that Mad Dog came to town we all went out golfing together. That was a nice way to say good-bye to Charlie and welcome Mad Dog at the same time.

Mad Dog and Charlie hit it off very well. The subject of Mad Dog replacing Charlie never came up. Both knew what was going on and both were professional enough not to have to discuss it. Instead, the conversation between the two centered around golf.

Greg Maddux is the humblest guy I've ever met. For someone who's achieved so much and who might be the best pitcher ever, he's very unassuming. Looking at him, you wouldn't know he's an athlete. Nor does he pound his chest and declare, "Hey, look at me, I'm the best pitcher in baseball!" He's a lot like the rest of us—he enjoys golf, goofing around, his time away from the field with his family. On the field, a completely different guy, he's extremely observant and intense.

When he first reported to camp, Smoltzie, Ave, and I knew right off the bat that he was going to fit in. He really just wanted to be a part of this team.

The hot topic in spring training that year was whether I was a little jealous about Maddux coming and taking over the top spot in the rotation. That was never a problem. I don't think Mad Dog came in and assumed he was the number one guy, and I know I never assumed I was it. Sure, I won the Cy Young Award and had won twenty games two years in a row, but we had Smoltzie and Ave and Charlie, who could be number one on a lot of teams.

Bobby said he made the choice to start Mad Dog on opening day because "We were playing against the Cubs, his old team," and not because there was a number one and number two designation. I think that fell into place naturally.

This was also a place where Leo had to weigh in: "I think they mesh together well. Tom Glavine doesn't care about labels or who's number one or number two. But I will say this, it's a great motivational tool because Tom Glavine doesn't want to play second fiddle to anyone. And there's not one damn thing wrong with that."

I suppose there's a healthy, friendly competition between us and it was never more evident than in 1993 when I was leading 11–2 late in a game and Bobby turned to Leo and said, "That's enough, let's save him for the next start. It's late in the season and we have to preserve his strength for the postseason." When everything is flowing and when I'm physically fine, I hate to come out of games, and maybe that first year with Greg, they wouldn't have said the same thing to him simply because they didn't know him that well. I said kiddingly to Leo, "What's the matter, don't you want me to catch Maddux for most innings pitched?"

In the end, who was number one, two, or five was a nonissue, and there was never preferential treatment of Greg. We were all quality pitchers and when it was our guy's turn to pitch he was the number one on that night. Ups and downs are inevitable through the course of the year, and at some point one pitcher is going to get more attention than another. That's just the way it is.

Why is Greg so great? You can begin to answer that question by understanding he has a tremendous amount of talent and a great ability to locate the ball in an awkward spot and not to make mistakes over the plate.

He's also the most observant pitcher I've ever seen, aware of every little thing that's going around the batter's box. For instance, he notices if the batter is taking different swings at certain pitches; or if the batter moves around the batter's box trying to make adjustments; or even what the guy on the on-deck circle is doing to prepare for his at bat! That's God-given ability.

I don't mean to imply that the rest of us aren't aware of our surroundings because we do pick up things during the course of a game. But Mad Dog has an extra sense or something. In the time I've known him, I've tried to absorb some of the things he sees on a given at bat when we're in the dugout watching the game together. Then, when I go out to pitch, I try to look for the things that Greg looks for. I find it very difficult to do so because I'm so intense and I have tunnel vision when it comes to pitching, so I tend to block out things around me.

Because I follow him in the pitching rotation, I chart all his pitches. Charting is recording each pitch to each hitter, what type of pitch and where it was located. It can be valuable in detecting tendencies of hitters, information you keep in the back of your mind when you go out there the next night. It's very helpful for me to see how he pitched a certain hitter because I would say our style of pitching is fairly similar. Greg is probably going to use more breaking pitches and I'm going to throw more change-ups. But the basic game plan is changing speeds and changing locations.

What's difficult at times is having to follow up one of his performances. I mean, he's pitched some games for the books. Game 1 of the 1995 World Series was obviously one of the best-pitched games in World Series history. There have been others, of course.

He can go out and pitch to twenty-eight, twenty-nine, thirty batters and throw first-pitch strikes to twenty-five of them! He gets ahead of an ungodly number of hitters, with an amazing strike-to-ball ratio. His domination is a pleasure to watch. And because I know him so well now, it's fun for me when I'm charting the pitches to call what he's going to throw next. More often than not, I'm right.

I've often been amazed at what I've seen from our pitching staff. Bad outings for this group are considered fair outings for other pitching staffs. Is it the greatest ever? Maybe I'm not the best person to ask and it's not easy to be objective. I've talked about it with Jim Palmer, with whom I play golf occasionally. He was part of the great Orioles staffs that had four twenty-game winners in 1971 with Jim, Mike Cuellar, Dave McNally, and Pat Dobson. We haven't done that yet, but come up with a better overall pitching staff in recent memory.

When we came together in '93, you could tell we were going to be very tough to beat night to night. You had Greg's stuff coming at you from the right side, and then another finesse guy coming in from the left side in me, and then Smoltzie, who throws really hard with a great curveball. The next night you're getting Steve Avery, who's throwing hard fastballs and hard-breaking balls from the left side. And then we had another lefty in Merck as our fifth guy, who threw ninety-plus with a change-up.

Take Smoltz, a terrific pitcher. The toughest thing for him to deal with has been the expectations of him. Every year somebody is picking him to be the Cy Young Award winner, the pitcher with the best stuff in baseball. You go out and try to prove that those things are true about you and in some people's minds you fall short.

Actually, starting the 1996 season 14–1, Smoltzie was probably the early front-runner for the award, but I'll say no more for fear of jinxing him.

As is usually the case, there was a tendency to get too caught up in results and not how he actually pitched. He'll go out there and pitch to beat the band and at the end of the game he'll have lost 2–1 or 3–2. He's been the most snakebitten guy on our staff since I've been there. If he makes thirty-five starts a year and he keeps his team in the game twenty-five times, then he's done his job and more as a starting pitcher. And there's no disputing the fact that he's our money pitcher—our go-to guy in the postseason. He's been awesome.

He not only has one of the best moving fastballs in the game, but his curveball is as good as anyone's. As many times as I can mentally say to a hitter, "Here comes my change-up, see if you can hit it," he can do the same thing with his fastball.

John is a typical power pitcher in that he does make mistakes over the plate and he tends to get hurt more than I or Greg would when that happens. That's because most batters are fastball hitters and his mistakes play more into their strengths.

He's survived trade rumors and fortunately they didn't take him up on his offer at the beginning of the 1995 season to move to the bull pen to be a closer. I don't know what kind of a closer he'd be. He's a nervous wreck at times. Being put in a tough spot every day, I don't know if he could live with that.

And he's too valuable to us, a right-handed power pitcher who gives you 230 innings per year. Try and find a right-handed pitcher who can do that for you year in and year out.

It's kind of scary to think how good Ave's going to be. Throw out what happened to him in 1995. When you look at what he's done overall in his first four years in the major leagues, he's just blowing people away. A lot of people forget that he's only twenty-five years old still, and to have already played four years and to have the complete package he has as a pitcher is unheard of. The only guy I can think of who was that complete that young was Doc Gooden.

I don't know what happened to Ave in 1995 because he never said a word to us about it. But the fact that he went through so much with his prematurely born son and the accompanying complications had to have some effect on him. Having a little baby who had all he could do to live and giving support to your wife through it all must have been extremely difficult. Being a father myself, I don't know if I could have handled it. To come to the park every day with that on his mind—it's impossible to think that wasn't bothering him.

To his credit, he never used that as an excuse. In fact, every time I would ask him how he was and how his boy was he would say, "Yeah, everything's fine." He never said he couldn't concentrate or anything like that. It proves he's mature beyond his years.

I know Ave had a problem with Leo in Colorado that was written about last year. When Ave struggles he tends to wander around the mound. A lot of times Leo will come out to talk to him and Ave takes off toward second base. It's like he's saying, "I don't want to talk to you, Leo, get out of here!" Leo will sometimes say jokingly and sometimes seriously, "Knock it off! When I come out there and talk to you, stand on the mound. I don't care if you listen to me or not, just don't make me look like a fool! I don't want to be chasing you around!"

Well, in Colorado, Leo started coming out to the mound and Ave waved him off. That was the final straw with Leo, and they had a shouting match. It looked worse than it was, and of course, as is the way with Leo, the next day it's forgotten like it never happened.

Ave was frustrated by the results and sometimes you want to be able to come out of something by yourself. That shows how competitive Ave is.

And so we entered the 1993 season with the Fab Four. With that comes added pressures. People think you're supposed to win every game and go 162–0. Well, obviously there are other things that happen, like maybe you don't hit one game or maybe one of us has a bad outing. After a 12–13 April, we didn't have too many bumps in the road. But neither did the San Francisco Giants. We anticipated the Giants would be a formidable opponent. It didn't take a genius to figure out why. Their lineup had Matt Williams, a great power hitter who also hits for average, three-time MVP Barry Bonds (who had left the Pirates), Will Clark, Robbie Thompson, and some guys who could really pitch—starter Billy Swift, and out of the bull pen Mike Jackson and Rod Beck.

It was the most dominating year we've ever had. We won 104 games after being as many as 10 games behind the Giants on July 22. There was never any worry for us. We'd been through it all before and we knew with our pitching staff we were going to stay in contention. Amazingly, though, heading into the final day of the season we were playing Colorado and in a dead heat with the San Francisco Giants.

And I got to pitch it. Because of the magnitude of the game I'd call this one one of the top five games I've been involved with. I think I felt more pressure in that game than in any game I've ever pitched in my career.

Here we are on the last day of the year and we've got to play one of the best hitting teams in baseball.

Any time I can keep my team in the game against a potent lineup I've done my job. I left in the seventh after Roberto Mejia, a second baseman, had taken me deep to reduce our lead to 4–3. Steve Bedrosian came on to get Alex Cole with the final out and then Greg McMichael held on to a two-run lead—after David hit his fortieth home run in the bottom of the seventh—to preserve the win. I probably didn't pitch the best game I could, but we won 5–3 over the Rockies and with it we clinched the divisional title as the Giants, who were in a flat-footed tie with us, lost to the Dodgers (who always seem to be involved in our fortunes one way or another) in an exciting end-of-the-season series.

The 1993 season was also the forum for one of my other top five greatest games. On June 16, 1993, at Fulton County Stadium, I threw only seventy-nine pitches in a complete-game 2–1 win over the New York Mets. It has become the challenge of our entire pitching staff to surpass this feat. I'm sure Mad Dog will throw a complete game with seventy pitches someday soon. As a pitcher you always look to minimize your pitches. Getting through a game with as few pitches as possible is the ultimate goal.

I had a lot of things going for me. The main one was that the Mets were swinging at a lot of first pitches. There were thirteen first-pitch outs. And there's luck. When a team is going up there hacking at you like that, there's a chance they're going to get on base a lot because some hits are going to fall in. But I kept those to a minimum and we played excellent defense that night. Also, I didn't walk anybody, which is a key to minimizing pitches, and a bigger key is I didn't strike anyone out! I never got deep into any count.

The performance almost rendered Leo speechless. He said over and over again, "I've never seen anything like that before."

At a certain point in each game, Leo, who keeps a count of pitches on his clicker, usually has Bobby guess the pitch count. After six innings, Bobby guessed around seventy pitches, but it was only about fifty at that point.

"I know there have been complete games pitched with fewer pitches, but there can't be that many. That was the lowest I've ever seen," said Bobby.

The only bad pitch I made all day was in the fourth inning when I left one too far over the plate for Darrin Jackson and he smacked a home run.

The entire game lasted two hours and nine minutes. I was asked if I was in a hurry to get somewhere.

I went out to a 7–0 start, pitched pretty well in the middle, and finished the first half 12–2. Right after the All-Star break I lost a start and the same old crap was starting up again that I was tired and headed for my swoon. I really got pissed off and everyone knew it. Especially John Smoltz.

Before I got to the ballpark one day he got hold of a dummy's head and took a blanket and stuffed it to form a body. Then he took a pair of my cleats and stuck them just under the blanket. So it looked like this thing was lying down sleeping. He wrote a sign that said, "Shhh! Tom is tired. He's sleeping."

That really loosened me up. And reporters in Atlanta got a big kick out of it and they laid off the tired bit from then on.

I finished the season 22–6 with a 3.20 ERA, my third straight twenty-win season, which was the most by a Brave since Warren Spahn won twenty games six straight years, from 1956 to 1961. Another meaningful stat was that we went 27–9 in my thirty-six starts, which means I kept the team in the game more often than not. I was named to a third All-Star team, but I didn't pitch, which, considering my last performance, was a break for the National League.

Mad Dog won his second straight Cy Young with a 20–10 record and a 2.36 ERA. He pitched eight complete games and allowed only fifty-two walks in 267 innings. A masterful year. Ave was 18–6 with a 2.94 ERA in another great year and a nice rebound from his 11–11 mark in 1992. Smoltzie was a solid 15–11 and struck out 208 batters in 243⅔ innings. Mike Stanton had a breakthrough year out of the bull pen with twenty-seven saves.

Offensively, we had a middle of the order that was devastating. Ronnie Gant hit thirty-six homers and knocked in 117 runs, David hit forty homers and knocked in 120 runs, and Fred McGriff hit thirty-seven homers with 101 RBIs overall.

Fred's advent was another stroke of genius by John. He gets Maddux to start the year and then trades for the big power hitter at the precise moment when we needed him. He took advantage of the San Diego Padres' fire sale and sent three minor league prospects to the Padres for Fred. The Padres had an excellent veteran team in 1992, a great lineup with Fred, Darrin Jackson, Gary Sheffield, who nearly won the Triple Crown, and a great shortstop in Tony Fernandez. But Joe McIlvaine, who is now back with the Mets as their GM (building a team that's eventually going to pose a big challenge in our division), was told by owner Tom Werner he had to get rid of $12 to $15 million in payroll.

Fred had been traded a few times, and because I didn't know him that well, I wondered whether there was something about his personality that led teams to trade him. Guys who get traded a lot oftentimes are either tough for the managers to handle or they're not that good for a team. But it was obvious Fred wasn't any of these. He's one of the quietest guys you'd ever want to meet. He comes to the ballpark and just wants to go out and play every day and make life miserable for pitchers. He's one of the hitters I often discuss strategy with. I'll ask him as a hitter what pitch he expects to see in a certain situation and that gives me a nice perspective on how to pitch a hitter of his type—a strong, powerful left-handed hitter with few areas of weakness in his hitting zone.

The night he joined our team for the first time was one of the strangest I remember in Atlanta as a player. I was scheduled to start against the Cardinals, so I went through my normal routine and then took batting practice. After that was over I went into the trainers room to sip a cup of coffee and relax when all of a sudden a security guard came rushing in yelling, "You guys had better get out of here—the stadium is on fire!" Thinking it's a prank, we didn't give this announcement too much credence and went about our business. Suddenly we hear an explosion! We run out to the field and look up and we see part of the press box and a few of the luxury boxes are on fire. The fire started in one of the radio booths when a Sterno can (used to keep food trays warm) caught on fire and spread rapidly, causing millions in damage. It took a couple of hours to put out.

Like a rain delay situation, I wasn't sure if I should get ready or wait to see what's decided. If the game had been postponed and I warmed up too much, then I might not have been available the next night. But the game was played and Fred made quite a debut in the cleanup spot. He hit a two-run homer, and that helped us come back after I spotted the Cards five runs and they led 5–0. We ended up winning the game 8–5, no thanks to me. But Fred went on a tear after that and our entire lineup had a different look to it. Now, you had to get through Gant, Justice, and McGriff in the middle of the order, and that required the type of concentration from a pitcher that would eventually wear him out.

I've often said that it was the night the ballpark caught on fire that the Braves caught on fire. It was one of those streaks where you keep winning and winning and then you realize, "God, we've won thirty out of our last thirty-two games!" We were playing great ball, with solid pitching, increased offensive production, and steady defense. And then we swept the first-place Giants at Candlestick Park in late August.

We just kept going and going, never really looking back or looking through the standings to see where we were. In mid-September we finally caught the Giants after they'd gone on a long losing streak and went up by four games before they turned things around and won eleven out of twelve. I'm telling you, it seemed like as great as we played we couldn't distance ourselves. From the fan's perspective, it was great because this was a race between two teams that wouldn't say die. But from a player's perspective, it can be somewhat exhausting to always know you have to play at the highest level.

I beat the Mets on September 19 to win my twentieth game. Three straight years of twenty wins was an achievement I was proud of, but I knew I couldn't get too high on myself until I won my last two starts. There's no reason to be happy about winning twenty if you lose your last two starts and cost your team the title. So I went out and beat Houston on September 29 and gave us a one-game lead, and then I won the final game to clinch the division. Those twenty-two victories then became meaningful.

In that last series of the season between the Giants and Dodgers, I couldn't believe we were actually rooting for the Dodgers. But we were behind them all the way.

While the final game of the year meant little to the Dodgers, it was a pride thing for them. Tommy was Dodger blue and through his entire life he was brought up to hate the Giants. So beating the Giants and knocking them out of the race was extremely meaningful to him and he got his team to believe the same thing. The Dodgers were out of the race, so this was their championship series, so to speak.

The other interesting theme was that Dusty Baker managed the Giants and Dusty had played for Tommy as a Dodger. I respect both of them greatly as managers. They have great methods of motivating their teams and both have been successful. And let's not forget that it was the Giants who had kept the Dodgers out of the play-offs in 1991, which had to be on Tommy's mind. What do they say about revenge, that it's a dish best served cold?

After we had done all we could do and won 104 out of 162 games, we stayed in the clubhouse long after our game was over and turned on the Giants-Dodgers game on the clubhouse TV. Outside in the stands, the fans were told they could stay and watch the game on Diamond Vision. It was a neat situation, where everyone was biting their nails and on the edge of their seats.

I was actually cheering when Mike Piazza—a guy who kills me— hit a home run off Dave Burba in the fifth. He led a charge that inning that produced three more runs, and the Dodgers were up 6–1. When all they had to do was hold on, Piazza came back and hit another three-run homer late in the game.

Because of the fight the Giants gave us, we all felt that this was a meaningful title.

And we just hoped we could keep our fans as excited as they were outside the stadium after the Dodgers beat the Giants that day. We had to prove to them and ourselves that we could follow up a great season with a successful postseason.

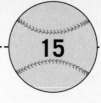

15

Twenty-four Morons and One Mormon

WE WERE A LITTLE TIRED ENTERING THE PLAY-OFFS. WHETHER or not that made a difference in the outcome is subject to debate. Personally, I thought it had to take something out of us.

It's hard to make people understand the intensity level of a September pennant race like we had with the Giants. Every night we were scoreboard watching. Every game was gut-wrenching. You'd be on the field and you knew that one mistake and you put your team in peril.

So it's not surprising that we walked into the play-offs a little flat. And maybe that sounds like an excuse and maybe people will say, "How can you not get up for the play-offs?" There's a difference between being excited about being there and being physically able to endure it.

You have to give a lot of credit to the Philadelphia Phillies. When you do the normal breakdown and preseries analysis you had to give us the edge in pitching, the offenses were fairly even, and we certainly had the edge defensively. But when I look at the six games of that series I have to admit that it was their defense that made all the difference to them. I'll bet you they made defensive plays they didn't make during the season.

They also had a great chemistry. They really made the most of their grungy image and John Kruk's characterization of them as "twenty-four morons and one Mormon [Dale Murphy]." Really in that way they were a completely different team from us. They were definitely the media darlings that year, just as we had been in '91. I think the media was probably a little sick of us at this point. It was like, "God, we have to go to Atlanta again!"

The Phils had a tendency to do things a little bit differently than most teams and they had some guys, like Kruk and Mitch Williams, who were a bit strange and off-the-wall. But I guess that's what made them tick. They got maximum return on their talent.

That's the beauty of baseball—that in any given year a team can come out of the blue and have a great season. But it wasn't at all surprising that it didn't last for them beyond '93 and even beyond the play-offs. With injuries in subsequent years they didn't have enough depth to overcome the fact they were unable to get career years from their big hitters again, nor from their pitchers.

They weren't a team we liked a whole lot. As I've already outlined in an earlier chapter, we'd had beanball wars with them earlier in the year. There was a lot of trash-talking from their side. They were a team we just wanted to beat and put in their place.

But they turned the tables on us.

Curt Schilling, a hard thrower who went 16–7 for the "Phil-thies," as they called themselves, seemed to set the tone for the entire play-offs when he struck out our first five hitters in the first two innings in Game 1 at Veterans Stadium. Nixon, Blauser, and Gant all succumbed to Curt in the first, and then McGriff and Justice both went down to give Curt the National League play-off record. Curt struck out ten in all. Because I had started the final game of the season, Bobby went with a rotation of Ave and Greg in the first two games, I went in Game 3 in Atlanta, followed by Smoltzie in Game 4. When you have a staff like ours it doesn't really matter what the rotation is.

Curt worked himself out of a couple of jams, where if we had gotten a hit at the right time, we might have won the game, because Ave pitched very well. We tied it 1–1 when Ave and Otis hit back-to-back doubles to score a run. (See, that's what I mean about a pitcher being able to help himself!) Then we took the lead in the fourth when the middle of our order—Ronnie, Fred, and David—all had a hand in producing the run.

But the game was tied when Kim Batiste, who had come in as a defensive replacement for Dave Hollins, took Mark Lemke's routine

Hockey was my first love—I knew how to skate before I knew how to throw a ball. I'm seven years old and ready for action. *Below:* I'm on the ice for my freshman year at Billerica High.

My brother Mike usually came along on game day. He doesn't look too thrilled standing next to me, but soon he'd be wearing a uniform of his own. *Below:* I'm hanging out with the high school team on the sidelines. Pitching at Billerica High set the tone for the rest of my career.

My family has been a big part of my success. My brother Fred, my sister Debbie, and my brother Mike, all dressed to kill. *Below:* My brother Fred joining Dad and Mom at Fulton County Stadium.

The 1987 Braves team picture. I'm not in it because I joined the team midseason. Despite the dog days, a lot of the guys managed a smile for the photographer. There were some terrific veterans on the team—Ken Griffey Sr., Graig Nettles, and Dale Murphy to name a few. *Top row:* Ted Simmons, Gerald Perry, Ken Oberkfell, Rafael Ramirez, Rick Mahler, Ken Griffey, Ed Olwine, Andres Thomas, Charlie Puleo, Graig Nettles, Damaso Garcia, Dion James. *Middle row:* Batting Practice Pitcher Jim Guadagno, Assistant Equipment Manager Casey Stevenson, Ozzie Virgil, Randy O'Neal, Bruce Sutter, Jim Acker, Paul Assenmacher, Gary Roenicke, Dale Murphy, Jeff Dedmon, Zane Smith, Bruce Benedict, David Palmer, Albert Hall, Trainer Dave Pursley. *Front row:* Traveling Secretary Bill Acree, Gene Garber, Coach Rich Morales, Coach Willie Stargell, Coach Bob Skinner, Manager Chuck Tanner, Coach Bruce Dal Canton, Coach Tony Bartirome, Coach Russ Nixon, Coach Al Monchak, Glenn Hubbard, Assistant Trainer Jeff Porter. *Batboys:* Jimmy Abel, Brad Phillips, Rick Gill, Edward Robinson Jr. (*missing*). (*Photograph courtesy of Joe Sebo for the Atlanta Braves*)

Braves Executive Vice President and General Manager John Schuerholz
shakes my hand at the press conference announcing my winning the
1991 Cy Young Award. This is one of the proudest moments of my life.
But, still, no championship ring.

Bobby Cox is one reason the Braves organization is one of the finest in baseball. He and GM John Schuerholz made us think like winners.
(Photograph courtesy of Joe Sebo for the Atlanta Braves)

Pitching coach Leo Mazzone is an excellent pitching coach, and I don't know where I'd be without him. His methods may seem unorthodox but they've helped create a top-notch pitching staff.
(Photograph courtesy of Charlie McCullers for the Atlanta Braves)

There was some nice stuff to say about my performance in my first All-Star game in 1991. Two shutout innings and only one hit. I did a lot worse in the 1992 All-Star game, allowing five runs in one and two-thirds innings. Not pretty. *(Bottom photograph courtesy of Barbara Bowen for the Atlanta Braves)*

Charlie Leibrandt was a veteran who took all the young pitchers under his wing, including me. He was a good man to learn from as well as a good friend. I was sorry to see him go when he was traded to make room for Greg Maddux. *(Photograph courtesy of Phil Davis for the Atlanta Braves)*

I don't think I need to point out the obvious, but Greg Maddux is the best pitcher in the majors, maybe the best ever. He is a master craftsman and—with him first in the rotation and me second—a tough act to follow. *(Photograph courtesy of Joe Sebo for the Atlanta Braves)*

Steve Avery has got ice in his veins. The kid rarely if ever cracks under pressure. *(Photograph courtesy of Joe Sebo for the Atlanta Braves)*

Looks like John Smoltz hit his stride in the 1996 season. I'm not surprised, though. This guy can throw some serious heat. *(Photograph courtesy of Joe Sebo for the Atlanta Braves)*

Some of the guys who have made winning easier for me and made the Braves champions: Fred McGriff (*top*), whose power has taken us to a higher level; Marquis Grissom (*middle*), the ideal leadoff man; Lemke (*bottom*) and Blauser (*opposite, top*), the perfect double play combination; Chipper Jones (*middle*), who's made third base his own; and Javy Lopez (*bottom*), like a rock behind the plate. (*Photographs courtesy of Joe Sebo for the Atlanta Braves*)

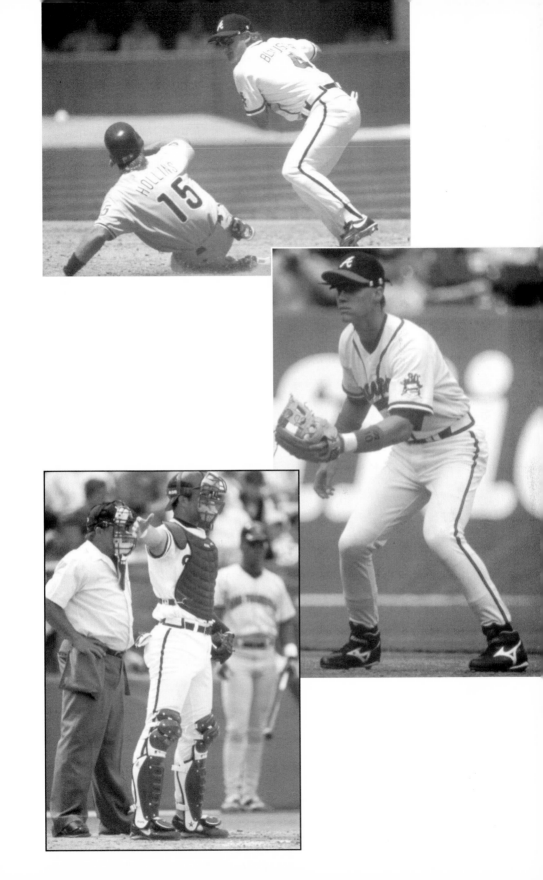

While I was doing my thing on the mound during Game 6 of the 1995 World Series . . .

. . . David Justice was doing his thing at the plate by smashing a home run that would be the only run of the game.

Mark Wohlers sealed the win, shutting down the Indians in the ninth. Many say Mark was the missing ingredient—the devastating closer we never had.

We won! There is no better feeling.

Braves President Stan Kasten and Bobby Cox hold the 1995 World Series trophy. These guys had worked long and hard for this moment.

Braves owner, Ted Turner, congratulates me on winning the 1995 World Series MVP Award. He was at every postseason game with his wife, Jane Fonda, cheering us on.

It's become a tradition for the president to invite the champions to the White House. We had a great time meeting President Clinton and presented him with a jersey.

The two people I cherish
most—my wife, Carri, and our
pride and joy, Amber.

double-play grounder and threw it away. We scored the tying run from there, but Batiste got his revenge in the bottom of the tenth when he singled to score Kruk.

It was a great story in Philly as the defensive replacement boots it and then becomes the hero.

But it was one of those games you just forget about and move on to the next one. In Game 2 we were facing Tommy Greene, an old friend from our early days with the Braves, and Tommy was 10–0 at Veterans Stadium, so everyone thought it was a great chance for the Phils to go up two games. Tommy had also pitched a great game against us in September, so we weren't looking forward to facing him.

Couple that with the fact that the Phillies pitchers have a great advantage at Veterans Stadium because the mound there is one of the worst in the league. It's hard to describe unless you're on the mound striding off it. It just has a funny feel to it—too steep, a more severe slope than Fulton County Stadium—and most of our pitchers have never been able to get used to it. I like a steep mound, but on this one it's hard for my arm to catch up to the rest of my body as I'm into my delivery.

But Tommy had one of those games that I've had a time or two when everything you throw up to the plate gets hit. Fred hit a long first-inning home run—the IBM Tale of the Tape measured it at 438 feet to the upper deck in right field, but it had to be longer than that—to give us a 2–0 lead.

Fred's homer was big for us. Our bench just exploded and the spirit we had been known for, but lacking, came shining through. It was exactly what we needed at that point after losing such a tough first game. The whole mood of our team changed. Suddenly, any sense that we were tired went away. We had the lead and we had Greg pitching. That's a confident combination. Blauser, Berryhill, and Terry all homered in the game and Greg took an easy win. In the third inning we strung together six straight hits against Tommy, and that's when we pretty much sewed it up and went on to win it 14–3.

When a team erupts like that it puts the next-day pitcher in a nice spot. Even though we had a day off between Games 2 and 3, our bats were hot and we were returning to Atlanta where our crowd would again act as the tenth man. I knew if I pitched a solid game and kept the Phillies down within reason, our offense would be able to do the rest. And that's exactly what happened. We won it 9–4. I went seven innings and earned my first play-off win. At last I got the monkey off my back. Those are things that you don't really think about but people kept throwing in my face. At least I didn't have to hear it anymore.

The best thing about that game is that I didn't walk anybody, and when you're in the postseason, that's key. I allowed two triples and Kruk hit a solo homer off me in the sixth inning to give the Phillies a 2–0 lead. But solo homers don't concern me unless, of course, they're hit in the ninth inning when we have a one-run lead or the game is tied.

As much as I thought we were going to keep up this offensive onslaught that had produced twenty-three runs in two games, I knew Philadelphia's pitching wasn't about to allow that. Instead, we went back to close, low-scoring games. Danny Jackson and Smoltzie hooked up in an excellent dual in Game 4, but Mark Lemke made an error in the fourth that we weren't able to overcome.

But you can't point the finger at Mark, who is probably the best second baseman in the league. Unfortunately, we had runners on base in seven of the eight innings Jackson was in the game but couldn't bring them home.

And the "Wild Thing"—Mitch Williams—also wiggled out of a couple of jams late in the game. In the ninth we had two on and nobody out, but we couldn't get it done. Ronnie hit into a double play to end the game. All in all, we were one-for-fifteen with runners in scoring position and, unfortunately, that isn't going to get the job done. And as eventful as Mitch made things, tip your cap to him for getting himself out of a tough situation on a night he didn't have a whole lot of strength. He had eaten something bad during the day and was suffering from food poisoning.

The next night we continued to play sluggishly. The Phillies defense was the reason they were able to leave Atlanta with a 3–2 lead in the series. Wes Chamberlain, who was normally a guy who would come out of their lineup late in the game for defensive reasons, made two throws that cut down key runners.

In the first inning he made a nice throw to the relay man, Kevin Stocker, who gunned Blauser down at the plate. Then in the second, Berryhill hit one to the wall in right and Chamberlain nailed him at second base. Then Pete Incaviglia, another outfielder not known for his defense, made a nice diving catch down the line in left field to rob us again. Still, while we trailed 3–0, we were able to come back and make it interesting, tying it 3–3 until the tenth when Len Dykstra hit a homer off Wohlers.

The loss really hurt our team mentally. After a while the emotion of being involved in so many tough, close games gets to you. We were very quiet in the locker room that night. We didn't want to say much to the reporters, and a lot of us just stayed away from the central part of the room and went into the lounges and trainers room just to escape the media. There are times when there just isn't anything to say. And this was one of them.

The Phillies were now in a great position. They needed one win to eliminate us. Our bull pen was being maligned for giving up big hits, but again, without their steady performance, 104 wins weren't possible.

The Phillies, who didn't lack for cockiness anyway, could smell the pennant. Fregosi was a perfect manager for that team. He pushed all the right buttons and had a way of getting them incredibly up and setting the tone of a "you against us" mentality. He said in the press conference after that game, "According to some people, we're not supposed to be on the same field with Atlanta." Well, they proved they belonged.

The waiting for the series to shift back to Philadelphia felt like an eternity. Then, we lost the finale, 6–3. Even with Greg on the mound, we just didn't have anything left.

I don't think I'd ever seen a more depressed clubhouse after the loss. You can accept losing, but when you're a team with our talent it seems everyone is gunning for you. Every time some team plays a key game against you, they're playing the greatest game they ever played to beat you. After a while that feeling is tough to deal with. As talented and professional as we were, we weren't superhuman. And in 1993, the Phillies were just better. And once we understood that we were able to let it go.

The Phillies went on to lose to the Toronto Blue Jays, who won their second straight World Championship. I remember thinking to myself how fortunate the Jays were to have experienced that two years in a row. It's weird that you can win 104 games and still not be the team that wins the championship.

We all knew the next few months of the off-season would be the worst we'd ever experienced in this new era. One more time, we had to go into spring training having lost a postseason and prove ourselves all over again.

16

A Stunted Season

AS A BASEBALL PURIST, AT FIRST I DIDN'T LIKE THE NEW AND expanded divisional format instituted in the off-season in 1993. I'm a guy who loves baseball the old-fashioned way. Don't forget, I grew up in a family that rooted for the Boston Braves and had to suffer through the Braves' move to Milwaukee.

But from a practical and business point of view, it all made sense. For the Braves to make three trips a year to the West Coast when we're located on the East Coast seemed crazy. I'm surprised with all the extra long-distance traveling we did that we performed so well.

I was concerned about damaging West rivalries with L.A. and San Francisco, but we were still playing those teams. And now it seemed we'd be able to begin new rivalries with Philadelphia, who beat us in the play-offs, and Montreal, with whom we shared a spring training complex.

This format had worked in creating late-season interest in the NFL and NBA, and now it was time for baseball to change and create more streams of revenue.

When we looked at the new East Division, we knew it wasn't going to be a cakewalk. The Phillies were tough, the Expos were the up-and-coming team in the division, loaded with excellent talent. The Mets and Pirates were rebuilding, but they also had excellent talent on the way, and St. Louis was traditionally a tough team.

Baseball was moving into the modern era, and we had to adjust to it. It was fun in that we were all part of history. Yet we were leery of the extra round of play-offs. You figure, a team that makes the wild card spot, which was basically the team with the best record other than the three divisional winners, could actually be the hot team coming into the postseason and knock off a divisional winner.

While bothersome, it turned out we would have been the wild card team in 1994 had a work stoppage not intervened and wiped out the postseason. Needless to say, I changed my mind about the format quickly.

The 1994 season was sort of a transitional year for us. Otis had signed with the Red Sox, and Terry Pendleton, our emotional and spiritual leader since 1991, was injured for more than forty games. Blauser also spent time on the injured list.

But the biggest blow was losing Ronnie Gant in the off-season in a dirt bike accident in which he fractured a leg in three places.

Ronnie liked cars, fancy and fast. There was a part of him that lived on the edge and he was a bit of a thrill seeker. But I didn't know one of his hobbies was riding an off-road dirt bike. If someone told me Ronnie had been in an accident without telling me the particulars, I would have thought he'd crashed one of his cars. He was gone for the year, and the Braves made a very difficult and painful decision by placing Ron on waivers for the purpose of giving him his unconditional release rather than pay him more than $5 million in salary.

Their thought process was, here's a guy who's meant a lot to the franchise, but how can we pay him over $5 million if he can't contribute the whole year and with his future also in doubt? I guess from a business viewpoint, it was a clear-cut decision.

I knew Ronnie's loss would be felt in two areas: his speed and his power. He was a thirty-plus stolen base man three years in a row and had stolen twenty-six bases in 1993. He'd also hit over thirty home runs three times and knocked in more than 100 runs twice. I just didn't know how we'd replace his talents. I knew it would be difficult to do it with just one player. We did have young outfielders like Tony Tarasco, Ryan Klesko, and an excellent all-around player in Chipper Jones coming up.

From an emotional viewpoint, Ron was very well liked on our team. He had started in our organization as a second baseman and even after he had made the Braves, he was sent all the way back to A ball to learn how to be an outfielder and improve his hitting. He was willing to do it, and he came back a much better player. Actually, a feared player.

Just when Bobby and our coaches decided Chipper, who came up as a shortstop, would go out to left field and take Ronnie's spot, he tore his interior cruciate ligament playing in an exhibition game against the Yankees March 18 in Fort Lauderdale. It was a huge blow for us because Chipper had hit .325 with thirteen homers and eighty-nine RBIs at Richmond in 1993 and everyone considered him one of the top two or three prospects in baseball. (Certainly we saw that potential come to fruition during the 1995 season when he took over the third base job after the Braves elected not to re-sign Terry Pendleton.)

There was some light, though. Between Klesko, a tremendously powerful hitter who hit seventeen homers in 245 at bats, and Tarasco, a good pure hitter, we had about twenty-two homers and sixty-three RBIs out of the left field position.

We also had a chance to watch the rise of Javy Lopez, who shared the catching duties with veteran Charlie O'Brien, one of the best defensive catchers in baseball. Javy hit thirteen homers and exhibited great raw power, which continued in 1995, and I think you're going to see big power numbers from Javy in the years to come.

It was the dawning of a new group of Braves players, again a tremendous compliment to Paul Snyder's efforts in the scouting department. Javy wasn't even drafted, but was signed by the Braves in 1987. Tarasco was also undrafted. When you can pick up people with that talent, then your scouting and farm departments are doing a pretty extraordinary job.

I wouldn't call 1994 a nightmare, but statistically it was my worst year since 1990. While most pitchers suffer a decrease in velocity on their fastballs as the years progress, just the opposite happened to me. In spring training my arm felt better than it had in three years. I don't know what to attribute that to. Some theorize the reduced innings in the 1993 postseason gave me a chance to rest more, but that's not proven by the numbers: In 1990 I threw 214⅓ innings; in 1991, 246⅔ innings and 17⅓ innings in the postseason; in 1992 I tossed 225 innings and 9 innings in the postseason; in 1993 I threw 239⅓ innings and 7 innings in the play-offs.

Anyone would love to go from throwing an eighty-two-mile-an-hour fastball to eighty-seven virtually overnight. Over the long run this was a good sign. But the added velocity led to mechanical problems. When you're a finesse pitcher whose change-up is your bread and butter, all you're trying to do with your fastball is locate it in the right spot, either busting someone inside or getting the hitter off balance. Suddenly with five miles per hour more, you start to think you can do more than that. Your whole thought process is thrown off, not to mention your release point.

So, for the first year since 1990, I allowed more base hits than innings pitched—173 hits in 165⅓ innings. I had the highest ERA since 1988 at 3.97, but my strikeout ratio was the highest it's ever been—140 strikeouts in 165⅓ innings.

My signature two-seam change-up got a little stale on me. It wasn't sinking as dramatically as it should, so I threw a lot of four-seam change-ups and in retrospect probably got away from my change-up more than I should have.

Typically, when I'm struggling with my change-up I wind up leaving it more over the plate than I like to. That's usually the result of dropping my elbow on my delivery or getting my wrist underneath the ball. The perfect correction for me is to throw the four-seamer. What that does is get me back behind the ball because if you're throwing it with four seams you've got to be absolutely behind it to make it sink. I went four or five games in '94 and threw nothing but four-seamers before I got back to throwing the normal two-seamer.

That's as much tinkering as I do with my change-up. Most of my other experiments are with my breaking ball and slider, where I'm constantly changing grips and trying to find something that might act a little differently to the hitter. My mechanics were so far off that this process was constant in '94 as I struggled to get comfortable.

The ironic part of the '94 season is that we got off to a good start. We had our best spring training record since 1966—20–9. I was 2–0 with a 2.37 ERA and it looked like I was going to pick up where I left off in '93 and capture my fourth straight twenty-win season. We won seven straight games on the road. We started 13–1. We were in a new division and in a new format, so we had something to prove.

I won three straight games twice, but I just had these ups and downs where I'd win a couple, then lose a couple. I threw only one complete game—on May 7 at home against Montreal, when I allowed just one run on four hits in our first series against the Expos. We took two out of three games and we thought, "Okay, this isn't going to be so bad."

Before the All-Star break we won eight out of ten, including a sweep of the Phillies in a three-game set at home. That was huge at the time because it was billed as the grudge match. But they were already having injury problems and it wasn't a fair matchup. We stayed in first place all the way through until a few days before the All-Star break, when we lost two of three to the Cards. On July 8, Bob Tewksbury pitched a beauty of a game and beat Mad Dog 2–0 at home, dropping us into a first-place tie with Montreal. By the All-Star break, we were 52–33, in second place by one game.

Mad Dog was 11–5 and was named to the All-Star game. He was joined by David and Fred in Pittsburgh. For the first time in three years I didn't make it. Nor did I deserve to. My All-Star break numbers weren't what people had come to expect. I was 10–7, but my ERA was 4.20. I really struggled in June, when in six starts I was 3–2, but I had an ERA of 5.17. I had the most problems with left-handed hitters, probably a result of leaving my change-up over the plate. They hit .323 against me, while righties were .255. Another odd flip-flop for me that year: The only teams I seemed to be able to beat were Cincinnati, Florida, San Diego, and St. Louis. Pittsburgh owned me, 0–2 and a 6.39 ERA.

It was discouraging. As a pitcher who has success, you think it's always going to be that way for you. All-Star games, World Series, Cy Youngs, twenty wins, all that stuff. This was the year I struggled. In a lot of ways it felt like 1990, a setback of sorts, but I knew I was a better and more accomplished pitcher.

We were able to come out after the break by winning three out of four against the Florida Marlins, which propelled us back into first place for a while. But then we lost five out of six to Pittsburgh and St. Louis and we dropped back into second place.

The Expos sure were tough. They had a great young team with strong hitters like Larry Walker, Marquis Grissom, Moises Alou, and Will Cordero. There wasn't an easy out up and down that lineup. Felipe Alou is a very good manager who gets the best out of a young team. They also had a very good pitching staff with Kenny Hill, Jeff Fassero, Butch Henry, and Pedro Martinez, and a lights-out closer like John Wetteland. They played us tough all season. They were the only team in our division we had a losing record against (4–5) and we lost two out of three to them in late July to move two and a half games out.

They got hot after the break and went 20–7, and we just hung around .500 at 16–13. On August 11, Game 114, with the strike looming, our season concluded in Colorado with a 13–0 win. Mad Dog pitched the shutout and we ended our season 68–46, six games back of the Expos.

At that point I don't know if we could have come back and overtaken them. That's as unknown as whether I would have been a good hockey player in the NHL. Would the Expos have trailed off? And would our experience and pitching staff have overcome a six-game deficit in the end? We still had some head-to-head games against them. Who knows, maybe my season would have had a resurrection of sorts if things had continued.

In late July Leo and I had a memorable confrontation, a big blowup between us on July 24, 1994, at St. Louis that tested our relationship.

Struggling with my control that day, I'd given up twelve hits in seven and a third innings. Among my problems was I went from doing what I do best—a fastball/change-up pitcher—to being the type of pitcher who just threw change-ups and if that doesn't work, to hell with it. I was experimenting and I was pitching a little bit backward. I was giving up a lot of cheap hits at crucial times. I'd have a good inning going and then I'd walk someone or give up a bloop hit.

We got out to a big lead and then I gave it up, but we overcame that and went up 7–4. I got a couple of quick outs in the eighth, but then I allowed a broken-bat blooper down the right field line, walked two guys, and it's suddenly a one-run lead.

I was pissed off—shaking my head, ranting and raving on the mound because I'd given up another blooper. Leo didn't see it that way as he came out of the dugout and started to give me a piece of his mind. He thought I should be pissed off because I walked two and started dilly-dallying around and got myself into trouble. After we walked off the mound and back into the dugout, one thing led to another and he started screaming at me and I started screaming back at him.

"It's not that damn easy to pitch," I yelled. "If it's so easy, why aren't you out there!"

"F—— you!" said Leo.

"F—— you!" I shot back.

This is going on right near Bobby, who's looking at us like we're both crazy, but never said a word, hoping we'd reconcile this on our own. Leo and I went back and forth for ten minutes in the dugout while everyone was quiet and wondering, "Why are these guys doing this?"

Finally it ended, I'm not sure who got the last "F" word in, but I walked into the clubhouse and didn't have contact with Leo until the next day when he talked to me like it never happened! I respected what he was trying to get across and he respected my frustration, but it was one of those things that both of us had to get off of our chests right then and there in the heat of the moment. Coaches, in general, do so much work with players and always harp on fundamentals that when those fundamentals aren't exercised frustrations build and if they're not dealt with right then and there, as Leo did, those problems bite you in the pants down the road.

All I know is that with the new format there were a lot of things to think about. With Montreal so hot for so long, we were thinking about getting in as the wild card and then taking our chances in the play-offs with our pitching. We were thinking we might have been the first wild card team to the win the World Championship.

Very early in the summer I knew there would be a work stoppage and warned guys of the possibility.

Right before the All-Star game, we had been discussing the possibility of boycotting it. But we opted to wait for several reasons, mainly because it's an event that fans look forward to and because some of the proceeds for the game benefit our pension fund. Had we known the owners would stoop to withholding their contribution to the pension fund, we surely wouldn't have played the game.

The whole reason for going on strike from the players' point of view was that we were trying to push something to happen. Typically, history dictated that whether it was a lockout by the owners or a strike by the players, it seemed to drive an agreement.

From our point of view, negotiations were going nowhere. If we waited until the end of the season with no agreement and we reached an impasse, we had absolutely no leverage. Something had to be done.

We discussed it internally at national meetings and in individual team meetings. There was a movement to just break it off at the All-Star break, but cooler heads prevailed. The most thoughtful suggestion was basically what we did: We waited as long as we could—to August 12—in the hope that we could get something done and then continue on with the season and the play-offs.

Obviously, it didn't work out that way.

I felt bad for Montreal. That was their year to do some damage with all of their stars. And it was the last year they were able to keep their team together because, inevitably, their ownership would just trade away players who were on the verge of making a lot of money, and they certainly had a few players who were on the brink.

And the Yankees were in first place in the American League East and they hadn't been in the postseason since 1981. Our team was looking to win a championship and get the monkey off our backs. There were also individual seasons that were threatening some of the greatest records in the game. Matt Williams, Ken Griffey Jr., and Frank Thomas had outside shots at surpassing Roger Maris's record of sixty-one homers in a season, and Tony Gwynn, hitting .394, had a great chance at being the first .400 hitter since Ted Williams hit .406 in 1941. Jeff Bagwell was threatening Hank Greenberg's RBI record.

So we were risking a lot. But these players were willing to risk their personal achievements for what they felt was right.

During the summer, as the strike raged on, there was a lot of discussion as to whether there should be postseason awards. Because the Baseball Writers' Association of America vote on most of the postseason awards, there was debate within the organization. But in the end, they decided there should be.

And with that there was no other choice for the National League Cy Young Award than Greg. He was 16–6 with a 1.56 ERA. Think about that. He took the art form to a new level. Pinpoint stuff. Every once in a while he'd start arguing with an umpire about a call.

I'd kid him after the game. "You have the nerve to argue! You get more calls than any pitcher in baseball!" Which he does. Greg is so pinpoint around the plate that it's very difficult for an umpire to call a ball on a borderline pitch. And once the umpire gives him the borderline call, Greg tries to stretch that strike zone out a little more. We all do that to a degree. But the respect that umpires have for Greg is completely earned.

Greg also worked very well with Charlie O'Brien, and Charlie stuck with him as his everyday catcher. Because Javy was so young and because Greg's method of pitching is a little more complicated than that of the rest of us, Charlie provided a nice stable target. Being a veteran, Charlie understood Greg's thought process.

For me, I didn't care who I threw to. I enjoyed Javy because he was a young catcher learning to catch the greatest pitching staff in baseball. And while it was probably neat for him, it must have been nerve-racking at the same time. All I wanted Javy to do was think along with me and provide a nice stable target behind the plate, and he did that. And again, his bat helped all of us at one time or another.

Maybe the strike ended all of our hopes of returning to the World Series, but it was a season in which we accomplished a lot of internal things. We got the youngsters—Lopez, Klesko, and Tarasco—going, David and Fred continued to have monster years offensively, and Lemke had the best season of his career, hitting .294. We also established a very nice fifth starter in Mercker, whom I really envied—on April 8 against the Dodgers at Dodger Stadium, he pitched a no-hitter. He walked four and struck out ten. It was really a beautiful thing to watch and we gave him the usual cold shoulder throughout the game so we wouldn't jinx him. He got the last eleven hitters in a row out and he was throwing smoke that day. That was only his twelfth major league start, as Merck had always been our middle reliever lefty out of the bull pen. To think that in just twenty-eight major league starts, he was involved in two no-hitters. The first one was the front end of a combined no-hitter on September 11, 1991, with Mark Wohlers and Alejandro Peña.

Merck went 9–4 with a 3.45 ERA. He struck out 111 batters in 112⅓ innings. He's a great guy on top of it, and he was instrumental as our assistant player representative in helping distribute information before and during the strike.

The off-season was much more hectic than the season. While we didn't win our division before the strike hit, nobody really won anything in the months ahead. It was a frustrating time in baseball, one that tested my personal convictions more than anything I've ever been through.

17

Striking Out

DOESN'T EVERY KID FROM BILLERICA GET TO HANG OUT OUT-side the Oval Office and rap about college hoops with the president of the United States?

Well, this one did.

I guess that was one of the benefits of being on the union nego-tiating committee that winter. There weren't many others. In fact, I can't recall a worse time in my life, a time when there was more stress on me than anything I could imagine on the playing field.

I felt like I was wearing the black hat. Talk-show callers in Atlanta were calling me every name in the book. I had never felt so hated. People said things to me that I can't print in this book, but suffice it to say that there were a lot of four-letter words tossed my way. I heard everything from "Glavine, you bum!" to "You're scum!"

Some people would yell out catchy things like, "Throw strikes, the strike is over!" I'd run to first and someone would yell, "You run to union meetings faster!"

I don't know that I would ever again feel strongly enough about something involving sports to go out and make a spectacle of myself. It requires more energy than I'd be willing to expend. Yet, despite the sense of mission and accomplishment, I can't think of anything that's ever hurt me more. I'd always enjoyed a great relationship with the fans in Atlanta. I'd been a quiet guy who always respected them and never said or did anything to offend anyone.

I'd won twenty games three years in a row until a 13–9 season in 1994. I thought I'd performed well for them. To hear your hometown fans say hateful, mean things was tough to deal with. Eventually I became thick-skinned and didn't let it bother me.

I was even criticized along with the other four players who came to the White House that night because I wasn't wearing the proper clothes to meet with the president. I had on a pair of golf pants, a sweater, and a blazer. I took the heat for not wearing a tie. That's because I didn't have a tie with me. Our meetings were day- and nightlong sessions in a stuffy conference room at some hotel. None of us were dressed in ties. The night the White House called asking us to hop in a cab and meet the president, I was ready to leave and go back to Atlanta. There wasn't time to get all dressed up. The president didn't mind, so I don't see why anyone else should care.

That was the moment when I realized people weren't looking at the issues anymore.

Early on I decided I needed to stand by my convictions. It was our union that was being wronged, not the owners. I just wish I and others could have gotten the message out better and convinced the public that it wasn't about money. It was about principle. The owners had a very concise message that they seemed to get out into the media a lot more easily and clearly, and that was, "The players want too much money!"

A Gallup poll in December revealed that 50 percent of Americans sided with the owners and 28 percent with the players.

And as hard as we tried to counteract it, we couldn't. It was a losing battle, and we were made out to be the villains. It was pounded into the fans' heads that it was the players who for the first time since 1904 were preventing baseball from staging a World Series.

We were the ones on strike, so that we would take the fall wasn't all that surprising.

Sometime during the negotiations, I started to be the player the media would run to for answers. Players' Association officials watched interviews closely and came to the conclusion they liked my answers. Every time the media called the Players' Association for an interview, those calls were referred either to me or David Cone. The next thing I knew, after every session, there would be a camera stuck in my face and I was on national TV.

I wasn't trying to be a spokesman for the players or a smart guy. I just looked at it as an opportunity to try and make people understand what we were trying to do. Inevitably the more interviews I did, the more people got sick of seeing me on TV and they associated me with the problem.

The more I tried to explain things, the more people got angry. I'd get asked questions that, quite frankly, I couldn't understand myself or that I couldn't divulge the answers to because they were confidential.

It seemed every time I made the comment "I don't think people understand the issues," it was being translated as me calling the fans stupid. I would never think that of them and I would certainly never say it.

I never had a problem with people disagreeing with us if they completely understood all the issues; then I would have loved to have debated them. And if we couldn't agree after that, fine, everyone's entitled to their own opinion.

But it quickly got away from that and the whole situation dropped to a personal level. Ninety percent of the things that were attributed to me I never said. That's when it became a problem for me.

I was listening to a talk show once and some guy called up saying I was driving around town in a red convertible giving the finger to people. One, I don't, and never have, owned a red convertible, and two, I wasn't brought up to act that way. I don't think I could ever be pushed enough to do something like that. That stuff—like the incident with Jack McDowell at Yankee Stadium in 1995 when he flipped off the fans after they were booing him—just incites the situation more.

I also remember the day after the strike, a TV reporter in Atlanta asked me if he could bring a crew to my house and interview me. I like this guy so I said, "Sure, come on." That day I get a call from the security gate at the country club where I live, saying there were more than twenty TV trucks waiting outside! I told the guard I was sorry about the chaos but that I had personally invited only one of them. The guard told me the trucks were blocking incoming and outgoing traffic and that I needed to do something.

The only solution I could think of was to send them to the country club, where I'd conduct a press conference in the gazebo.

I was trying to be accommodating. That night, I'm watching one of the TV stations and they're portraying me as a rich, greedy ballplayer who called a press conference at the country club! I couldn't believe it! I was just trying to be nice to everyone and take care of everyone's demands with one press conference and they turned it around and made me look like someone I definitely wasn't.

I kept getting asked after every bad game I pitched after the All-Star break whether the potential for a strike was affecting my performance on the field. That had nothing to do with it. I wish I could have used that as an excuse. I think I left the team one day to go off to a meeting in New York, but other than that I'd spend maybe a few minutes on the phone every day. It probably amounted to three or four hours a week on the phone. That's not going to affect how you pitch.

The real aggravation was spending all the time we did talking to reporters about it. Every day after the All-Star break it seemed I'd get questions like "What do you hear? What do you think is going to happen? Are you going to get anything done?"

I'm often asked what I would have done differently, or what I would do differently if I were placed in that position again. And it would probably be that I wouldn't make myself as available for interviews.

There were media people I'd cooperate with and then I'd find out they were ripping me on the air or in the newspapers. That bothered me. I was trying to be cooperative and answer their questions as best I could, and they were turning around and letting me have it. I don't think I ever said anything that was offensive to anyone I was trying to represent or that was offensive to the Atlanta Braves organization. I was really careful about that.

A comment I made during a TV interview was interpreted completely wrong and it had me characterizing Phil Niekro as greedy if he tried to return as a replacement player. I never called Phil greedy. I was asked what I thought of former major leaguers like Dennis "Oil Can" Boyd returning to baseball as replacement players, and there was speculation that Phil had called the Braves inquiring about returning. I said whether it's Oil Can or Phil, major league players have benefited from the system in the past and for anyone to return as a replacement player would be shortsighted of them. If their sole reason for breaking a strike was financial gain, then they should be the ones considered greedy, not the striking players.

That's a long way from calling Phil Niekro greedy. But that's what people heard because of edits and recuts, etc. Phil is very popular in Atlanta, so naturally I took plenty of heat for the comments.

The strange thing is, I like Phil a lot. I know he tried to call me after the comments came out and I kept missing him. And as I'm doing this book, I realize I've never had a chance to explain my comments. I hope we're able to get together and clear the air.

But the more interviews I did the more redundant the questions became and the more redundant my answers were. People got sick of hearing it.

I'll still go to meetings and be involved. That will never change. But in the future I'll just go back to my room, call my players and the player reps around the league, and take care of that side of things.

Another bothersome issue was charges by the media and fans that the chief counsel of the Players' Association, Don Fehr, was leading us down this long, dark path and we were following him blindly. I found that offensive.

By saying we were following Don blindly, they're telling me that I'm a stupid jock and that I don't have a mind of my own. I'm not going to lie and tell you I understood the ins and outs of the salary cap or most of the components of the sliding luxury tax. But I knew enough that once you did the numbers, there wasn't a big difference between the luxury taxes proposed and the salary cap. The luxury taxes were just window dressing for a salary cap. And I didn't need Don to tell me that or to order me to go out in public and say that on TV. I understood that for myself.

I'll be the first to admit I didn't fully understand some of the legal issues and we were relying on Don a lot to fill us in and educate us on what some of the legalese meant. But it wasn't a case of just asking Don questions and then dropping it.

We asked a lot of the other staffers from the union questions as well. Oftentimes we would kick Don out of the room and ask our lawyers the same questions we'd just asked Don and ask them to explain things to us in terms we could understand.

And I'll be totally honest, Don's explanations and interpretations didn't vary much from the lawyers'. So either these guys were all lying to us or what they were saying was the truth.

Don got a bad rap. He didn't come across well because he speaks like a lawyer, which is sometimes hard for the average Joe to comprehend. We had the same argument with him all the time. "Don, tell us in English!" When you're as intelligent as he is, perhaps it's difficult to speak simply. And Gene Orza, who did a great job, talks too fast, so we'd have to say, "Gene, slow down!"

I always thought Don was in a difficult situation because he represents seven hundred baseball players and he can't really jump up and say that he's a fan of a certain team. Sometimes that gets mistaken for not loving the game of baseball. I know he loves it because he often attends games around the country and sits in the stands and enjoys himself like a fan.

That same charge could be brought against a lot of owners, too. Many of them are businessmen who have made their fortunes in other businesses, so how much do they love or understand the game? I'd have to question that with the same energy.

In the spring of 1992, I started hearing rumblings about a work disruption, but we were able to avoid it and keep pushing back our negotiations with the owners toward a basic agreement. It seems like these things always have to go to the last minute. We'd been willing to discuss a new basic agreement for some time, but the owners didn't seem interested in talking at all.

It didn't really sink in that we were moving toward a work stoppage until the spring of 1994. The writing was on the wall. All our attempts to negotiate were met with delays from the owners. We were prepared but they couldn't seem to get on the same page. They had spent most of their effort and time realigning the divisions to three divisions per league and creating a new tier of play-offs.

There was a lot of jockeying for position during most of 1994. We were steadfast in our belief that we were not going to give up anything the owners had negotiated and agreed upon in previous negotiations. That was the basic premise we stuck with all along. We'd be completely satisfied with leaving things alone.

The owners, meanwhile, were definitely trying to appeal to the public that some of their franchises were on the brink of financial ruin. We said, "Okay, let's open up the books and see what's going on." But they never did that.

My feeling was and has always been, if a franchise can't exist in a certain market after years of losing money, then it's obvious the fans in those cities no longer want to support the team. There are many markets dying to get a baseball franchise who can guarantee all types of revenue up front and brand-new stadiums that make the clubs a fortune.

We've seen that with the Colorado Rockies and their beautiful new ballpark, Coors Field. The Cleveland Indians rejuvenated their franchise by building Jacobs Field, and the Baltimore Orioles might be the richest organization in the game today because of the millions of revenue they bring in every season at Camden Yards.

There are gold-mines-in-waiting all over this country. Certainly a franchise shouldn't move without making every attempt to stay. It's tough on the loyal fans to watch their team moved out from under them, but a businessman has to make tough decisions for his good and the good of the franchise, and sometimes moving is the only solution. It bothered me when the owner in San Francisco was shot down when he wanted to move to Tampa and have a built-in revenue-producing system.

One moral issue drove me throughout this process and that was I wanted to make certain the basic principle of freedom was kept intact.

I understood that the owners were trying to save money. But I never thought they had to have a new set of rules in place to do it, and their actions of the last two years have proved that they've been able to control their costs yet still make respectable bids for free agents.

All the players ever asked is that the owners attempt to solve their problems on their own and not attempt to take back what the players have earned through negotiations over the years.

I know that it takes a great deal of creativity; revenue sharing among large-market and small-market teams is probably one answer. But that was never our problem to fix. If the owners didn't want to spend money, then they didn't have to do it. Nobody is holding a gun to their heads.

What's important to the players and to me is the right, at some point in the career of any baseball player, that he be able to choose where he wants to play. And that has nothing to do with money.

I don't think that most people realize that through most of our careers, we have no say in where we're going to play. You're drafted out of high school or college and you spend X number of years in the minor leagues—on average about five years—and then you get to the majors and you're basically the property of the team for six more years before you have a choice. That's eleven years before you have the right to choose. I'm not sure people understand the frustration of that.

And when the argument was raised that even under a salary cap free agency would still flourish, that simply isn't true. Even though you have twenty-eight teams, only six or eight teams are going to be able to afford a big-time free agent under a cap.

What if those six or eight teams aren't the teams I want to play for? Our freedom has to be maintained. In 1992 I had the right to say, "I like it in Atlanta and I would like to sign a long-term deal to stay here but if I can't come to terms I'd like to be able to play someplace else, someplace of my choosing."

I always felt, and I'm not speaking for the other players, the owners were trying to break our union. Whether that's right or wrong, that's just my opinion.

I based that on things I'd heard from reputable, reliable people. This was more of a battle to gain control over the players because in the owners' minds the players had gained too much control over the years. I don't know if it was the sole purpose of the fight, but I think it was part of it. After all, these owners are successful businessmen, and like everyone else in life, they have egos. I think they felt, "Who are they as employees to be telling us how things should be done?"

I first took over as the player representative in 1990 after Murph decided to give it up. I had been in the big leagues almost four years and there was a lot of stuff I didn't understand.

We had an insurance plan I didn't know anything about. I had no idea what kind of coverage I had. I had no idea how much our pension plan would pay me after I retired. I didn't know about our investment plan or any of the rules of the basic agreement.

And I thought, if I'm going to be around here for a few more years, I'd better get a decent grasp of this stuff and how it affects me. I figured the best way to do that was to become a player rep, which would force me to understand the issues so that I could educate the other players.

And quite honestly, in 1990 I was probably the only guy who could have taken over that job. The union actually prefers that a pitcher take on the responsibility because it can be too time-consuming for the everyday player. I was a veteran who had a future with the team and I was a pitcher, so I was elected.

In spring training of 1991, I started speaking out on what I thought was the lowballing of a few zero-to-three-year players who weren't eligible for arbitration.

This is part of the problem with our agreement and why I'm not sure players would agree on four-year free agency if we agreed to give up arbitration. I think the owners would do anything they could to put the screws to zero-to-four-year guys if that happened. I could see it happening a little that spring. We had eight unsigned players in early March—with March 7 the contract renewal date that year. Guys like Smoltzie, Greg Olson, Tommy Gregg, Blauser, and Merck were being offered salaries far below their market value.

Almost every day these guys were asking me questions about it, and all I could do was call the Players' Association office and get some advice on what to do. And really there wasn't much we could do. The Braves had this policy, which had been brought in by John Schuerholz, that players with zero to three years' experience couldn't compare themselves to players with similar experience from other teams. I just spoke out and thought that was unfair.

John spoke to me about it and I gave him a lot of credit for that. He nipped it in the bud before it became a big issue. He told me his side of the story, and I think that's when the business side of the game really started to dawn on me. Sometimes things aren't as cut-and-dried as they seem. For a general manager to do his job well, he has to tick off people once in a while. I think all of the guys wound up negotiating fair contracts. I spoke out and I let them know I wasn't pleased, and I think by talking, John and I developed a mutual respect for one another.

In 1993, I was elected the assistant National League player representative. There was a movement by our association then to get younger guys involved on the negotiating committee since it comprised a lot of guys who were at the ends of their careers. When I was nominated, I never envisioned I would have to serve on a negotiating committee. I was pretty naive about it, but sure enough there I was right smack in the middle of the whole thing.

By the beginning of August 1994, things were heading down the path of no return. We had our conference call to set the strike date. Once we agreed on the date, all of the player reps had to go back to their own teams and take votes. We held a meeting after batting practice one day and I explained to everyone what was going on and we approved the August 12 date in a 25–0 vote.

Believe me, it was a horrible task to have to tell players we were actually about to vote on a strike date and that the game of baseball would be shut down. I don't think it all really sunk in. I felt a little sick.

There was some discussion. Most of it stemmed from the fact that some guys wanted to be able to collect their paychecks until

October 2. I tried to explain to them why it was important that we strike on August 12 and why we didn't want to wait until the end of the season: It was the best date to stimulate an agreement. We didn't want to be blatant and strike at the end of the season and lose out on postseason, but we didn't want to strike early, like say the All-Star break, because that would give the sides too much time and thus they would drag their feet.

With that completed, the next few days were spent trying to make sure I had everybody's phone number so I could track them down and keep them informed.

There was a strange feeling in the clubhouse because you knew you had six weeks left in the season, but in reality, there were just a few days left and I was only going to pitch one more time in 1994.

At the time I think everyone thought we'd be back in a week or two, but it obviously didn't work out that way. We were in Colorado playing the Rockies, and when the clock struck midnight, August 12, we were in the air returning to Atlanta. A lot of teams were caught in visiting cities and had to provide their own transportation back to their homes.

When we returned to Atlanta, a lot of guys started cleaning out their lockers. Because I live so close, I just took a glove and some spikes so I'd have something to work out in. It was a weird feeling packing our stuff in the middle of August.

I went home that night and went to bed. I talked to Carri about it the next morning and I warned her that it was going to be a busy winter. Carri was pregnant with our first child, and the one thing I wanted to do more than anything was to be there for her.

It seemed from August through February I was gone at least two weeks out of every month, or ten days home, ten days away. I probably did more traveling during that winter than I did during the season.

There were meetings in New York City in October. William Usery was named the federal mediator and the person who reported directly to President Clinton. In November we went off to Virginia for a couple of meetings, and in Rye Brook, New York, on November 10 we received the owners' salary cap proposal, which didn't do a thing for the players and took back all of the things we had fought for.

Around that time, Richard Ravitch was essentially ousted as the chief negotiator and replaced with Boston CEO John Harrington. This was no surprise to us because it's been almost a tradition that the negotiator who starts as the lead man is usually ousted. Mr. Harrington is a likable and well-respected man and considered one of the most knowledgeable of the owners, and we thought this appointment might bring us closer. But that didn't help either.

In late November in Leesburg, Virginia, the owners started to bring up the possibility of using replacement players, which brought on a lot of anger and furthered the gap between us. Here we were trying to get something done and then they're threatening us with scabs.

In early December we had our players' meeting conveniently located in Atlanta. It was a meeting just to talk over the current state of matters amongst ourselves.

It was interesting to see how players were reacting. I know Lenny Dykstra said things about having to go back to work at some point. In Boston, Mo Vaughn said he didn't like the way the players were coming across to the public. That wasn't something I could disagree with. But overall we presented a unified front.

On December 10, we presented a new proposal to the owners at Rye Brook. Basically, we offered to give up arbitration for four-year free agency and there was a tax on payrolls over $52 million so teams would be able to control their spending. They didn't go for that.

The owners implemented their new system—four-year free agency, no more arbitration, but with a salary cap. That's when we instituted our signing freeze. And then, after the owners' system was revoked by the National Labor Relations Board, the owners implemented a signing freeze on February 5.

It was back and forth. You do this and we do that. It was a mess. Nothing was getting resolved. And that's the way it went most of the winter.

Another interesting meeting occurred not far from my home, in Marietta, Georgia, on December 21 when Terry Pendleton, Brett Butler, and I visited incoming House Speaker Newt Gingrich at his Sixth District office. I live in Mr. Gingrich's constituency in Georgia. He came to a lot of Braves games over the years, as has former president Jimmy Carter.

At the time, we were trying to have the antitrust exemption overturned for many reasons, but the immediate problem was that the antitrust exemption gave the owners a legal right to implement their salary cap. I thought getting it overturned would put us on a much more level playing field in that we'd be able to have our day in court, giving us more of an option than just striking.

That thought process suffered a blow the last week of January when the appellate court ruled that antitrust laws can't be used to stop the NBA owners from imposing rules during a collective bargaining agreement. Don disagreed that the ruling had any bearing on baseball.

The Speaker listened to our concerns and made us feel quite comfortable. He was certainly up on the issues and understood the arguments for or against a given proposal. I don't know whether he agreed with us or not, but he listened. Our hope was he'd go back to Congress and present our concerns. But in the end, discussion about the repeal of the antitrust agreement was put on the back burner.

I was getting worried about Carri late in her pregnancy. She had a few complications that left her bedridden for a few days at a time. I was always concerned that the baby would come early and I'd miss the birth and I'd never forgive myself.

Amber's birth on January 24 made everything a little more bearable, and her arrival put everything into perspective. I now had a family. I was a dad. I knew I could come home at the end of the day and I'd have a wife and a baby girl waiting for me. My life had a whole new meaning, and the personal attacks stopped affecting me as much.

I left for Washington just a few days after Amber was born, though. Luckily, I had family staying with Carri to take care of things, which eased my mind a bit. The owners had made a new proposal and we went to Washington to negotiate it, but for some reason we didn't see the other side for days.

What a waste of time! Carri would call and ask me what was going on and I'd say, "Nothing." Then she'd ask, "Then why aren't you coming home?" I said, "I have to be here in case something does happen." It was all pretty frustrating and I didn't have much of an answer for her, because I didn't know myself.

In early February, just two days before the deadline imposed by President Clinton for both sides to reach an agreement, we presented a new proposal to the owners. We were proposing a four- or five-year basic agreement. We had rejected their proposal the day before and it looked like this one would get zapped as well. After a quick glance, Harrington told reporters, "We've taken a preliminary look, and we don't see any meaningful movement."

We revised our proposal of December 22 and we tailored it to coincide with the revenue sharing.

We offered to end salary arbitration and accept a form of free agency after four years. We recognized the owners' demand for $58 million in revenue sharing and came up with a "three-tier" tax rate that would provide it.

We also proposed that the current benefit plan continue as is, especially as it affects nonuniformed players. We agreed to go along with expansion in 1997 and the approval of the players' participation in the growth fund to the tune of $30 million. We even proposed that a new commissioner be named immediately, with the caveat that it not be someone who currently runs a ball club.

This was met with more thumbs-down from the owners.

I was frustrated. On February 6—the president's deadline—Usery met with Clinton in the White House for forty-five minutes and told him that the last four days of talks had gone nowhere.

Usery and Secretary of Labor Robert Reich got together and tried to solve the problem, but despite the strong tone of the president's message to Usery to get it done, it wasn't. The deadline was extended another day and still nothing.

Basically, I think we could have agreed on issues like salary arbitration, free agency, and stuff like that, but we just couldn't get together on the tax stuff.

The owners wanted a high tax on revenues for clubs who go over a threshold. So what's that? That's a salary cap. They were asking for a 75 percent tax on the amount of payrolls between $35 million and $42 million, and a 100 percent tax on the amount above that.

With no agreement in sight, it was about 3:00 P.M. on February 8 and I was sitting in the hotel, ready to take off and go back to my family. President Clinton had press secretary Leon Panetta call the hotel and invite six players as well five owners and lawyers from both sides to come and visit.

This is where the kid from Billerica got a little nervous. It was great to be going to the White House. I'd always wanted to be in there. But I'm not sure under those circumstances. I didn't think that the president would be able to solve this dispute anyway.

I think President Clinton was searching for a way to bring the two parties together in hopes that his influence would settle it. But we were a little apprehensive about it. We were all thinking, "What are we going to do if the president tells us something that we don't want to do? Will we say no to the president?"

In the end he recommended the sides agree to binding arbitration. We agreed with that, but the owners said they would only agree to it under certain conditions and we said, "Uh-uh. Let's just go to binding arbitration and whoever wins, wins." I think we were willing to do what the president asked of us, but the owners weren't willing to take that chance.

But the greatest thing was just being able to hang out outside the Roosevelt Room and Oval Office with the president. We spent about an hour in the hall. Some of us were trying to peek into the Oval Office, but we weren't allowed in there. President Clinton was out in the hall talking to us about various sports topics including college basketball, golf, baseball, you name it. All of us—David Cone, Jay Bell, Scott Sanderson, Cecil Fielder, and Terry Steinbach—got to ask questions and make comments. It was something I'll never forget.

Even though I haven't voted in recent presidential elections and I consider myself a conservative, I understand now why the president was elected. In that one hour it was very obvious what tremendous people skills he has and how charming he can be. On February 26, 1996, during spring training, our team was invited to the White House, where I got to speak to the president again, and I presented him with a Braves jersey. Would my relationship with him spur me to vote for him in the next election? I'm not sure. But having met him, my respect for him has grown tremendously.

The nice part about the whole winter was that I was able to get to know some of the players that I play against and am supposed to hate. I had a new respect for Orel Hershiser, Scott Sanderson, Terry Steinbach, Jay Bell, Joe Girardi, and David Cone. They were the core group that went to every meeting, and we became pretty close. Everywhere we went we always found the time to work out and throw. Sometimes we'd play catch in empty hotel ballrooms. I tried to get Girardi to squat down so I could throw to him, but he wouldn't. But catch was fine.

It was also a chance to speak to Orel about pitching because he's so knowledgeable about the game. He's a guy I've loved to watch over the years because I always thought I pitched like him, but from the left side. Listening to his experiences in big games against some of the best hitters in the game was valuable in understanding how he pitched certain hitters and why.

It took a large commitment from all of the players to fight for this cause. Some of them, like me, had pregnant wives. Others had kids they were leaving at a time of the year when they should have been home with them. I respected their efforts and the time they gave it.

And we had a lot of back-and-forth at our meetings. We all gave a lot of input. When we broke up into negotiating sessions, I did very little talking. I just sat there and listened and tried to absorb everything that was being said. I left it up to our representatives— Don, Gene, Steve Fehr, Mike Weiner, Lauren Rich, all of our lawyers—to do the talking. Certainly, every now and then one of the players, whether it was David or B. J. Surhoff or Jay Bell or Orel, would ask something or say something.

I have to admit, I was somewhat intimidated by the owners because they are all very smart businessmen. I didn't want to say something that was viewed as stupid and I was still a relatively young player—twenty-eight at the time—and I thought it was best to keep my mouth shut, take good notes, and not come off as an idiot.

It was a little awkward for me to have Braves CEO Stan Kasten across the table representing the views of the other side. Stan was quite vocal, along with David Montgomery of the Phillies, and later, Jerry McMorris of the Rockies. Stan understood the NBA salary cap inside and out as a result of also running the Atlanta Hawks, so he was always asked for his viewpoint on trying to implement the cap in baseball, as was Chicago White Sox owner Jerry Reinsdorf, who owned the Chicago Bulls. Montgomery was very good with numbers. Jerry McMorris was a guy that we felt as players we could talk to and Don could talk to, so I think his inclusion was a great thing. And while John Harrington was quiet in those meetings at first, he really took over and became much more vocal at the end.

I have to say this about Stan—he was great throughout the whole process. We disagreed on a lot of things, but we had made a pact before we started this process that we weren't going to let it affect our relationship. I know Stan did a lot to calm down the fans in Atlanta who were on my case, by saying things in my defense. And that had to be tough for a guy on the other side. I'll always appreciate that.

I tried very hard during all these months not to burn any bridges with the owners because I still had a long way to go in my career and who knows, I could be playing for some of them someday. I might not have agreed with what they were doing, but I respected them and I treated them so. I didn't want to get into a personal war with anyone, but simply focus on the issues. I think we did that.

I really wish that Bud Selig had become more involved. He was, after all, the acting commissioner, and I think if he had weighed in a little more on the issues it might have helped. I guess he had his own reasons for not getting involved, which is part of a larger issue—why is there no commissioner? I'd love to see both sides come up with a candidate who can serve both sides, rather than owners having the only say. After all, it's a game whose biggest product is the players. Why shouldn't we be represented by a commissioner as well as the owners? Isn't this supposed to be a partnership?

In the end, the owners lost about $400 million and the players about $250 million. At press time there is still no basic agreement, but at least there are behind-the-scenes discussions, mostly away from the media, that might lead to an agreement. At the normal start of spring training, players had to suffer the indignity of watching replacements at spring training camps. Most chose to ignore them.

18

Putting the Pieces Back Together

I WISHED THE BRAVES HAD TAKEN THE SAME APPROACH AS THE Baltimore Orioles, the only team not to field a replacement team, and said the heck with it, we're not going to subject our fans to this.

But that didn't happen. I didn't follow the replacement season too closely because I was busy at the negotiating table and busy talking to our players. I was completely opposed to scabs, so more than anything, I just wanted to keep my eye on who was participating and what former major leaguers may be involved.

There were also a couple of guys I played minor league ball with—and I don't want to mention their names—who phoned me and talked to me about playing as replacement players before they did it. That was a difficult situation for me because I came up with these guys. All I tried to do was listen to what their reasons were for contemplating a return to baseball, which generally had to do with money.

A lot of teams sold these men a bill of goods. They told them they'd be paid the minimum salary and they would get bonuses for signing and then bonuses for being on the replacement rosters. And they were, in large part, assured that if they performed well they had a chance to stick in the organization.

I couldn't sit there and tell these guys not to do it, being in the financial position I was in. They had a chance to make some quick money, a better chance than they had of making it anywhere else.

And I certainly wasn't the type of guy who went around threatening would-be replacements with bodily harm or verbal abuse. I just told them I didn't think the decision would be that beneficial to them. I told them about the ramifications of being a replacement player if they were fortunate enough to stick on a major league roster when the regular players returned and the possible segregation they would have to endure. I tried to show them both sides of the coin. I didn't try to change their minds.

I know we had six replacement players who stuck in our minor league system after the strike. I made it clear to management that it was going to be disruptive if these guys came up at any time during the year. I couldn't guarantee that we'd be able to hide our feelings just because we were in a pennant race. Crossing the picket line was an important and emotional issue to us. And luckily, we never had to deal with it.

The saddest aspect of the whole thing was the death of a Brave replacement player in West Palm Beach during spring training. That was shocking. I couldn't help but think that he should never have been in a position for that to happen. If we had just figured this stupid thing out, then it could have been avoided. It put a lot of things in perspective for everyone. For as much animosity as there was between major leaguers and replacement players, I don't think anyone wanted something tragic like that to happen.

On March 31 in New York, a federal judge validated what we'd been saying all winter: The owners were guilty of unfair labor practices. A federal injunction restored the old work rules and we all got to go back to work. Was it a glorious day? Not really. It was great we were able to play baseball again. But there was still no agreement in place.

The next couple of days were hectic in trying to get everyone ready to return to work, but it didn't take long.

I reported to spring training a few days later, and please forgive me if I was a little paranoid after the public beating I took. But every time I'd hear my name called out, I expected an expletive to follow. Thankfully that didn't happen. I'd hear "Glavine!" or "Mr. Glavine!" and I'd turn around and it was just a kid who wanted an autograph.

Maybe it was that the spring training crowd is more laid-back, but there was a softer side to the fans than the ones I'd heard on the talk shows.

It was important for us as a team to spend as much time signing autographs for the fans as possible. The fans had been the ones most screwed throughout the strike and we owed it to them to accommodate them any way possible. Players around baseball felt the same way. The Red Sox were excellent in dealing with this. Early in the 1995 season, they held a FanFest outside of Fenway Park and more than thirty thousand fans came out to meet the players and get autographs. The club opened the ballpark, and long lines of fans came through to touch the Great Wall of Fenway on what was a rainy day.

The strike definitely took its toll on attendance around baseball, but fans slowly but surely came back. In spring training I didn't see any great drop-off in fans who came out to watch us.

Bobby and Leo handled the start of spring training perfectly. Just because the training period was cut in half, it didn't mean we were going to push guys to get ready in three weeks. In other camps, teams were going with four-man pitching rotations and their starting pitchers were going five innings right out of the gate.

Bobby and Leo weren't about to run this like a boot camp. Their concern was trying to get everyone in shape, but not at the price of injuring someone. Bobby took things slowly. We stayed with the philosophy that you go two innings in your first appearance of the spring and gradually build up. We didn't have time to build up to seven or eight innings, so Leo told us to build up to five and when the regular season began we'd go five innings our first time out.

Bobby took the same approach with the position players. So when camp broke we were healthy and, except for a couple of minor things, we stayed healthy all season.

On April 14 I made my first start at West Palm Beach. I was a little apprehensive because I thought, "I haven't heard much in the way of boos, but now I'm in a game I'll probably start hearing them." But I didn't hear one, not when I was introduced and not after I came out of the game. In fact, people were cheering. I pitched well, so maybe that had something to do with it.

Besides the normal stiffness and soreness among some of our pitchers, Mad Dog caught the chicken pox. Nobody knew at this point whether Mad Dog would have to miss opening day and so I readied myself for that possibility. But my availability soon came into question when I got hit with a line drive off the left shoulder in the fourth inning of an exhibition game on April 18 by Marlins second baseman Quilvio Veras.

It's too bad because I was pitching a shutout and I felt great. Any time a ball hits your shoulder you get a little anxious because that obviously is a pitcher's livelihood. I knew a few minutes after it stung me that it wasn't going to be that bad, because it hit the muscle and all I had was a pretty bad bruise.

Mad Dog recovered in time to get enough work in to start the opener at home against the Giants on April 24. Bad publicity from the strike took its toll. Only 32,045 came out to Fulton County Stadium to watch the greatest pitcher in baseball.

During the opening day introductions, I was booed. Here they were. Atlanta is a big nonunion town, and here I was the union man being scapegoated. I guess I was mad more than anything. I stood by my convictions more than ever, and at that moment I was willing to take it. I certainly wasn't going to say I regretted it. I wasn't going to hide in the corner. I was proud of the work I did for the players, and whatever people thought of me was secondary. I wasn't a coward. And I wasn't going to start being one.

We had a great opening day, a 12–5 win, getting a big day from Fred, who went four-for-five with two homers and five RBIs, and David, who went three-for-four with an RBI. Mad Dog pitched like Mad Dog. Five innings, one run, one hit, five strikeouts. I went home afterward knowing the pressure was on. I was pitching the next game, and if they were booing me in the introductions, imagine what they would do if I messed up.

At home Carri and I talked briefly about whether she should come to the game, and we both agreed she should. I warned her I might get jeered and things might get ugly. But she didn't seem fazed. She had been at every one of my games and she wasn't about to stop. During the game people said things and Carri shot back with a few words of her own. She wasn't about to back down. Her indignation during our conversation got my dander up. Nobody was going to run me out of the place I'd spent my whole career. The same people who had booed me had cheered me at one point or another and I was going to make them cheer for me again.

When I was warming up, there had to be five or ten guys standing behind me in the bull pen, just hammering me. Things like "You greedy scumbag! How much money do you want! Here's a dollar, does that help!" It was strange to see people literally throwing money at me! Not to mention offensive and hurtful.

*   *   *

I started out great. My first two pitches to leadoff hitter Darren Lewis were strikes and I got him to ground out. Then I allowed a double to Robbie Thompson to left field—not unusual for Robbie, who throughout his career has hit me at a .420 clip—twenty-one-for-fifty with eight doubles, three homers, and six RBIs. I got Barry Bonds to ground out to third base. But with two outs, I walked Matt Williams, and Glenallen Hill doubled to right field, scoring two runs. Hill is another one of my all-time nemeses. Two of them in the same lineup! Hill is eight-for-eighteen (.444) against me with a homer and five RBIs, and his slugging percentage off me is .722. When I throw anything, it's no surprise to him.

I could hear the boos. The very thing I wanted to avoid, I'd done. But like any other time when I've given up first-inning runs, I tell myself to hold them right there and not surrender any more. I went out and pitched four more shutout innings, gave up only a Kurt Manwaring single in the fifth, and my day was done. There were fewer boos as I left the game. In retrospect it wasn't as bad as it could have been. I know if I'd struggled that day I would have heard more and I would have stayed the whipping boy all season. But we went on to win it, 6–4. Lemke and David hit homers, and even though I didn't get the decision, I survived my first game.

Amid all of the strike news it was another season when John Schuerholz and Bobby made some subtle changes to bring us to a new level. Not long after the players went back to work—April 6— John made a huge deal with the Expos, sending Tarasco, Roberto Kelly, and right-hander Esteban Yan to the Expos for Marquis Grissom and cash. What we got was the best leadoff man in the National League, one of the fastest men in the game, a great center fielder, and the consistent leadoff hitter we hadn't had since Otis left us.

Even though Marquis had some nagging leg injuries, he was a gamer. He missed five games all year, stole twenty-nine bases, and hit twelve home runs. I think we saw his full ability in the post-season when he started to heal, and I can't wait to watch in 1996 because he's going to get back to the guy who once stole 154 bases in two years for the Expos.

Beyond that, the only questions we had was who our closer was going to be and what we were going to do for a bench.

We acquired Dwight Smith, who became a good player off the bench and a good guy in the clubhouse. Later Schuerholz really balanced our bench by adding left-handed hitter Luis Polonia and then right-hand-hitting outfielder Mike Devereaux, both of whom did incredible work for us late in the season and in the postseason.

Rookie Brad Clontz emerged from spring training as our closer, but eventually handed those duties to Mark Wohlers. Brad went 8–1 with a 3.65 ERA in fifty-nine appearances after just a half year at Triple-A in 1994.

Though there was talk about Smoltzie going to the pen, Clontz won the job in spring training and wisely Smoltzie remained a starter. However, I just knew Mark was eventually going to be the guy. He was throwing better than I'd ever seen him. He had command of four pitches and his velocity was incredible. Mark's confidence really started to grow and I know at one point he turned to Leo and said, "I'm going to be your closer before the year is over and you're never going to have to worry about it again." By about mid-May Mark took over the job and rattled off twenty-one straight saves. It was just lights out almost every time he pitched. He gained about twenty-five pounds to give him more power through his legs and it really helped him. He struck out ninety batters in sixty-four and two-thirds innings! You don't get much more dominating that that.

Mark's emergence gave us an excellent young bull pen, with workhorse McMichael, the funky sidearm delivery of Clontz, Pedro's great stuff from the left side, and Mike Stanton, who was with us until the trading deadline on July 31 and was then traded to the Red Sox.

Stanton was certainly a fixture with the Braves for a long time, but he never lived up to the promise of his first year with us. Later on we rented Alejandro for the stretch run and again he was awesome for us in the play-offs. Alejandro hadn't been with us since 1992, but he had spent the last couple of years injured and then had stints with Pittsburgh, Boston, and Florida before coming back to us. Alejandro is a heckuva guy to have around during crunch time, and for short stints like Octobers he becomes a money pitcher. He'll probably touch them all before he retires. He was re-signed by the Marlins after the 1995 World Series, but who knows, we might see him again someday.

We were, once again, a very solid team. The Phillies were chasing us for a while. Our lowest moment all season came in early May when we lost four straight games at home to them. They held a four-game lead over us as late as June 30. But we went on a nine-game winning streak from July 1 to the All-Star break, sweeping the Phillies, Dodgers, and Giants to go 43–25, putting us four games ahead.

We only held three team meetings the whole year—the traditional one at the start and then one in June when we were struggling, and finally one before Game 6 of the World Series. They were all effective. I called the June meeting after what seemed like a week's worth of debating with Lemke and Blauser over calling it. Lemke and Blauser are the two guys who act as my sounding board. When things aren't going well, I always go to them and say, "So, what do you think? Do we need to do something?" Like I've said throughout this book, team meetings are great when they have a purpose and we don't call them very often. Unless Bobby calls one, which is rare, we usually make it players-only. That way different guys can get up and speak what's on their minds without fear of what Bobby or a coach might think of their comments.

And in that June meeting, a lot of our players spoke about what they felt was a lack of intensity—a complacency that we needed to overcome. And we did.

I didn't make the All-Star game again, but I was very happy with my season. I was 8–4 with a 3.49 ERA at the break and went 8–3 with a 2.70 ERA after it. I had another year of problems in the first inning, allowing twenty-five runs in twenty-nine innings, which to this day I can't explain. But I truly believe that it was my best year. When I say that, people roll their eyes and don't believe I mean it.

I think the turning point for me was after the June 10 game at home against the Cardinals. I was breezing along for six innings—held them to one run—and we had a 3–1 lead. Then, all of a sudden in the seventh inning, everything went to hell in a handbasket. I gave up four runs and we lost the game, 7–3.

I started to do some soul-searching after that one and tried to figure out what the problem was. I determined it was concentration. From that point on I started to focus on pitch-to-pitch and not think ahead to two innings beyond. I trained myself mentally all week when I did my side warm-ups with Leo and when I was watching the games.

We went out to Colorado, which is not the greatest place in the world to pitch. It's hard to get a good grip on the ball there because you can't produce a natural flow of sweat on your fingers to put on the ball. The air is thin and the balls fly out of there quite easily. As a pitcher you have be very careful you don't leave many pitches over the plate because a routine fly ball will be a home run. I've seen it happen.

Not only are you battling the environment in Colorado, you're battling their lineup, which is the most potent in the National League. They hit 134 of their 200 homers at home.

I gave up six singles. Ellis Burks made it to second base a couple of times, but never scored.

My focus was 100 percent on the hitter I was facing. There was no looking ahead. My mind didn't wander. And I'll tell you, that's a team where it's easy to look at who's coming up next. There's no break in that lineup. My ability as a pitcher really reached a new level after that game. It's not that I went out and won every game after that, but I felt good about my concentration level, which is key in pitching.

The shutout was the first one ever at Coors Field. We won 2–0.

For me to go in there and apply the lessons I'd learned from the Cardinals game and come away with a shutout was something I was very proud of. It was the best game I pitched until Game 6 of the World Series.

The other reasons I feel I was a better pitcher in '95 than in '91 or '92 was that in those years I was primarily a fastball/change-up pitcher. I'm still that and I still feature those two pitches and mix in the breaking pitch and slider. But there were times in '95 when my fastball or my change-up just wasn't working. When that happened in the earlier years, I didn't have a plan B. I would just stick with them and try different grips, as I mentioned before. Now I was able to make adjustments game-to-game and even inning-to-inning. If the change-up wasn't working, let's go to the slider or the curveball. Throw a breaking pitch in a change-up situation. It's almost like a southpaw boxer who all of sudden changes to the conventional style of boxing and kind of messes up his opponent, who's used to seeing him punch with his left hand.

I had an exceptional fastball on the outside part of the plate in '95, which is exactly what I had going for me in '91. But what I'd do to push a hitter off the plate was, instead of using the fastball in, I'd use the slider in to set up my other pitches. Really, I didn't have to go to a plan B very often because my change-up was consistent and my fastball was still coming in in the mid-eighties, but when I needed to do it, it was available to me and it became a successful part of my arsenal. I think sometimes those subtle adjustments can mean the difference between winning seventeen instead of fifteen, or twenty instead of seventeen games. That's what made me a better pitcher over the last five years: winning a game when I don't have my best stuff.

A season of intermittent booing pretty much came to an end by August. On August 10 I had one of the great thrills of my life when I homered off John Smiley in the sixth inning of a game against the Reds in my 536th major league at bat. It tied the score 1–1 and we went on to win it, 2–1. I was so pumped up by my pitching in that game that it put some extra punch in my bat.

It was a dream of mine. I remembered the ball I hit at Billerica that kept heading deep into the afternoon in center field. This one was hit toward left center. Hitters always say that when you want to hit a homer you pick a spot in front of the plate and you try and hit the ball before it gets there. That's what I did.

I ran around the bases at a brisk pace because I didn't want to show up John. I hate when hitters take a slow trot around the base paths when I'm pitching and when they make a big deal out of it. I just went right into the dugout and took my seat and started toweling the sweat off me. The crowd, amazingly, wanted me to take a curtain call. I came out, tipped my cap, and I guess I knew then that the mending had taken place and the healing was over. The fans and I were friends again.

On August 21, I struck out Doug Drabek to earn my 1,000th career strikeout. I'm not a strikeout pitcher, so maybe it didn't mean as much to me as it would someone else. But I guess 1,000 of anything is a neat accomplishment. It signified consistency to me and maybe longevity. You wonder if you're going to play long enough to be in that position.

I think what bothered me most about the entire season was my final start. I know the game didn't mean anything, but when it's your final start and you're heading into the postseason, you need it to be fundamentally sound.

I lost to the Mets, 6–3, and I was pissed off. I went four innings and allowed six runs, and all the good things I'd accomplished with concentration level and so on all seemed to go out the window with that start. The Mets hit a lot of bloopers and stuff, but it just bothered me that my concentration level wasn't quite there. It also cost me a chance to finish the year with an ERA of under 3.00, which I take great pride in.

Yet, I ended with a 16–7 record. Greg had another dominating season, a 19–5 record with a 1.63 ERA, and he was for sure the Cy Young winner again, for a fourth straight time. *Sports Illustrated* wrote that Greg was the best pitcher since Walter Johnson. Ave struggled with a 7–13 record and Smoltzie was 12–7 but with a 3.18 ERA.

Mercker contributed seven wins and once again it was a great year for a great pitching staff.

We were off to the play-offs again. I think the shortened 1994 season made us hungrier as we entered the '95 postseason. We also entered the championship season very confident that we were the best.

19

Climbing the Rockies and Seeing Red

BOBBY COX AND JOHN SCHUERHOLZ CERTAINLY HAD RESERVA-
tions about the new format. Bobby reasoned, "It's going to be hard
from here on out to build a dynasty. With three rounds of play-offs
there's going to be a great chance that somewhere along the line the
team that's supposed to win it all doesn't. Really, you have to win
four times—your division and three play-off rounds. That's pretty
hard to do."

Schuerholz wasn't fond of the best-of-five format, specifically
saying the owners needed to revise it and make it seven games.

Sure, there were fears that a team like Colorado with their potent
lineup could get hot and curtail the play-off hopes and dreams of a
team that dominated its division. Like us. Thankfully, that didn't happen. Anyway, you can't play scared. You have to have supreme confidence in yourself individually and as a team every time you step
out onto the field.

You can't listen to what's being said on the talk shows or in the
media. Everything is broken down so minutely, and in the end, most
of the analysis isn't worth a damn. You can't play the game on paper.
The more you play this game the more you understand that. Even
the players talk about that stuff.

"Hey, their bull pen is tough."

"They have a much better hitting team than we do."

"Their starting pitchers have been hot lately."

There are endless things you hear and think and feel and after you go on the field you realize that even if a team is hot at that moment, you can beat them and turn it around. Same way with a hitter. A guy might come into a series ten-for-twelve in his last three games with three homers and eight RBIs or whatever. But if you're pitching your game and everything is clicking, he doesn't have a chance to hit you.

It's like in '91 we always heard that eventually the clock would strike midnight and we'd turn into a pumpkin. Well, eventually it did. But not before we took it to extra innings of Game 7.

And the Rockies probably felt the same way. So they're the wild card team and they're playing the team with the best record in the National League. I looked down all of the "matchups" and we beat them here and there. And I said to myself, this is going to be a tough series. And it was, even though we won three games to one. The games were close.

We had beaten Colorado in nine of our thirteen meetings during the regular season. Ellis Burks and Dante Bichette wore out our pitching during the season. Ellis hit .436 with four homers and ten RBIs and Dante hit .426 with one homer and eight RBIs. Our offense had outslugged them, hitting twenty-one homers to their thirteen, with Blauser, Justice, Lopez, and McGriff all hitting three apiece.

If the theory was true that good pitching beats good hitting, then we'd know right away in this one.

The first three games were one-run games and we won two of them. A lot of reporters were calling it a "great series." In Game 1, Mad Dog pitched seven innings and allowed three runs—a quality start at Coors Field. He was really upset that he left a pitch over the plate for Castilla, a former Brave, who took him deep for a two-run homer. Greg didn't make many other mistakes.

We won 5–4. Chipper hit two home runs and made the play of the game when he dove and stopped a grounder heading into left field to prevent a big Rockies rally in the eighth inning. We all got a scare when Chipper banged up his left knee and also hurt his lower back on that play. That was the knee that kept him out the entire 1994 season. But Chipper went on to have a great series.

I still believe that Chipper should have been the rookie of the year in the National League over Hideo Nomo, given his all-around play and importance to our team. Nomo had a great year for a pitcher in his first major league season, and I'm the first to rise to the defense of pitchers when people say they shouldn't, for example, win the Most Valuable Player Award. But his story, as the first pitcher to defect from Japan and pitch here, created a media swarm and ultimately far more attention than Chipper ever received; thus Chipper was runner-up.

I guess people looked at our statistics in that round and thought our pitching wasn't up to par. But given the circumstances of Coors Field and that lineup, I think we pitched very well. Greg may have allowed nineteen hits in fourteen innings, Smoltzie, our Mr. October, may have gotten roughed up in his Game 2 start, and I may have allowed three runs in Game 3. But I'm telling you, our pitching kept us in all of those games and allowed our offense to pull out two out of three.

One of the controversies of the series was Rockies manager Don Baylor putting twelve pitchers on his postseason roster. Some consider that too many, since teams usually go with nine or ten. In Game 1 he ran out of players and had to use pitcher Lance Painter as a pinch-hitter in the bottom of the ninth with the bases loaded and two outs. Poor Lance had to face Mark, who threw twenty-four pitches in that outing, twenty of them at over 100 miles an hour. I guess Lance was the best hitting pitcher the Rockies had because he had seven hits and three RBIs in forty at bats. Needless to say, it wasn't much of a contest. I'm not sure that anyone had a chance against Mark in that situation, because the smoke was coming off the ball.

Everybody was all over Donnie for making that decision, but he has to construct his team the way he sees fit. With that lineup, you're not going to do much pinch-hitting anyway, so you don't need a lot of players. And he probably felt he needed more pitching because with Bret Saberhagen hurting he might have to use the bull pen more often.

We beat Bret twice in the series but Bret wasn't himself. He had been taking cortisone shots all week and it was amazing he was even out there.

In Game 2, our offense provided some heroics with a four-run ninth inning. Fred, Mike Devereaux, Chipper, and Mike Mordecai all struck for key hits. Mordecai, who knocked in the game-winner, is one of those great stories of determination after a long minor league career. Huge for us in the postseason, he showed the knack of being a clutch player all year, hitting .437 with runners in scoring position. We've had players like Mike and Francisco Cabrera who have come out of the blue to win big games for us. They're just as much a part of our history the past few years as some of the everyday players and pitchers we've had.

I pitched okay in that game. It wasn't vintage June 16, the game of the year for me, but I shut them down for the first five innings, which I thought was a good sign.

I was keeping the ball down and out of the strike zone, out of the reach of their big hitters. Against this team you don't want to fall behind ever, but especially not early, because usually they'll find a way to score later. And in this game, they did.

I had a precious 3–0 lead after five thanks in part to a couple of solo homers by Marquis. In the sixth, things kind of fell apart for me. Blauser committed a throwing error, and Bichette hit a soft single that fell into center field. You tend to give up a lot of bloop hits at Coors Field because the outfielders have to play deep to go back for those routine fly balls that tend to drift toward the wall and oftentimes go over it.

Before I knew it, there were base runners all over the place. Walker then took me deep. I mean deep—442 feet into the right field mezzanine to tie the game at 3–3. I was just a little too conscious of trying to get ahead of him on the count, and as a result I lost sight of making a quality pitch. I was trying to go after him with a fastball away, but instead it stayed down the middle of the plate and he made me pay for it.

It turned what was a well-pitched game into a pretty good game. The best part was that we won it and Alejandro got the win for the second time in the series.

We returned to Atlanta and the fans weren't really into it, the consensus being that bad feelings lingered after the strike. Another theory was our repeated failed efforts in the postseason had worn off the novelty. Fans were definitely taking a wait-and-see attitude. Understandably, they didn't want to get all excited again only to be disappointed.

Smoltzie really wanted to end the series quickly, but maybe he was too eager. He came into that game with a 5–1 record and a 1.94 ERA in ten postseason games. Smoltzie threw pretty hard but leadoff hitter Eric Young and Vinny Castilla hit two-run homers. He lasted five and two-thirds innings and gave up five runs. Unfortunately, it was one of those games our bats couldn't rally in like they had in Games 1 and 2.

In the finale, in Game 4, Greg gave the Rockies a 3–0 lead on Dante Bichette's three-run homer to center. Dante hit .588 (ten-for-seventeen). And then Greg buckled down. He held them in check the rest of the way and we went on to a 10–4 win, thanks to a huge pair of homers by Fred. But Chipper provided the big hit—a two-run double in the third inning when we overtook the Rockies, 4–3, and then rolled on from there. The incredible stat on Greg is that only twice in 1995 did he allow more than three earned runs in a game. One of them was May 17 against Colorado, when we lost 6–5.

Marquis was unbelievable, going five-for-five in the final game after hitting three homers in the first three games of the series. Marquis was primed for this because after struggling, like I said, with a bunch of nagging injuries, he hit .303 in September.

Having conquered the new preliminary round, we moved on to the National League championship against the Cincinnati Reds. All we heard about was that it was going to be tough to contain their speed. It was, but we did. We called a lot of pitchouts, which kept their faster players close to the base. We also heard they were throwing three lefties at us to counteract McGriff, Justice, and Klesko and to make Chipper bat right-handed. Except for Game 1, that didn't work either.

That we beat them four straight games was a shock. They had good pitching, speed, and power, but we seemed to catch them in a slump.

We had beaten the Reds eight games to five in the regular season. I was 2–1 with a 1.86 ERA against them during the season, and in my career, I was 13–1 at Riverfront Stadium and had given up only twenty-five earned runs in 111⅔ innings. I love pitching there. Riverfront Stadium isn't the best ballpark for a pitcher—the ball carries well—but home plate is fairly close to the backstop so you feel like you're on top of home plate. That makes it comfortable. Which is unusual because ballparks tend to have mounds that have been tailored for that team's pitching rotation.

They also have the type of hitters in their lineup—like Ronnie Gant and Reggie Sanders—who are conducive to my type of pitching. I've always been able to handle the power hitters, fooling them with my off-speed stuff and getting them to chase bad pitches.

Reggie Sanders had a nightmare of a series, a carryover from his last game against the Los Angeles Dodgers in the preliminary round, when he struck out five times in a game. He started our series zero-for-twelve with eight strikeouts before he finally smoked an infield single in Game 3, but was two-for-sixteen with ten strikeouts overall. Ronnie wanted to beat us badly, openly admitting he held a grudge against our organization for releasing him so soon after his accident. I couldn't blame him. I probably would have felt the same way and I would have searched for any incentive to get my adrenaline pumping for such a big series. And there was a potential grudge match in Barry Larkin versus Greg, who had a little feud going after Greg hit Barry with a pitch in a game on September 16. Barry accused Greg of throwing at him. It was defused before the series started when Barry approached Greg and said there were no hard feelings. Those are two pretty classy players right there and it was good to see them bury the hatchet.

One of the sad stories of the series was the attendance in Cincinnati. They couldn't sell out, with over sixteen thousand empty seats in Game 1 and almost ten thousand empty seats in Game 2. Some blamed it on the strike, others blamed Marge Schott and the way she runs her team, saying that fans are sick of her as an owner. If that was the reason I can't blame them. I don't like her insensitivity to people, including her players, or her social and political views. Like most people, I was appalled by her comments that Adolf Hitler "just went a little too far." How can anyone think like that? Imagine the people who have suffered because of Hitler's actions—doesn't she stop and think about that? It must be tough to play for the Reds because of her, and I hope I never have to do that. I've had the good fortune to play for Ted Turner my whole career.

You saw a lot of him on TV over the past few postseasons, snuggling up with his wife, Jane Fonda, doing the tomahawk chop. It was a pleasure to see them enjoying the Braves and celebrating with us.

His presence at the games has never added pressure to us on the field. In fact, quite the opposite is true. He's had some classic locker room visits, which have loosened us up.

I'll never forget Ted's speech to us in the summer of 1990. He walked into the locker room, which is something he hasn't done that often over the years, and proceeded to shoot from the hip.

"I know I'm not at the ballpark very much, but quite honestly, the way you guys are playing reminds me a lot of a friend in the hospital with cancer. It would be hard for me to go see that friend of mine in the hospital and it's awful hard for me to come watch you guys play," he said.

Another time in 1992, he walked into the clubhouse before the second game of the play-offs against the Pirates. He told us how proud he was of us. We had gone to the World Series the year before and nobody had given us a chance to get there. And here we were in the postseason again.

Right before Game 7 against Pittsburgh, he visited again.

"You know what? It's not like you guys are going out there in a life-or-death situation. It's not like anybody's gonna get killed out there tonight. It's not like this is a war that's being fought. You guys are going out there to play a BASEBALL GAME!

"Go out there and play the best you can. Have some fun! I hope to God you win, but if you don't I've made a lot of money over the past two years and I don't care!" Typical Ted. He always found a way to put sports in the proper perspective.

When Ted comes to the ballpark he comes to have a good time. It's a getaway from the hustle and bustle of multimillion-dollar deals. He doesn't want to have another business problem to solve at the ballpark. He's involved with enough of those on a day in and day out basis with TBS and CNN. This is almost comic relief for him. Hopefully, not to the degree of World Championship Wrestling, which he owns.

You can see in his voice and in his eyes that he truly loves being a baseball team owner. I'm sure there's a hard side to him, a tough businessman side. Anyone who can work out a $7.5 billion merger with Time Warner has to have some toughness. But I know that as an owner of our team, he spends a lot of money. At the same time, he doesn't give John or Stan carte blanche. There's a budget and guidelines and they stay within those guidelines. But not at the expense of the team.

His treatment of us goes beyond paying the players well. He makes sure we have first-class travel and first-class hotels. When we need new bats, we get new bats. If you want a new hat, you get a new hat. Maybe that doesn't seem like much, but you wouldn't believe what players go through to get the proper equipment in other cities.

He's not squeezing a penny. You hear guys come over from other organizations and complain about how brutal it is. You hear all of the stories about Marge Schott and the Reds and all of the things that go on there. The Braves take care of the smallest details so all the players have to go out and worry about is playing baseball.

Every spring training he throws us a big party, and you haven't lived until you've been a part of one of those.

The more you hear about the way it is in other organizations the more you realize how lucky you are to play for the Atlanta Braves. I've never been with another organization, but I can't think of another owner I'd like to play for more than Ted. We know that even if he's not at the ballpark, he's keeping track of us, whether it's between business deals or when he's relaxing at his ranch in Montana.

Here's a guy who once came out of the owner's box to manage a game in 1977 when the Braves were amid a seventeen-game losing streak! So he's got that funny side to him and he always gives us a laugh and loosens us up before a tough game.

He's been smart enough to be hands-off with the baseball team. He's hired the best people in the business to run the organization— Stan and John and Bobby. Ultimately, however, he's the man everyone answers to. And we know that he wants a first-class operation. That's just the way he does business.

He's not around to the point where he's yelling at managers and general managers. Guys aren't afraid to go out and make a mistake on the field because Ted is watching. We're not afraid to go out and play aggressively, and it's because we're not afraid that we've been so successful.

I can't say that I know Ted really well. I think it's gotten to the point where he doesn't have to look at the name tag above my locker to know who I am and he doesn't have to turn to Bobby for an introduction. He knows my name and he knows my face. And because of the strike, we were able to speak one-on-one a lot more and I think we got to know each other a little bit.

I would classify it more as a respectful business relationship than anything else. Respect is the key word. What made going on strike so difficult for me was having to be on the opposite side of the issues with Ted. But I think what made it easier is that Ted told our entire team, "I don't have a problem with the way things are going. I can run my business the way things are." So I knew that Ted wasn't necessarily in complete alliance with the other owners.

Yet, he had to do what he had to do, just like I had to do what I had to do.

Ted called me the day before the strike hit in Colorado.

"I'm sorry it's come to this," he said. "I hope and pray that by midnight tonight we can get something done and avoid this. I know it doesn't look good. But I just want you to know before this starts, there are no hard feelings, and you can tell the rest of the players that. I understand that you guys are doing what you have to do.

We're doing what our constituents want us to do. When it's over, no hard feelings."

I know that he still feels that way because I've had subsequent conversations with him and our relationship has never changed. That goes for Stan and John as well. Stan sat with me before the labor situation started and he was on the opposite side of the table and he said to me that this wasn't a personal battle and that we were gonna be friends and respect each other. He was true to his word.

It's neat for all of us that Ted and Jane Fonda, an actress everyone respects, come to cheer for us and are such diehard fans of our team. Jane has a lot of fun at the games, and when we won it all she was in the locker room spraying champagne and getting soaking wet with the rest of us.

I think it's fun to see your owner and his wife letting their guard down. It was nice to see that the owners and the players were finally enjoying something together after such a long and bitter fight the winter before. It was a sign to me that the two can exist together and be part of the same goal and dream. It's a shame that not every team can have that moment with their owners because it really does bring you so much closer together as an organization. You truly are a family, and though maybe you've had some problems along the way, at the most tender moments you come together. And that was our moment.

Forgive my digression on Ted, but mentioning Marge just set me off. We were talking about Cincinnati and their not having the ballpark jammed pack and the city buzzing. It was strange, almost as if we were playing in a start-up league or something.

That first game was a dogfight. Pete Schourek is a tremendous pitcher, and for eight innings we couldn't get a man to second base. We trailed 1–0. As feeble as we can look sometimes, when we get to the late innings in the play-offs, we shift to a higher gear. Practically possessed, we can sniff out a win. It's just amazing. It got to be the ninth inning and Pete still seemed to have a lot left. We tied it when Chipper, who plays like he's been in the league forever, delivered a clutch single. And then Fred singled and Chipper went to third and scored on David's grounder.

It's 1–1. Our defense did a great job. They turned five double plays—a play-off record—and got me out of some incredibly tight spots. Bret Boone knocked into two double plays and the fourth-inning one was crucial because the bases were loaded with one out after they scored their first run on Barry Larkin's triple and Ronnie Gant's infield hit.

Jerome Walton hit into a double play to end the fifth, and after I allowed Barry another extra-base hit, a double to lead off the sixth, I got Benito Santiago to end the inning with a 5–4–3 double-play ball. You sure don't want to put as many people on base as I did, but when you're getting outs on the ground, then that's your way out of a bad situation.

After allowing a double to Hal Morris to lead off the seventh, I was able to squirm out of that jam by retiring the bottom of the order and striking out both Mark Lewis and Schourek to end my night.

We held them down the rest of the way. Alejandro came on and mowed them down in the eighth. Wohlers threw gas in the tenth—twenty pitches, three strikeouts. He struck out all three batters with different pitches: Bret Boone on a slider, Jeff Branson on a split-finger, and Eric Anthony on a fastball. A real testimony to the coming of Mark Wohlers as a pitcher.

In the top of the eleventh, Mike Devereaux began his heroics in that series with an RBI single, which eventually led us to a 2–1 win. Obtaining Mike was a huge factor in balancing our lineup off the bench. He had been an excellent player for the Orioles and then earlier in 1995 hit .306 for the White Sox before John obtained him.

McMichael got out of trouble in the eleventh when he got Sanders to knock into the fifth and most important double play of the game to end it.

The second game was also great. More fans showed up, evidently sensing the series might be exciting. Javy starred. He made a huge block of an 0–2 change-up McMichael threw in the dirt in the ninth inning in a 2–2 game with a runner at third. Then in the tenth, after Mark Portugal threw a wild pitch on an 0–2 count allowing the go-ahead run to score, Javy put the icing on the night with a three-run homer.

David has said, "Javy Lopez has more power than anyone on this team." And he might be right.

Smoltzie pitched seven strong innings to keep us in the game, and if it wasn't for a throwing error he made in the fifth he might have held on to the 2–1 lead.

Charlie O'Brien is known for his defense, but his three-run homer in the sixth led us to a 5–2 win behind Mad Dog's excellent performance in Game 3. Chipper also had a two-run homer earlier in the game. Greg pitched seven shutout innings before he allowed a run. Bobby made a tough but smart choice by going with Ave in Game 4 instead of me on three days' rest. There was really no point to that. We were up 3–0 and Ave deserved a start. Even though he had a tough season, he came on at the end, and the best thing we could do was improve Ave's confidence with a solid outing.

Ave threw six shutout innings and our bats exploded again, enough for a 6–0 win. We turned three more double plays and turned eight in all in four games. Devereaux hit a three-run homer and was named the play-off MVP.

It was the first time in ten years a team had swept the National League play-offs. Here we were, a team that always seemed to extend our play-offs and World Series to the limit, and we won seven out of eight games from the Rockies and Reds, two very powerful teams.

The confidence we had after these series was really high. A 1.15 team ERA in four games went a long way toward making us feel that way. The best part was we had a chance to recuperate. Because we won so early, we had six days to let everything rest and heal. David, who had a problem with his knee, certainly needed the time. Unfortunately, Jeff had a bad ankle injury he couldn't come back from and he missed the World Series, which was a tough blow for Jeff after all he'd been through. Psychologically, too, we didn't have to deal with the pressure of continuous must-win situations.

As to whom we preferred to face in the American League, we didn't really care. I thought Boston and Seattle were two teams who would be potentially difficult. I was, in a way, hoping for Boston for the hometown reason, but I didn't want our hitters to be subjected to Tim Wakefield again, especially after the year he had. And Seattle's story kind of reminded me of our story in 1991. For the first time, that community rallied behind their team. They had such a powerful lineup and probably the best player in the game in Ken Griffey Jr. and the best left-handed pitcher in the game in Randy Johnson. Having to face Randy three times in a seven-game series? No thanks.

We were content that it was the Indians. Even with the new round of play-offs, in the end, the best two teams made it to the World Series. And that's the best anyone could have hoped for.

20

None but the Braves

I WAS GLAD THAT THE BEST HITTING TEAM IN BASEBALL—THE
Cleveland Indians—was opposing the best pitching team in baseball—the Atlanta Braves—in the World Series.

Part of me hoped that it would be a great series like we had
against Minnesota in 1991 so the fans would forget the ugliness of the
strike. And I think that did happen. In the end, the game did return to
the fans. We provided a lot of entertainment with close and exciting
games and individual performances that will be forever frozen in
time. Mad Dog in Game 1, for instance, was the definition of perfect.

There were a lot of ironies for me. My high school team's nick-
name at Billerica was the Indians. My brother Mike plays for the
Indians organization. And Dennis Martinez and Orel Hershiser were
two pitchers I respected as much as anyone in this game. Watch
them pitch closely sometime and you'll get quite an education.

The Indians also had two Hall of Famers in Eddie Murray and
Dave Winfield. Belle had compiled the most incredible statistics in
years over a 144-game schedule. We only hoped that he had calmed
down from Game 3 of the first round of the play-offs when Red Sox
manager Kevin Kennedy had his bat checked for cork. I don't think
we ever thought about doing it, deciding instead to let a sleeping
dog lie. Anyone who can hit a couple of opposite-field homers as
Belle did in Games 4 and 5 is a hell of a talent. Someday maybe he'll
wake up and treat people a little better, too.

And the Indians were a nice story. Because of the strike they weren't able to participate in the postseason after forty-one years of suffering with lousy and pathetic teams. Finally, they had produced a great core of players and surrounded them with veterans and role players who made them so potent they won 100 games and lost only 44. John Hart, the general manager of the Indians, did a terrific job in bringing that organization together.

And their ballpark was absolutely beautiful. It was a place you wanted to come to play baseball. But like Coors Field it was a hitters' ballpark. Make a mistake and you pay.

Our well-deserved and hard-earned World Championship began at Fulton County Stadium. With the new Olympic Stadium being built across the street and an opening scheduled for 1997, moments here were becoming precious. As much as we're all looking forward to playing in a new stadium, there are great memories here. As a staff, the Fab Four had conquered the Launching Pad. It was a ballpark that provided a challenge to our pitching staff, and more often than not, we won.

Greg Maddux versus Orel Hershiser is about as good as you can get for an opening game. I charted his pitches that night, and Greg hit every corner, located every pitch almost perfectly. It was absolutely amazing to watch him go through the Indians' lineup.

Greg admits that he got a great scouting report from his brother, Mike, before the game. Mike had a nice season pitching for the Red Sox in middle relief and as a spot starter, and really knew that Indians lineup inside and out. I think that really helped Greg focus in on certain tendencies of hitters even more than a normal scouting report would.

In the first inning, Rafael Belliard, who played in place of the injured Jeff Blauser, showed some jitters when he botched Ken Lofton's routine grounder. Obviously, Lofton was a player we'd keyed on in pregame meetings. The message was simple and clear: Keep him off the base paths. After Greg struck out Omar Vizquel, Lofton stole second and stole third, but Greg, calm and cool, got out of it with a couple of ground balls that Raffy scooped up and made the play on.

Lofton scored the run, but Greg retired thirteen straight batters without blinking. He threw ninety-five of the most magnificent pitches you'll ever see, sixty-three for strikes. Jim Thome singled off him in the fifth, but then twelve more guys were set down before Kenny Lofton's double in the ninth. It was just an unbelievable performance. Greg could have been the first pitcher since Jim Lonborg for the 1967 Boston Red Sox to throw a one-hitter in the World Series. But Lofton's hit eventually led to a second run because he was attempting to take two bases on a groundout. And by the time McGriff spotted him and threw the ball too high to third base, Kenny scored Cleveland's second run.

Fred popped the big hit of the game for us—a second-inning home run on the first pitch Orel threw, tying it 1–1. Fred said, "Orel and Greg are a lot alike in that they throw strikes all of the time. I knew I was going to get a first-pitch strike and I got a fastball that was a little bit over the plate."

We got to Orel in the seventh. He walked two batters before Mike Hargrove came out and replaced him with Paul Assenmacher, which was controversial. Apparently, Orel told pitching coach Mark Wiley he was done and that the Indians would be better served with Assenmacher. Mike Hargrove said later, "If we had our druthers, I'd rather have had Orel face one more hitter." We wound up scoring a couple of times, once on a nice suicide squeeze by Raffy, giving us a 3–1 lead.

Orel, whose seven-game postseason winning streak ended, never divulged why he came out of the game, and right now I guess the point is moot.

As usual, I was faced with having to follow Greg Maddux. If I could pitch half that well, I'd be doing cartwheels. Things worked out okay, despite my being a bit rusty. After all, here we were on October 23 and it had been ten days since my last start. Being well rested is fine, but there's a fine line between lots of rest and too much rest. And I think I suffered from that. Nonetheless, we won Game 2, 4–3.

I was into the seventh, battling my butt off against Martinez. The game followed a typical pattern for me: Eddie Murray hit a two-run homer in the second inning after an Albert single and that's when I found my resolve to end the deterioration. I got the last three outs of the second, retired the side in order in the third, put a couple of guys on in the fourth but got out of it, and then survived the fifth when we made an error that produced a jam.

I allowed three hits, two runs, and three walks through six innings, and that was all. Luckily our offense tied it in the third when we took advantage of Martinez hitting Marquis with a pitch and an error and scored on Chipper's sacrifice fly and David's RBI single. We went ahead, 4–2, on Javy's big homer in the sixth. It wasn't the worst performance but it certainly wasn't my best. I was fortunate in that we got good work from our bull pen with Greg McMichael and Alejandro, who got Belle to pop up behind home plate with a runner at third in the eighth inning, and then Wohlers came in and got the last four outs to preserve what became a one-run game.

It was a big performance for Mark. He'd dreamed all his life of pitching in a World Series and winning it, and he was halfway there.

We flew to Cleveland for the off-day and we knew this was going to be the Land of the Unknown. We had been warned about the intensity of the crowd and that it was going to be so loud we wouldn't be able to hear ourselves think. We heard and read all the hype—how the Indians were going to come back and squash us. This and that, the usual posturing. We weren't going to try and do too much here. We wanted a win. If we got at least one we could go back to Atlanta for the final two. But for a lot of us we would have loved to have ended it right in Cleveland. We just didn't want to take anything for granted after so many frustrations. On the flip side, we wanted to win it for our fans, too.

In two games, we got good starting pitching—Greg and I held the Indians to a .096 batting average—our bull pen was excellent, our hitting was timely, and our defense was decent.

We'd been in hostile environments before and done okay. Game 3 was Smoltzie versus Charles Nagy. The windchill made it feel like twenty-nine degrees at game time, which is absolutely tough to pitch in. Smoltzie from Lansing, Michigan, and Charlie from Fairfield, Connecticut, were certainly used to the elements. We got a quick first-inning run, but Cleveland responded for two runs in the bottom of the first. Nagy really settled into a nice routine, while Smoltzie struggled. In two and a third innings, he allowed six hits and four runs. But our offense kept coming and coming. It was back and forth. There was no intimidation factor involved here at all. Both teams were battling. Cleveland needed to win to survive emotionally, and we were trying to get the win to take a huge advantage.

It was 5–5 in the eighth when Devereaux, who had come into the game to replace Ryan Klesko, who contributed with a homer in the seventh, gave us the lead with a single against Julian Tavarez, driving in Chipper with the go-ahead run. In the bottom of the eighth the Indians just wouldn't give up. Sandy Alomar, who played most of the series with a pinched nerve in his neck, doubled off Wohlers to drive in Manny Ramirez. But Mark escaped further harm by retiring the next two batters. So it's 6–6. Extra innings.

In the bottom of the eleventh, the Indians finally pulled out their first win. Carlos Baerga doubled and, after an intentional walk to Albert Belle, Eddie Murray singled him in to win it, 7–6.

The crowd went crazy, and it was a good win for the Indians. Those hard-fought wins can do a lot for a team's confidence and it can put a damper on the team that lost. We were still up 2–1 and it was important that we put our stamp on this series in Cleveland.

Bobby again decided he wanted to use all four starters. "I want to be able to use my starters with a proper amount of rest," said Bobby. So Ave got the nod rather than Greg on three days' rest.

The press again had a field day with Bobby. They calculated that by not pitching Mad Dog in Game 4, we couldn't use him in Game 7. But people still don't understand that when you have four starters like we do, any one of them can pitch a big game and win.

Again, it was a great move. Ave had clinched the National League play-offs with a 6–0 win against Cincinnati in the fourth game of that series. He was pitching well again. His confidence was back. You could just see by the way he walked around the clubhouse and kidded around with us.

He looked to me like the kid who walked into the 1991 postseason and just dazzled. He was the guy with the cap pulled down over his eyes and oblivious to everyone. You could set a firecracker off next to him and he wouldn't know it. That's how focused he was again.

A lot was made of the cold conditions, and Ave, being from Michigan, like Smoltz, suggested, "I hope we get a little snow, too. I'd rather pitch when it's cold rather than when it's hot. When it's cold you don't have to worry about dehydration."

Feeling relaxed and pitching on a cold night, just like he wanted, Ave threw six excellent innings—one run, three hits. He allowed a solo opposite-field homer to Albert. No big deal. It was a 1–1 game, a pitching duel with Kenny Hill, who was nasty in his own right.

It was neat to see all of the New England guys who participated in the World Series. Mark and me for our side and Paul Sorrento from Peabody, Massachusetts, Ken Hill from Lynn, Massachusetts, and Charlie Nagy from Connecticut.

We broke the game open in the seventh when after one out, Marquis drew a walk and Luis doubled him in, making it 2–1. Then after an intentional walk and a passed ball and after Fred's strikeout for the second out, David really hung in there against a very tough Assenmacher and singled to right center, scoring two runs. We were up 4–1.

If people accused us of having bad bull pens in all of the previous years, they couldn't make that claim now. Throughout the postseason, whether it was Peña, McMichael, Borbon, or Wohlers, we seemed to get the job done. McMichael relieved Ave and even after Thome pinch-hit for Alvaro Espinoza and doubled to left field to open the seventh inning, the Indians couldn't get him across. We made it 5–1 when Freddie and Javy hit a pair of doubles in the ninth. And although Manny Ramirez homered off Mark in the ninth, it was a three-run lead that Mark and finally Pedro, whom we called "Microwave" because he warms up just about every inning, were able to hold.

Up 3–1, we had Greg pitching Game 5, up against Orel again. This was a case where no one gave the Indians a chance to win.

The Indians did a little soul-searching. They held a team meeting. The subject I'm sure was "We can beat Greg Maddux, he's only human." If I were holding a meeting I know that's what I would say.

Orel said before the game, "If Greg is as magnificent as he was in Game 1 in Game 5, then he deserves to beat me." Greg wasn't as magnificent, but he pitched very well. I wasn't sure what the Indians were doing differently. There were suggestions that the Indians were moving closer to the plate so Greg couldn't get the outside strike. Whatever it was, it worked.

Mad Dog walked Omar Vizquel in the first inning, something you're not going to see Greg do that often. After Baerga made the second out of the inning, Albert, apparently keying on the outside pitch, went the other way and hit a two-run homer.

This really got the crowd crazy. The best hitter had beaten the best pitcher, and beaten him with a good pitch!

The fireworks started moments later. Greg came inside to Eddie Murray on an 0–1 pitch and brushed Eddie back. Eddie became indignant, accusing Mad Dog of throwing at him.

Mad Dog just stood out there as calm as could be and took the verbiage that was being targeted toward him by Eddie and the Cleveland dugout. Eddie made a move toward the mound, more for effect, I think, than anything else, but Charlie O'Brien was there to step between him. Soon the benches and the bull pens cleared and appeared on the field, as Charlie kept jawing at Eddie. But peace was restored soon after.

Orel was yelling from the bench to Greg, "You're better than that!" Greg ignored that and everything else that was going on. He just wanted to get to the next pitch. The Indians claimed this fired their team up. Maybe it did. It was kind of silly because we're not out there throwing at anyone.

Tim McCarver, the NBC color commentator for the series, was right on when he said, "That's just part of the game. He's [Murray] been around long enough that he should know that. I think Eddie is trying to intimidate Maddux, but he came right back in there." Mad Dog came right back inside on Eddie, showing and proving that he's tough as nails.

Eddie ended up walking. But Charlie made a nice snap throw to first base to pick Eddie off, which is exactly what Doggie needed.

The score was 2–0 until the fourth when Luis Polonia again got a big hit for us, a solo homer on a hanging breaking pitch. We tied it after five, but Thome, who really came on at the plate, smacked a single up the middle on a 1–2 change-up, followed by another RBI single by Manny Ramirez. Later, Thome hit a home run off Brad Clontz and the Indians were on their way to a win.

Orel helped himself with his fielding in the eighth. We had two on when Marquis smashed one back at Orel, who was able to stab it for the out and then doubled off Mordecai at first base to end what might have been a fruitful threat.

Everyone made a big deal of the fact that Greg had lost and if the Indians could beat Greg they could beat the rest of us. With Greg losing, he would not be able to return for Game 7. Blah-blah. All I wanted to know from Greg was whether the Indians had made some serious adjustments or was it that his location was off. Greg assured me it was the location. He advised me to go out and pitch my game and not worry about anything else.

Everyone had their own opinion about who the pressure was on.

Orel: "I think the pressure is on them."

Bobby: "We just have to go back to Atlanta and win a ball game."

All I knew is that I wanted to be in this position. I'm sorry Greg didn't win it, but I had been the guy in waiting for a long time. I'd been the guy who was supposed to pitch next and never got the chance. Now it was in my hands.

We returned to Atlanta, took part in the off-day workout. I tried not to make this any different than any other game I was about to pitch.

I tried to stay businesslike and focused. From day one of the 1995 season we were on a mission and that mission was to win it all. Finally.

We all sensed, I think, that we were going to get the job done that night. John Schuerholz told reporters, "We'll be creating new memories after Game 6."

After the triumphant moment that I tried to describe at the beginning of this book, I got a chance to reflect and think about all the great players who have come through here and all the great players who never got a chance to win it. So this one was for Murph, for Bobby Horner, for Jim Acker. Pick a name. This one was for all the Atlanta Braves who struggled in this city for so long, and I hoped they enjoyed Game 6 as much as I did.

We had finally arrived.

21

A Pitcher's Diary

THERE'S MORE TO WINNING TWENTY GAMES AND THE CY Young and World Series MVP Awards than going out there for seven to nine innings and throwing a baseball. The conditioning work you do months before the season begins and days before and after game day is vital to your success or failure.

I'm not a power pitcher, so I don't need to have the big powerful legs and the big butt that can drive off the mound and create incredible thrust toward the plate and velocity on the ball. But I do need strong legs to put power behind the pitch and take away the stress on my shoulder. Roger Clemens is the perfect example of a guy with incredible strength who puts all of his weight behind the ball and thus is able to generate speeds of ninety-five miles an hour with no problem.

I'm built like a regular guy. I'm not going to win any weight-lifting contests or bodybuilding championships. That's not my intent. I don't have a huge chest or big legs, but I think I'm as strong as I need to be for what I do and for the type of pitcher I am.

My weight rarely fluctuates, so I stay in the 185-pound range most of the season, though there are times I'll start losing weight in the middle of the summer because the heat and humidity can often take seven or eight pounds off me in any given start in 90- or 100-degree heat. Like everyone else, I tend to gain some weight around the holidays, but it doesn't stay on me very long and it definitely burns off in spring training. It doesn't hurt that I've just been blessed with great metabolism and don't need to do much to stay at the weight I feel most comfortable at.

Some say pitchers don't have to be in the best condition in the world because they're not position players, but I don't believe that's true.

You have to be able to field your position and get a good jump off the mound on a slow roller. For instance, quickness is a big asset for a pitcher. It can mean the difference between winning and losing. If you're not in shape and you have trouble fielding a ball because your stomach is in the way, that could be costly to you and your team. It's not fair to your teammates to be out of shape. And it's also dangerous—if a line drive is hit right at you and you're not quick enough to react to protect yourself, that line drive could end your career. When you're in shape the quickness and agility come a lot easier.

I've pretty much stuck to the same kind of regimen through most of my career. In the off-season, I'll take a solid month off after our season has ended. I give my body a chance to recover from the punishment of a long season—and for four of the last five years our seasons have run long and as a pitcher I've thrown a lot of innings in that time. So rest is vital. I often wonder how beneficial it is for some of the younger guys to pitch a full season and then go off to winter ball. I never did it, even though I was asked a lot and even urged by the Braves to do so. Looking back, I'm glad I didn't because it's an awful lot of wear and tear on a young pitcher's arm.

December 1 is usually a signal to get going with a workout routine. The workout is a combination of what I feel works for me and what the Braves advise. Our strength coaches, trainers, and doctors keep a close eye on us and suggest the areas where we need strengthening in the off-season. For me, it's been getting my shoulder stronger and trying to put a lot of muscle in my back because the pitching motion can really do a number on it.

You go through years where you might need to address different areas of your body. But the past couple of years I've been pretty healthy, so I've been reluctant to change anything. Sure, once in a while I look in the mirror and I think I'd love to have a bigger chest or maybe I should reduce some of my body fat—which is probably about 13 percent—but like they say, why fix what's not broken?

I've been fortunate to be able to design a gym in my home where I do the majority of my workouts. For about a month, until

January 1, I work out with heavier weights, which aren't geared at all toward pitching. I focus on strengthening my back muscles and try to add more strength to my shoulders. My leg workouts are also done with heavier weight at first—squats and leg curls to really build some mass on my legs.

When I say heavier weight, it probably isn't that heavy for a lot of people. I bench-press about 160 pounds. I'm very careful with bench-pressing since it really doesn't do anything for my pitching and probably does more damage than anything because the nature of the movement puts a lot of pressure on the shoulders. Without a good shoulder, I've got no career. But I do it because as a person you have pride in the way you look and you want to have a toned body.

Fortunately for me, I'm really limber in my shoulders and legs, so the weight lifting doesn't make me too muscle-bound where I can't stay loose. My chest is a different story, however. After lifting for a while, I feel a little bound up in there and you don't want to be that way as a pitcher. I want to be as flexible as possible. I do three sets on the upper body, reducing the repetitions from twelve to ten to eight and increasing weight with each set. Usually if I can get through three sets pretty comfortably, then I'll go up in weight.

Primarily, I'll do work on my shoulders, back, and then biceps and triceps. It's important to make sure I balance off my routine by working both sides of my body equally. Balance is one of the most important aspects of pitching, which I'll get into later. I usually work the quadriceps, hamstrings, groin, and calves. Those seem to be the parts of the legs that take the most punishment during the year, either through pitching movements, sudden movements off the mound, or running out of the batter's box down the line (and running around the bases if you're lucky enough to do that).

If you have tired legs you're going to come out of the game before you want to. In so many cases for pitchers, the legs go before the arm and they're forced to leave the game. So they're important.

Since legs are the strongest part of the body, I usually increase the weight for my leg work by several pounds. I also decrease the reps to where I do fifteen, twelve, and ten, again increasing the weight gradually.

During the off-season, Mondays and Wednesdays are upper-body days and Tuesdays and Thursdays are lower-body days. I also run on a treadmill during the lower-body days—two to three miles at a nice steady pace of about eight minutes a mile.

I start running more when I get outside. To be honest, that's one area where I'm very lazy. As a pitching staff we don't do a whole lot of running, probably less than most staffs, but I think we do enough of it to keep our legs in shape. In every other area of my workouts, I'll push myself, but with running I only do what I feel I have to do. It's just so boring to me. To make it interesting I alternate between distance running and interval running (hard at one speed, slow it down, bring it up). Interval running is designed to get my heart rate going and adjust my breathing level, which for me is more beneficial than if I went out and ran a mile.

Usually, by the middle of January I'm ready to start throwing. There's about a month to go before spring training starts, so by watching what I eat, reducing fat intake, and hitting my workouts hard, I'm able to be at a workable weight. I cut down on snacks and fast foods—and that's tough because I love fast foods. I'm not the chicken-and-fish type. Actually, I shouldn't admit this being from New England, but I hate seafood. What I do is, if I go out and have a steak and baked potato, I cut back on the butter on the potato and I don't eat dessert. Something that simply works pretty well for me.

Leo usually has a pitching camp in Atlanta about a week before spring training starts, just to see what kind of shape everyone is in. He watches us throw lightly on the side, which helps him prepare for spring training in terms of how hard he should push some pitchers and back off on others.

The frustrating part about the winter workouts is it seems no matter how much working out you do and how much running you do, when you hit spring training and get into that Florida heat, you don't feel like you're in good shape at all. It takes you a couple of weeks to adjust to the point where you feel you're in decent enough shape to start the season.

The heat and humidity is great for you. It loosens the body and helps get you in shape by improving your endurance and stamina. I know that pitchers who train in Arizona sometimes complain they don't sweat enough because of the dry air. That's a real problem because you have to work extra hard to get a sweat going and sometimes you might overexert yourself trying to lather one up.

When the season begins I go through an entirely different type of workout routine. The day after I pitch is normally my heavy workout day and my heavy running day.

I focus on my legs, using machines to do two or three sets of fifteen reps of various exercises, including squats and leg presses.

I play catch in the outfield, which Leo requires, just to loosen up my arm and get that bad blood (that's what we call it, but we mean stiffness) out of there. The second day is spent doing more light rotator cuff stuff, sprinting with the rest of the pitchers in the outfield, then working on the side with Leo off the bull pen mound.

I don't put an exact time frame on my throwing. There might be times when I throw for ten minutes and other times when I throw for twenty. Some of that time is just standing talking to Leo about mechanics. Time varies because the purpose is to gradually get my arm back in pitching shape. Essentially, I throw to the point where I'm loose. I'd love to be able to throw all four pitches on that day, but if I can only throw two of them comfortably, that's fine. It's knowing when enough is enough. I ask myself, "Do I feel loose and do I feel like I've accomplished what I set out to accomplish?" If the answer is yes, then I leave and head to the clubhouse for a little R and R or I get a rubdown from the trainer.

The day after I pitch is also the day I love to play golf. This doesn't sound like it should be part of a regimen, but it's very therapeutic for me. Usually, I play with the other pitchers, and we get a chance to escape baseball for a while and spend a nice day at a beautiful country club, walk around, and relax. I find that I feel a lot looser in subsequent days after I play eighteen holes.

Our golf games are pretty competitive because we have good golfers. Smoltzie is the best, but I usually shoot in the high seventies to low eighties. It's funny: I love golf with a passion, but it's a sport I haven't been able to conquer, unlike baseball or hockey. Maybe I haven't devoted enough time to it. I started playing when I was a junior in high school, but never really played that much until I got to the big leagues.

Golf has also provided me with my biggest embarrassment. In 1992, Charlie Leibrandt, Smoltzie, Bret Saberhagen, who was in with the Mets, and I went out to play at the Country Club of the South in Atlanta, which is where I live. We got to the sixteenth hole and we'd all taken our first shots. There was a temporary stone walkway that separated the creek and the sixteenth fairway. When I stepped on one of the stones I fell through! Before I knew it I was standing in water about neck-high. I knew there were snakes in there, so I scrambled out as quickly as possible, slipping over the stones to get out, and that was quite the trick.

The three of them were just standing there stunned. They didn't say a word.

Finally, Smoltzie asks, "Are you all right?"

I said casually as I stood soaking wet, "Yeah, I'm fine."

As soon as I said it, they burst out laughing. The worst part is I lost my sand wedge and it's still in there. At least my house was located on the sixteenth fairway and I was able to change into dry clothes, get new cleats, and rejoin them on seventeen.

Thankfully, this has not become a regular routine.

After a relaxing day of golf, I get back to work on the third day. I do more repetitions on my light-weight work with my shoulder and with five-pound dumbbells I use on about a dozen different exercises involving my shoulders and back. I throw on the side again, but try to make it shorter than the previous day, and then I do more sprinting in the outfield.

Then on the fourth day, I'll play catch for a little while with Leo and go over all of my pitches with him. He watches my mechanics as we throw to make sure they're fine.

Sometimes if things are going bad, we'll sit down and watch some video. Video is the rage around baseball with other teams, but we don't use it all the time, maybe even less than most teams. That's probably because Leo is so good at detecting the flaws by sight.

The way our rotation works, I follow Greg; therefore, I'll chart his pitches. Basically I keep track of what pitch he throws to what location and what the result was to each hitter. This helps me and other pitchers in noting certain characteristics about the hitters.

There are certain hitters who play against both right- and left-handed pitchers, but oftentimes because Mad Dog is right-handed, I'll have to face a right-handed hitter that I didn't see while I was charting.

In that case, I'll look at an old box score that might have their lineup against a left-hander that's similar to me and study how that lineup did. At times, I'll grab some of Leo's meticulous records on hitters around the league and go through them, and also go over what the scouting report might say about the tendencies of a certain hitter—whether he's prone to chase an off-speed pitch, or whether he's hitting well and right on the off-speed stuff. All of that information is readily available to our pitchers if they feel they need it.

To be honest, I'm not the type who pays a great deal of attention to the scouting reports, because I know what I need to throw to get the hitters out. Just because the report might say something like "He likes the ball low and inside," that doesn't mean I can't throw it low and inside and still get him out. I'm not going to succumb to the hitter. My feeling is that when I'm throwing my pitches well, I can throw him everything he wants and likes and he's not going to be able to hit it.

Leo preaches that to our entire staff. We do not ignore the scouting reports, but like Leo says, "All they tell you is what you can't do." Leo says we like to live on the edge. We go after the hitter and pitch it where they like it and dare them to hit it off us.

It's the greatest rush there is to know you're pitching so well and you're in such a rhythm that when a guy steps up to the plate you're saying to yourself, "There's no way this guy can get a hit off me." There are moments when I feel that way.

It's not so satisfying that I'm out there laughing at the guy or smiling at him. I would never show anybody up like that. You have to realize that the flip side of that is going to occur, too. The same guy you feel will never get a hit off you in one game might come back in another game and you can't get him out, either because he made the adjustments against you or because you just stink that day.

The toughest hitter in the league for me is Tony Gwynn, but I'm not alone in that. He's just the best hitter, period. You can throw him a pitch that might be unhittable to 95 percent of the hitters in baseball, and he'll find a way to do something to hurt you. He's a difficult hitter to throw to because there are no patterns to his hitting style. He thinks along with you and he has such incredible bat control and bat speed he's able to react to whatever location and whatever speed you're throwing at. When you get Tony out you feel you've accomplished something.

All the training and practice would be meaningless without sound mechanics. There have been endless books written on pitching mechanics. Some of them are really complicated and make this whole process of pitching something that can only be understood by the rocket scientists at MIT.

There is no one formula for success, but each one of us has a different method of attaining the final goal of being able to throw a baseball at the maximum velocity your body will allow, with the maximum movement your delivery will allow, and throw the ball in a way to create the maximum deception so the hitter is kept off balance and can't figure out what's coming up to the plate next. Piece of cake, right?

Like I said, there is no set way to pitch. It's whatever feels comfortable for you. Growing up, I watched Luis Tiant and I'm sure all of the pitching experts were saying, "Don't try this at home!" when Luis would practically turn his body to second base before he delivered the ball. I doubt that any one of us would feel comfortable with that delivery. But it worked for Luis.

The hitter had little idea of where the ball was coming from because Luis hid it so well and for so long. It created a certain amount of deception. Juan Marichal was known for his high leg kick, so the hitter had problems finding where his release point was. Most pitchers can't kick their leg up that high and still have an idea of where the ball is going.

When I go out and teach pitching to kids, number one I tell them you've got to do what's comfortable for you, whether it's a high leg kick, no leg kick, no windup, whatever. The key to my entire delivery, however, is balance.

If you're getting so far back one way that you're going to fall over, or when you're thrusting toward home plate and you're so far ahead of yourself that you can't stay on your feet, then you're not balanced and therefore you're not going to be able to have your best control.

When I'm making my delivery, I'm thinking about keeping my front shoulder driving directly toward home plate. Then there's a pretty good chance I'm going to be in a good position to unload the pitch and have all my momentum going toward home plate.

The other thing you have to be comfortable with is how you release the ball. Some guys are straight overhand, some are sidearm, and there have been pitchers in the league like a Dan Quisenberry or a Todd Frohwirth who come in almost submarine style. My delivery is three-quarters overhand, which means I'm a little bit off to the side. I guess if you were to extend your arm straight up and draw a forty-five-degree angle in there, that's where I'm comfortable throwing the ball from.

It takes a lot of practice to stay consistent with your release point. It is the single most frustrating aspect of pitching that keeps major league pitchers up at night. You want to get very familiar with exactly where that release point is and do your best to release the ball from that spot consistently.

I've found that one of the best ways to find a comfortable release point is by picking up a baseball and pretending you're an outfielder. Catch a fly ball and pretend there's a runner heading for the plate and you want to throw him out. Don't even think about it. If you can get somebody to watch you, they'll tell you where you released the ball and that's where your natural release point is.

There are obviously times when something throws that release point off. It can really range to pitching on an unfamiliar mound or, on any given day, you might just be too quick on your windup so you're getting out in front of yourself a little bit.

On some days your delivery might be too slow, often as a result of being too conscientious about locating your pitches too perfectly. Everything slows up and you find yourself aiming the ball.

When you find—and keep—your release point you're going to get the best results on your pitches and your best location.

It's somewhat important to hide the ball from the hitter as you deliver it, but not at the expense of losing a balanced delivery. It doesn't make sense to do something quirky in your delivery to hide the ball at the expense of location and movement. It's ultimately those two things that will get a hitter out. Even if he sees it a little better coming up to the plate, you're going to get the hitter out if you have the right location and movement on the ball.

Sometimes when everything is flowing well for me, I make a more conscious effort to hide the ball, but if I'm off a little bit I say the hell with it! I couldn't care less how good the hitter is seeing the ball because I'll conquer him more often that not.

Everybody approaches the hitter differently, too. Like I've said, I'm not Roger Clemens or Randy Johnson. I can't usually overpower the hitter. Everything I'm doing to a right-handed hitter is on the outside part of the plate. The reason I can be effective to right-handers is that I stand on the opposite side of the rubber.

Most left-handed pitchers either stand on the first-base side of the rubber or in the middle. To my knowledge, I'm one of the few and perhaps the only left-handed pitcher in baseball who stands on the third-base side of the rubber. That's one of at least two unique things I do, the other being the way I grip my change-up.

When I was pitching on the first-base side of the rubber years ago, I felt like I had to bring the ball back over the plate to get it on the outside corner and that I would miss ten or twelve inches off the outside corner just because of the angle I was delivering the ball at. On the other side of the rubber, it gives me a better angle to the outside corner and it's more conducive to the way my change-up moves.

Now, if I were more of a breaking-ball pitcher, it would probably be better to stand on the first-base side of the rubber so I could throw more across my front leg to get a better break on my pitches. But breaking pitches are not my bread and butter.

When I was younger I couldn't throw the ball straight because I had all of this natural movement on the ball. If I stood in the middle of the mound, I found that I naturally missed the corner of the plate, away. And so my dad told me that if I kept missing there why not move over? And suddenly the pitch that was moving six inches off the corner was hitting the corner for a strike.

I also didn't use my legs as much in high school as I do now, and I don't bring my hands up over my head anymore. Just bringing my hands to my chin and eliminating all of that extra hand movement during delivery gave me more consistency and more strikes. The less movement, the less chance for things to go wrong. Simple is best.

When I start my delivery and turn my foot sideways to the mound and get into position to drive toward home plate, I just try to be balanced. A good way to know if you're balanced is to stop your leg kick at any given time; you should be perfectly balanced on one foot. I concentrate on keeping my shoulders square going to home plate, with a little bit of a hip turn. I keep my right back pocket as a guideline as far as my hips are concerned. I want to turn enough that my hip is facing the hitter or facing home plate but not so much that the hitter sees my left pocket.

There are other things that have to happen depending on the type of pitcher you are. Because I throw a change-up, I have to make sure my arm speed is the same speed coming to the plate as when I'm throwing a fastball. My fastball, nowadays, is probably eighty-five to eighty-seven miles an hour, but the change-up should be slower—ten miles an hour slower so the hitter sees the arm speed, but the ball comes out of the hand slower, which plays havoc with the hitter's timing.

I have command of four pitches, which I think is a must in the big leagues if you're a starting pitcher. I can throw my fastball, which sinks naturally. If I locate it properly it's effective for me after the hitter is looking at change-ups and breaking balls. So while my fastball isn't a blazing one, it seems a lot faster to the hitter after he's seen my curve, change-up, and slider.

There's a prevalent pitcher's school of thought that you have to pitch inside, meaning you have to throw it in, in, in and knock hitters off the plate and that's the way you're going to get hitters out. That's not the way I pitch.

I do use the inside part of the plate—if I'm throwing a hundred pitches a game, I'm going to come inside about ten times. (But most guys think you have to come in there twenty to thirty times and sometimes more.) You can't just be away, away, away so that's all the guy is looking for and so he's not conscious one bit of the inside pitch. If you did that the hitter would be crowding the plate a little more every time up and he'll eventually get a hit. So that's why I do feature the fastball inside every now and then. By doing that the hitter has to recognize the fact that if he crowds the plate too much I'm going to bust him inside. When I come inside and it's called strike three, they act like the ball almost hit them and they look at the umpire saying, "How could you call that?"

This philosophy was hammered home to me one day when I had a chance to speak with Sandy Koufax at a charity dinner after a golf tournament during the strike in the fall of 1994. Sandy said, "I hardly ever pitched inside, but you have to get guys out on the outside part of the plate and that's where I pitched."

On the mound I'm not constantly thinking about how to fool the hitter, but in key spots I say to myself, "What do we want to do here? What pitch do I want to throw and what location would be the most effective in this situation and for this type of hitter? Is this a spot where I want to do something different?"

But you can really overdo it with that stuff. You try and outsmart the hitter so much you wind up outsmarting yourself.

When you get right down to it, hitters usually know what I'm going to do or have a real good idea about what I might do. So every once in a while you provide a new wrinkle. Maybe you throw them a fastball in a normal change-up situation. Or maybe throw the slider when they're expecting a fastball. What you do all depends on what's happened in the previous at bats with that hitter. You try and think back, "I struck him out with a change-up away on 1–2. It's 1–2 now, should I try it again, or should I try maybe a fastball inside and give him a completely different look?"

But again, I don't go through that thought process on every single pitch. While a lot of pitchers do that, I've always believed, and maybe a lot of the so-called pitching experts out there will think I'm crazy, that the less you think about out there the better off you are. When I'm on my game—meaning I have a nice smooth balanced delivery, my location is great, my change-up is biting the outside part of the plate, my fastball is working great and sinking, and my other pitches are on—I know exactly what pitch I want to throw and where I want to throw it. I get the ball back from the catcher, I get the sign (if it's what I want to throw I begin my delivery, if not, I shake it off until I get the pitch I want), and I throw it. Nice and simple. That's why I say, you don't have to be Einstein to pitch. You have to know yourself, however, and have the confidence in your ability and know that you can conquer the hitter with the stuff you have.

When I'm going bad I don't try and break it down to the nth degree either. There are only so many things that can go wrong. If I'm getting hit hard it's probably because I'm struggling with my mechanics and leaving my pitches out over the plate, hanging there fat as a basketball. If I get hit hard and my mechanics are great, but my pitches are just over the plate, I work on location. And there are those days when I'm making a ton of mistakes out there like I did in the eighth inning of Game 6, but they're hitting the ball right at people or they're swinging and missing for some reason.

I try to tell myself that during the course of a year—over thirty to thirty-five starts—everything is going to even out. That's not to suggest that when I get my butt kicked I don't care. I care as much as anyone and I get as mad as anyone. It's just that I won't beat myself up over it. You're facing the best hitters in the world and every now and then they're going to have a great day against you. Sometimes you have to tip your cap to them and say to yourself, "Things will be different the next time." And there's always a next time. That's the beauty of baseball. You may have to wait a full season, but you'll get a chance for your payback.

The wonderful thing about our team is that I have so many resources available to me. I not only have the best pitching coach in the game, but I can also pick the brain of Mad Dog. Don't think I'm shy about going to Mad Dog and asking him, "What did you see? What was I doing wrong?" And don't think he won't offer suggestions or ideas. When someone is struggling we all get involved and we try to find a solution.

I talk to Greg a lot obviously because of the success he's had, having won four Cy Youngs, but also because we live close by in the same development and we ride to the park together all the time. We're constantly talking about pitching and how we feel we want to approach a certain team and what changes we might want to make. So every once in a while, we'll go over a team and say, "Mike Piazza knows we're going to do this, so let's see if we can pitch a little backwards and trick him." In my case, that usually doesn't work with

Mike because he's always owned me and probably always will. But every now and then it makes a difference. If you do that one time during a game, or maybe in four at bats you pitch the guy backwards three out of the four times, maybe that will confuse him. That's the kind of stuff we can take advantage of and the stuff that Greg is good at analyzing.

It's the same with our hitters. Clarence Jones is a terrific hitting coach, but we also have top-notch hitters like Fred McGriff and David and Marquis, who know a lot about their business. And don't think I don't go over to C.J. and ask him what a hitter would be thinking in this situation. Sometimes when I'm not pitching and just watching the game I'll get up close to him in the dugout and say, "So, runners at first and second, one out, what pitch do you think that hitter's looking for right now?"

And it's not that you take anyone's opinion as gospel. Ultimately, you're making the decision on what to throw. There are times even during the game that you're shaking off the catcher because you just don't want to go down the same road. There's nothing wrong with that as long as you aren't shaking him off every other pitch, otherwise you and your catcher have a little problem.

I've been lucky over the years that I've been able to throw to very good defensive catchers who understand the game. When I came up we had Ozzie Virgil and Bruce Benedict, and they were excellent at calling games. As a young pitcher, I certainly relied more on their expertise with the hitters and rarely would I shrug them off.

Greg Olson was an excellent receiver and a guy who really took over a game and made you feel confident about your stuff. And Damon Berryhill, I thought, was the very best receiver. He called the best game of anyone who's ever caught for me. He seemed to be thinking right along with you. I know that Clemens has said in the past that Damon, who played for the Red Sox in 1994, was also the best catcher who has ever caught him and I know Roger asked that Damon catch him all the time.

But I had no problems throwing to Javy Lopez. He's a young catcher still learning the league and the pitchers on the staff, but I thought he did a terrific job in the World Series and he's going to be a good one. With Javy, I try to help him out by keeping things simple, which is the way I like them anyway. He pretty much knows now what I want to throw in a given situation.

*   *   *

Game day isn't unlike other days. I'm a little quieter, but I'll still goof around with our trainers Dave Pursley and Jeff Porter and our clubhouse managers Fred Stone and Casey Stevenson, and sometimes the pitchers take part in putting contests in the clubhouse. As the game draws closer I'll get quieter, but if someone wants to speak to me or tell me a joke, that's okay, too. I'm not going to conduct lengthy interviews before I pitch, but I'll answer a question or two from a reporter.

Preparation, instincts, and physical and mental conditioning are a big part of this game. Without taking these seriously, you can't pitch in the big leagues. And I realize that the longer you play, the more you have to do because there's always someone new trying to take your job.

In many ways our staff is a throwback to the old days of baseball when everyone always talked about the game in general, strategy, mechanics, grips on pitches, situational pitching. We talk about the opposing hitters. I don't know if other teams do it to the extent we do, but we do it because we love to talk about the game and that's one of the reasons we're so into what we do as a staff. I know you're saying: "Talking baseball is the reason for your success?" I don't underestimate it. The more you talk, the more ideas you get, the more you learn. We motivate ourselves with mental games.

For instance, we have fun with a first-pitch contest, where Leo keeps track of every first-pitch strike our staff throws. Given the atrocious state of pitching around baseball early in the 1996 season, more pitching staffs should find ways to motivate their pitchers to throw strikes. We take great pride in that.

And finally—and I don't take this for granted—we've had stability in Atlanta since mid-1990, which helps with the mental part of the game. And now that we've had a taste of success, we're champing at the bit to do it all over again.

22

To Have a Dynasty

AFTER WINNING A WORLD CHAMPIONSHIP, A CY YOUNG AWARD, and twenty games three times, what's next? I often hear that nothing could possibly motivate me enough to excel and win another championship. Well, that's simply not true.

What's wrong with winning two of everything or three of everything? I've been called greedy before, I guess, but I think you would all agree that this is the type of greed that's the most fulfilling.

I entered the 1996 season still thirty years old. The way I pitch and the way I take care of myself, I could pitch another five or six years if I wanted to. But I don't know. When I was twenty-seven or twenty-eight years old, I didn't feel as good as when I was twenty-nine. Hitters will tell whether you should keep pitching. I don't foresee being in a situation where I'm thirty-five and I need two more years for three hundred wins or something and hang on.

Because it took us so long to win a championship, I'd like to win it three times or four times to make up for all the tough times, and all the times we got to the postseason and didn't win it.

If our front office can keep our pitching staff together, we're going to be a good team for a long time. They did a great thing signing Fred McGriff to a four-year deal. Fred is a huge part of our offense and a leader in a quiet sort of way. John Schuerholz went out and re-signed Marquis long term, too. Because the Braves do have a budget, they had to draw the line somewhere, and they decided to draw it with Merck.

Merck was a big part of the Braves and a good friend and I'll never forget him. John had to make a tough decision, and he figured with Jason Schmidt and Brad Woodall on the way, one of the two could take on the role of the fifth starter. I wish Kent the best in Baltimore. That's a great situation for him and maybe now he'll get to be the starter he's always wanted to be. You know you have a great situation when Merck can't crack your front four. He's got a world of potential, and as he begins to stretch out his innings to become a starter, you're going to see the great stuff he has in Baltimore.

We're a young enough team that we could build something of a dynasty here. We have Ryan Klesko's emerging power, and Javy Lopez will become one of the top catchers in the National League in years to come. I'm convinced of that. We've already seen his great natural power. His game calling is ever improving, and he should probably take that to a new level this year as he gets more and more familiar with the hitters in the league.

We have Woodall, who pitches a lot like I do—a finesse lefty—and hopefully I can help him make the adjustments he needs to make to be a winning pitcher in the majors. Jason is a lot like Smoltzie—a hard-throwing power pitcher—and I know Smoltzie will help him along. And Terrell Wade is another promising pitcher in our system who could break into our rotation in 1996. Mark Wohlers has emerged as one of the premier closers in the league. The search is finally over.

We have a great young player in Chipper Jones, who signed a four-year, $8.6 million deal in spring training. John Schuerholz called him a young George Brett. And there's no doubt he's the centerpiece of our future. There's no telling how great of a player he'll become.

I think he had such an excellent rookie season—.265 with twenty-three homers and eighty-six RBIs—because he had a chance to hang around with us in 1994 when he was injured all season. He had a chance to watch the games and study the pitchers, and it gave him a good idea of what major league ball was all about. Come to think of it, he also managed to elude our rookie initiation.

Every year we make our rookies go through an initiation as our way of officially accepting them as our teammates. Last year we got Mike Mordecai and Ed Giovanola as well as Schmidt and Woodall. At different times we made them dress up in bright red polyester bell-bottom trousers, a red-and-white pinstripe shirt, and size-thirteen god-awful platform shoes. We pick an airport like Montreal, for example, where the players have to go through customs. And after a few moments of humiliation the initiation is pretty much over.

We have a lot of fun with it. It's become a Braves tradition. I'll have to make sure that Chip becomes a part of it in 1996.

I know in a way it must be difficult for our prospects to look up and see that there's a World Championship team up above and there are four starting pitchers in the way. But I've always said that if you belong in the big leagues, you'll be here no matter who's in the way. The other great thing for our prospects is that they've come up in a great organization that grooms their young talent the right way. They have the best instruction.

It'll be interesting to see how long the Braves can keep Ave, Greg, Smoltzie, and me together. If we're together the rest of our careers, then we'll keep winning.

The 1996 season should provide an interesting challenge, and early on it was shaping up like 1994 when the Expos challenged us. They were doing it again in first place and leading us by a couple of games, but we were also hot. Our pitching staff had an ERA of under 3.00 the first quarter of the season, and Schmidt was doing well as the number five starter. Ave was rebounding well from an off year, dominating hitters again, and Smoltzie looked much like he did the second half of 1991. It was fun to see that the hunger was still inside each and every one of us and that we had a team like the Expos to keep us motivated.

The game keeps finding new ways to market itself for the next century. One thing that is expected to be enforced is that the low strike is going to be called. That's great for me because that's where I throw the ball anyway. But I've always felt that you'll never get the current group of umpires to change their way of calling balls and strikes no matter what the rules are. It's conditioning. Maybe a new generation of umpires will be groomed in the minors to call that pitch a strike and then things will finally change.

Also, in the winter of 1995, interleague play was adopted for the 1997 season. I'm still debating whether I like the concept. Certainly, I look forward to the opportunity to pitch at Fenway Park. And it will be exciting for the fans to see the other league on a limited basis. I'm just worried whether those fifteen games against the other league will impact a pennant race. As it currently stands, the NL East will play the AL East, NL Central against AL Central, and NL West against AL West. The AL East is traditionally very strong. That means we would play tougher teams than Los Angeles and Colorado have to play against the AL West. That's the part that bothers me.

And how much interleague play will we eventually have? Hopefully it's limited to the fifteen games. A taste of it is nice, but I'd rather see more games played interdivisionally. I think that would create more intense pennant races, which is great for the fans.

Mad Dog, I'll say it yet again, is the greatest pitcher in the game today and it would be great to watch him produce several more twenty-game and Cy Young seasons and then enter the Hall of Fame. The more I'm around him the better I can be. You can't help but learn about pitching watching him day in and day out.

In the nineties, I've won more games than any pitcher in baseball—ninety to Greg's eighty-nine. I don't know what that means exactly. Am I the best left-handed pitcher in the game? I can't answer that. Randy Johnson is a very imposing, intimidating presence and he throws a baseball harder—with control—than any southpaw in the game. Obviously, I can match my statistics against anyone. And I'm sure the writers and the fans will choose my proper place in history.

I'm often asked how much longer I want to pitch, and I think that all depends on the health of my left shoulder. So far it's held up quite well, and as the years go by maybe I'll find new ways of getting the hitter out. That could mean another five years of tormenting Leo, or Leo tormenting me, maybe longer, if I'm healthy.

The other factor is whether I'm still enjoying the game. I can't imagine ever not wanting to play baseball, but sometimes as the years go by and the traveling and being away from your family catches up to you, that all enters into your thought process.

I know I can improve upon 1991 and 1992 and even 1995, when I thought I pitched the best of my career. As a pitcher, I'm just hitting my prime.

The last year on my contract is 1996. The team has an option for 1997, but I know we'd like to negotiate a long-term deal so I can spend the rest of my career in Atlanta.

If that can't happen, I would look first to Boston. That would always be my first alternative, and I stress the word alternative. If that couldn't work out then maybe I could be part of an expansion team. That would be fun.

I'm not going to sweat the contract, and if the subject doesn't come up and the Braves simply exercise the option on my contract, that's fine. Having been through the labor war, I understand the economics of baseball more than ever. Sometimes tough decisions have to be made and I know one of these days I'll be a victim of one of those decisions.

But my heart and soul is in Atlanta. This is where I make my home, where Carri and I will raise Amber and her future siblings.

I hope that after all this time has passed, people no longer hold me responsible for the strike. I would do it again to fight for what I think is right. That's the way Fred and Millie Glavine of Treble Cove Road raised me.

And finally, it's been said that it's hard for a Yankee to go south and mix in with the natives. All I know is there's nothing like the southern hospitality of Atlanta. I hope you've enjoyed my ride through time.

See you again in the World Series.

The Top Five

Here are some lists of the things that make the game of baseball a challenge and a pleasure.

Five Toughest Hitters I Face
1. Tony Gwynn (San Diego)
2. Mike Piazza (Los Angeles)
3. Barry Bonds (San Francisco)
4. Robbie Thompson (San Francisco)
5. Mark Whiten (Philadelphia)

Five Favorite Ballparks to Visit
1. Wrigley Field (Chicago)
2. Coors Field (Denver)
3. Busch Stadium (St. Louis)
4. Jack Murphy Stadium (San Diego)
5. Dodger Stadium (Los Angeles)

Five Favorite Pitchers to Watch (not including our staff)
1. Randy Johnson (Seattle)
2. Jimmy Key (New York Yankees)
3. Hideo Nomo (Los Angeles)
4. Ramon Martinez (Los Angeles)
5. Orel Hershiser (Cleveland)